# Reviews from *Sacred Places Around the World*
## *first edition*

"... the ruins, mountains, sanctuaries, lost cities, and pilgrimage routes held sacred around the world." *(Book Passage* 1/2000)

"For each site, Brad Olsen provides historical background, a description of the site and its special features, and directions for getting there." *(Theology Digest* Summer, 2000)

"(Readers) will thrill to the wonderful history and the vibrations of the world's sacred healing places." *(East & West* 2/2000)

"Sites that emanate the energy of sacred spots."
*(The Sunday Times* 1/2000)

"Sacred sites (to) the ruins, sanctuaries, mountains, lost cities, temples, and pilgrimage routes of ancient civilizations."
*(San Francisco Chronicle* 1/2000)

"Many sacred places are now bustling tourist and pilgrimage desti-nations. But no crowd or souvenir shop can stand in the way of a traveler with great intentions and zero expectations."
*(Spirituality & Health* Summer, 2000)

"Unleash your imagination by going on a mystical journey. Brad Olsen gives his take on some of the most amazing and unexplained spots on the globe—including the underwater ruins of Bimini, which seems to point the way to the Lost City of Atlantis. You can choose to take an armchair pilgrimage (the book is a fascinating read) or follow his tips on how to travel to these powerful sites yourself."
*(Mode* 7/2000)

"Should you be inspired to make a pilgrimage of your own, you might want to pick up a copy of Brad Olsen's guide to the world's sacred places. Olsen's marvelous drawings and mysterious maps enhance a package that is as bizarre as it is wonderfully accessible. The historical data and metaphysical ruminations make it an intrigu-ing read. So pick a mystical corner of the world, be it Mount Shasta, Delphi or Borobudur, and plan out a pilgrimage real or imagined among the Tungus shamans of Siberian Russia, the ghosts of Mohenjo-daro, the Muslim faithful at the Grand Mosque in Mecca, and more." *(San Francisco Examiner* 1/2000)

# Reviews from *Sacred Places North America*

"An interesting book for both the armchair and the adventurous traveler, this (book) is recommended." (*Library Journal* 4/2003)

"The book is filled with fascinating archeological, geological, and historical material. These 108 sacred places in the United States, Canada, and Hawaii offer ample opportunity for questing by spiritual seekers." (*Spirituality & Health* 3/2003)

"A revealing, useful, and enthusiastically recommended guide for the vacationer seeking to fulfill their spiritual as well as their recreational yearnings." (*Midwest Book Review* 2/2003)

"World traveler Brad Olsen has compiled a book that documents 108 destination spots for 'feeling the energy' of our spiritual historical roots. Pilgrimage is one way we can find ourselves and this book will provide a guide." (*Twin Cities Wellness* 3/2003)

"The book's chapters correspond to ten regional sections of the U.S. and Canada, which are further subdivided into specific U.S. States and Canadian provinces. No less than 38 of the 50 United States are revealed to contain sacred sites — some of which are very public and easy to access, such as the House of David in Michigan, and some of which are more obscure, like Shiprock, 'the stand-alone neck of an ancient volcano core' in New Mexico. But never fear: Olsen provides lucid and detailed directions, as well as tantalizing and historically well-informed essay-portraits, for each destination. The book is also peppered with excellent maps, illustrations, and photos." (*Fearless Books* 2/2003)

"For travelers who prefer destinations with spirit ... juxtaposing local folklore and Native American legend with scientific theories to provide context." (*Orlando Sentinel* 2/2003)

"It's an odd lot, the places that have a way of touching your heart: mountains and homesteads, caves and monasteries, lakes and pathways. Author Brad Olsen has recognized that variety in this bringing together of 108 places that stir the soul. Many of the destinations mentioned come as no surprise in a collection of the hallowed: Ohio's Serpent Mound, Wyoming's Yellowstone, Colorado's Mesa Verde, for instance. But other entries serve as a delightful reminder that there is room in our hearts to expand the definition of sacred: Massachusetts' Walden Pond, Michigan's House of David, and Tennessee's (and Elvis') Graceland, for instance." (*Chicago Tribune* 4/2003)

"Olsen maps out obscure destinations brimming with intrigue and history, places where you will not have to fight thousands of tourists. You'll find lots of maps, drawings and photos. It's a travel guide for the individualist." (*Ashley Tribune* 3/2003)

# SACRED PLACES

# AROUND THE WORLD

Second Edition

# 108 DESTINATIONS

Written, photographed, and illustrated by

## BRAD OLSEN

## CONSORTIUM OF COLLECTIVE CONSCIOUSNESS

www.cccpublishing.com    www.bradolsen.com    www.stompers.com

# Sacred Places Around the World:
# 108 Destinations

second edition

Library of Congress Cataloging-in-Publication Data:

Olsen, Bradford C.

Sacred Places Around the World: 108 Destinations / Brad Olsen

   p. cm.

Includes index

ISBN 1-888729-10-4 (Pbk.)

1. Spirituality—Guidebooks. 2. Travel—Guidebooks. I. Title

Library of Congress Catalog Card Number: 98-092920

Printed in Canada.

10 9 8 7 6 5 4 3 2

**Front Cover Photos:** (c) 2004 Brad Olsen (Golden Buddha, Darjeeling, India; Forbidden City, Beijing, China; Montserrat Monastery, Spain).

    (c) 2004 Trevor Zimmer (Sphinx and Great Pyramid, Giza, Egypt)

# 108 SACRED PLACES AROUND THE WORLD

# TABLE OF CONTENTS

# ECHOES THROUGH THE AGES

In the midst of planetary turmoil the peoples of the world are awakening. Accompanying this mass awakening, the voices of our ancestors beckon forth the truths of their Ages. In the Essene and many other ancient traditions, an *Age* is a period lasting 2000 years during which the whole of humankind encounter life-trials through which we, as a collective group, progress.

At the beginning of each new Age, therefore, we—the body-human—are given a new lesson-plan, and our lives, and lessons, continue. So has the human experience progressed through "the Ages."

Without fail, each Age has had its enlightenment periods, and fortunately for us, the bodhisattvas and Christ-conscious beings of past eras have sought to share their experience with future generations of humankind ... us!

In the case of our most ancient civilizations, the broad range of knowledge accumulated through observation and experiential trial-and-error was passed on through oral tradition. The Modern Age, on the other hand, has the people of earth preserving memories in print, virtually and in Time Capsules destined for future eyes.

In the past, mass paradigm shifts in human belief have caused huge amounts of ancient wisdom to be shunned, disregarded, or outright destroyed—much of it to remain lost forever. Truth, it has been said, "begins as heresy and ends as superstition." Indeed, the innate human fear of the unknown has caused entire societies to withdraw from truth.

Fortunately for us, the voices of our ancestors are not so easily squelched. Indeed, it is their voices you hear as you visit the spiritually significant locations described in this book. Each cries forth to teach, warn and compel future generations toward *Right Action*. Through their artifacts we can learn what they learned as they worked, prayed, and meditated through life.

So, as you proceed on your quest for Self, look to the wise among us, whenever and wherever they lived, and remember: *truth exists absolute,* no amount of subversion or denial can effect the purity of its nature.

Be blessed and go forth.

**—Mark J. Maxam**
**Author and Publisher**

# AUTHOR'S KARMA STATEMENT

Society today has corrupted man. All seem to be caught
up in the search for money, fame and power. But a
smaller few of us have kept the values of the old world
and try to live this way. We come to the mountains and
commune with nature. We visit the relics of mankind's
glorious past to remember our own. We have not lost
sight of God and moral reasoning. Therefore, with our
quests, I can safely say we are bettering societal values;
we are helping future generations.

—*anonymous journal entry,*
*Mount Shasta Base Camp*

H uman civilization in the 21st century can be defined by diversity and duality.
One-fifth of the world's population is Chinese, another fifth Muslim. A hundred million of us are homeless children living in extreme poverty. More than two
percent of the human population is mentally retarded. There are over 10,000 spoken
languages. Yet, a perception of some form of God pervades 95 percent of our religious
belief. In essence, all religions of the world are valid, as each one shares insight into
the divine. This communing of humans with the "oneness" of the universe has led to
the building of countless places of worship around the world. In this modern age,
some of the sacred places described in this book are especially relevant to certain religions but not to others. Some are forbidden to enter while others are open to all.
Some are museums, World Heritage sites, national parks or tourist destinations on
private land. Some are completely inaccessible or forbidden to enter. Nevertheless, in
my humble opinion, I feel as we collectively ascend from polarity consciousness into
unity consciousness the relevance of these spiritual sites become even more profound.

For better or for worse, we are entering a new era on our little blue-green planet. It
is apparent the earth is grossly overpopulated and our overwhelming presence is
beginning to disrupt the natural order of things. October 1999 marked the birth of
the 6-billionth human being, and by 2050 CE there will be 8.5 billion of us riding on
this planetary spaceship. Every 110 hours the world population adds another million
people more than those who have died in those same hours. Despite planetary population growth of nearly 5 billion people in the past century alone, our origins come
from a single source. Evolutionists determine we are all Homo sapiens, a strain of
hominids emerging onto the planetscape some 150,000 years ago. According to this

9

model, we are generation number 7,500 from the time our species originally evolved on the African savanna. That would make us about the 500th civilized generation, counting back 10,000 years to when early farmers settled down in primitive communities and thus began our first perceptions of sacred places.

## "As above, so below" –Hermetic Axiom

As people become more aware, they also become positively attuned to their surroundings. This inexorably leads to interpersonal perceptions of sacred places. Visiting the sites in this book I found myself opening to many new insights—both concerning the world in general and myself. I came to realize that there are major issues challenging our collective survival. Quite frankly, there has never been a time in history when so much lay in the balance. Within a few decades we must save the natural world from utter destruction; disarm ourselves to prevent nuclear holocaust; and we must urgently rise to the calling that all life on this planet is extremely valuable. To advance we must confront ourselves as the master tenants of earth and rise to the challenges of a new millennium. We must discard old, destructive ways of thinking and reinvent ourselves as the unified human race. Despite urgings from certain organized religions to the contrary, we must realize the consequences of overpopulation and decrease our impact before we consume the planet into oblivion. There has never been a more important time in history when all people must come together in harmony and respect. We can survive this challenge, and to do so we must learn to cooperate and share amongst ourselves and with those who are less fortunate. Indeed, we are all one and everything we do to another we do to ourselves.

## Why the Number 108?

Numbers, it can be argued, carry as much significance as letters. Numbers convey a different method of communication altogether, forming the basis for commerce and all the sciences. Numbers are deeply rooted in many cultural traditions, oftentimes contemporary with a civilization's original literary works. Such is the case with the number 108 in most East Asian religious cultures. 108 is the number of beads on sacred *mala* necklaces worn by millions of reverent Buddhists and Hindus. To them, the number 108 is associated with the precessionary cycles of earth and the cosmos above. If a Buddhist or Hindu pilgrim can endure a trip to the most sacred mountain in Asia, the inhospitable Mount Kailas on the Tibetan Plateau, one is on a true path to *nirvana*. If that same pilgrim can manage 108 circuits around the base of Kailas in a single lifetime, their entry into heaven is assured.

For a transcendentalist book like this I found myself looking for instruction and guidance from many varied sources. I sought out experts on the subject of sacred sites, whether it be world travelers, Native Americans, or anyone else with an intuitive sense into the power of place. Every Wednesday night at my old San Francisco artist warehouse called the CCC we hosted a yoga class for our friends. My occasional yoga instructor, a mystical kind of guy named Antoine, traveled to India frequently and upon his latest return inquired about my current writing projects. I told him what I was compiling and he offered me some information on the subject of clustered water, the kind often found emitting from holy wells. Antoine asked why I choose the standard number 101 for the first edition of this book instead of a revered number like 108. Without a good answer for Antoine other than most readers would probably associate better with 101 (maybe not?), I agreed with him and decided to make the "Sacred Places" book series based on a strait 108 spiritual destinations. Since then, I have seen the number 108 appear again and again—on highway signs, advertising billboards and in spirituality books—but that's not necessarily relevant. However, I will share one nifty mathematical formula: 2 squared multiplied by 3 cubed equals 108.

## Custom Drawn Maps

The artistic technique of illustrating maps or charts is called cartography. The information contained within maps was a highly protected secret in ancient times. Not until the 19th century did the physical properties of the planet at last become common knowledge. In antiquity the best cartographers were usually travelers themselves, studying shorelines, weather patterns and mountain ranges; trying to accurately convey their knowledge in maps for other explorers and sea captains. By way of contrast Amerigo Vespucci, the man who loaned his first name to identifying the continents of the New World, was not an explorer but merely an "Age of Discovery" cartographer who put his prominent signature over the landmass of North America.

Following the age-old tradition of cartography, my maps are hand drawn from other source maps. It would have been easy enough for me to completely create the maps digitally, but I feel the hand drawn look better enhances my writing and adds a personal touch. Usually I worked on the text, maps, and illustrations simultaneously during production, going from one to the other. I included many additional minor sacred sites in the maps that I was not able to include in the textual 108 described sites. The maps are designed to identify as many spiritual sites with spiritual significance as possible. I eliminated most modern cities and highways unless necessary for point of reference. I tried to use an eclectic assemblage of maps reflecting the long heritage of diverse cultures in the world.

## Cultural Diffusion

It was said a long time ago that life is sometimes stranger that fiction. Who we are as a collective civilization will one day surface and encompass many different people in very anomalous places. Just as the Greenland Vikings are finally being accepted in academic circles as being the original "discoverers" of North America, evidence of other significant migrations is surfacing in various corners of the world. It would therefore be reasonable to assume that each group would have brought with them unusual cultural traits that influenced and eventually blended with native populations. In writing this volume it was necessary for me to engage in some supposition unconfirmed by conventional archaeology. If I have surpassed the usages academic historians consider acceptable, I have done so in an effort not to mislead anyone. A footnote from Gibbon's *History of the Decline and Fall of the Roman Empire* explains how the master historian grappled with this dilemma. Gibbon writes: "I owe it to myself and to historic truth to declare that some circumstances in (what follows) are founded only on conjecture and analogy." The perspective of Cultural Diffusion is new and open to many different interpretations. Mine is the voice of a lifelong world traveler.

*—Brad Olsen*
Consortium of Collective Consciousness
San Francisco, CA
2004 CE

The Dating System used in this text is based upon the modern method of using Before Current Era (BCE) instead of Before Christ (B.C.), and Current Era (CE) rather than "in the year of the Lord" *anno Domini* (A.D.). Those unfamiliar with this dating system should take note that 1 B.C. is the same as 1 BCE and everything then counts backward just the same. Similarly, 1 A.D. is 1 CE with all the years counting forward to the present, or Current Era. To assist in universal understanding, all measurements of length, distance, area, weight, and volume are listed both in the old British standard and the metric system.

# INTRODUCTION TO
# WORLDWIDE SACRED PLACES

**It is only with the heart that one can see rightly;
what is essential is invisible to the eye.
—Antoine de Saint-Exupéry, The Little Prince**

In the depths of the human spirit resides an inclination to follow the same paths long venerated by our ancestors. Travel is food for the soul, especially when that journey takes us to where our hearts illuminate. Journeys to sacred places touch upon that which is vital to our humanity. These trips open our minds to the world around us, our collective history, the cosmos above and also to each other. When we arrive at a spiritual destination, we find ourselves closer to our own individual reality, not only in time, but in space. Something magical happens at a sacred place that triggers an unconscious memory. To learn about the world of sacred places is to learn about ourselves.

## Sacred places represent the essential spirit of humankind.

Planet Earth is shrouded in third-dimensional physical wonder—both natural and human manufactured. All over the world we find the remains of pyramids and temples sprawled across the landscape like ancient scientific instruments, placed along a precise geometric grid pattern. These landmarks of ancient civilization also correspond to distinct characteristics on the mantle of the Earth. Fault lines, volcanoes and mountain ranges, above and below the ocean, bisect the planet. Certain intersections between and through these geologically active zones create intense "acupuncture" points. This network is called the Earth Grid, and "ley lines" are the energy paths between powerful points. Mystic mountains, caves, vortex regions and various unexplained natural formations have long enchanted humans as powerful energy spots. These points and intersections are the locations where humans first erected temples, pyramids, shrines, churches and cities. This invisible energy web also correlates with known areas of anomalies in gravity and space-time, such as the Bermuda Triangle in the Atlantic Ocean and the Four Corners region in the southwestern United States. It has been postulated that different dimensions exist simultaneously and that an electromagnetic web of energy interlocks all things on this planet.

### What is a Sacred Place?

As discussed individually, each natural and human made sacred place has some discernible quality. Sometimes it's the design, the physical proximity of the site, the building materials used, or the shape of the monument. How the sacred site inspired, or continues to inspire, a religious movement is reviewed. The most important quality is the feeling these sacred locations evoke in people. We all venture to sacred sites, knowingly or unknowingly, to satisfy the human spirit's desire for communion with ourselves and our collective humanity. Every sacred place has its own unique prominence. The following are some determining factors:

## Gaia, Ley Lines and Geomancy

The ancient Greeks were the first to describe the planet as a living "mega-organism" on which we all depend. The "Gaia Hypothesis" put forth by the Greeks has come back in popular thought, as well as in the collective mind of scientists. Gaia is the Earth represented as a single living, breathing entity with both memory and intent. Making up this body throughout the world are electromagnetic energy paths, or ley lines, which connect to the greater Earth Grid and interact with vortexes above, at and below the surface of the planet.

In the 1920s, an English gentleman named Alfred Watkins coined the term "ley lines" in his book titled *The Old Straight Track*. Watkins discovered a huge grid of flowing energy lines connecting ancient sites, pathways and geographic markers (mounds, holy wells, ponds, depressions in hills, etc.) all over southern England, primarily in

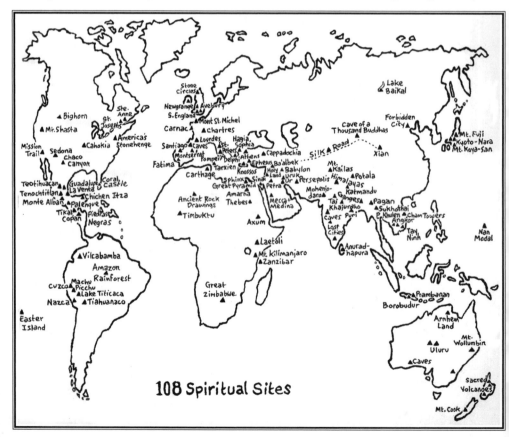

108 Spiritual Sites

Herefordshire. Some of these ley lines, Watkins noted, dated from the Neolithic period and they denoted the location of Britain's many churches, shrines, villages and town squares. Although called lines, Watkins and other geomancers began to perceive these lines as three dimensional, similar to tubes. Sometimes the lines would interact and combine with stronger vortex energy.

Geomancy is the art of divining earth energy and detecting ley lines. Modern geomancers describe two kinds of electromagnetic energy lines that the planet uses as part of its nervous system. The first is a straight line, or yang line, which intersects the planet much like the latitude and longitude lines on a globe. The second type is curvilinear, or a yin line, which resemble the twists and turns of the natural environment. Geomancers have discovered that most of the sacred sites around the world are built upon the intersection of yang lines. Where three or more yang lines cross, one can almost always find a sacred well, place of pilgrimage, cathedral, temple or pyramid. Where yin lines cross, on the other hand, there is an accumulation of negative energy. People staying for an extended period of time over intersecting yin lines can feel nauseous or worn down. There are really no good or bad energy lines, however; they are all part of the planets' system of regenerating living power.

### Vortexes and the Noosphere

Vortexes are subtle earth energy centers located along strong ley lines in various locations around the world. Vortexes are viewed as funnel-shaped and created by a whirling fluid, or by the motion of spiraling energy. The energy resonates within and strengthens the inner being of every person coming within a quarter-mile of them. The power emanating from the vortexes produces some of the most remarkable energy fields on the planet. Notable vortexes worldwide include Peru, Mexico, Egypt, England, Italy, Greece, India, and Sedona, Arizona.

As the next science of nature and the mind emerges, receptive people will begin to tap into a new paradigm of amazing human abilities. One of those abilities is the perception of the planet's living vitality. The ancient Greeks called the planet's vitality "Gaia" and the Hindus knew it as "Mother"—the one living force that sustains all life on earth. The placement of significant sacred places on an etheric web of ley lines encompassing the planet can be seen as an effort to tap into Gaia energy, in order to feel and understand it and so to live better lives. This noosphere, or "mind layer" as Teilhard de Chardín describes it, consists of all points surrounding nature, or actually is nature, and Chardín maintains that this etheric web is the cogitation between matter and human consciousness. In the noosphere construct, humankind's inventions, institutes and ideas are in perfect parallel with the living biosphere and upper atmosphere of our planet. Yet, before intuition of the earth's energy web can spread to all humans globally, a critical mass of advanced beings must trigger change by visualizing the noosphere. Until then, "Myth is an act of faith in a science yet unborn" as Levi-Strauss postulated.

## Mountains

Hundreds of mountain ranges cover the planet, including those protruding from the sea and those below the ocean's surface. While elevations and physical characteristics vary widely, it is only a few individual mountains that resonate with a discernible aura revered by spiritual seekers. These pristine peaks are the ones worshiped through indigenous folklore and ancient religious texts. Pilgrimages to sacred mountains have been taking places for thousands of years, and shall continue as long as people believe in their power.

"From time immemorial the mountains have been the dwelling place of the great sages. Wise men and sages have all made the mountains their own chambers, their own body and mind." So spoke Dogen, the 13th century founder of the Soto Zen tradition, a faith famous for its communing with nature. There are countless mountains around the world, but only a few are considered holy by cultures past and present. These sacred peaks have long been regarded as homes to immortal gods: For the Greeks, it was Mount Olympus; Buddhist and Hindu deities abide at Mount Kailas; the Kurds worship Mount Madai; and the Hopi regard the San Francisco Mountains as the legendary residence of the Kachinas. The Kachinas are Hopi gods who are said to live underground in the mountains, much like the Lemurians inside Mount Shasta. Several other sacred mountains are keystones to indigenous religions, including Mount Kilimanjaro, Mount Fuji, and the many impressive peaks in New Zealand and the Himalayas.

## Sacred Caves

Before early humans started building freestanding structures, they resided in caves. Here, in the dark caverns of Europe and Asia, the first signs of religion began to be formulated. Survival of the clan depended on hunting and fertility, and most prehistoric artifacts represent this concern. Later, as religion evolved, certain caves and grottoes took on spiritual connotations — adorned with religious icons or acting as a safe house for sanctified texts. Notable sacred caves include: Cave of a Thousand Buddhas in China, Saint Michael's Grotto along the European Saint Michael's Line, Ellora and Ajanta Caves in India, and the many prehistoric caves in Southern France (Lascaux) and Northern Spain (Altamira).

## Pyramids

Pyramids and ziggurats are the original permanent monuments constructed on the planet. Remains of very old pyramids in Xian, China and Tiahuanaco, Bolivia suggest an interaction with the Great Pyramid in Egypt, which incorporates a profound understanding of the Earth Grid. Atop Central American pyramids and Middle Eastern ziggurats began the first practices of advanced religion.

Perhaps no human built object in the world can better represent our collective vision of the cosmos than a pyramid. A faultless geometrical shape precisely

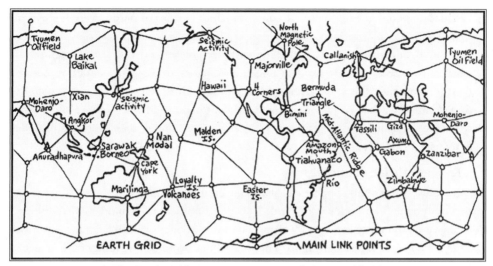

▲ The Earth Grid connects many sacred sites worldwide.

positioned where strong energy lines intersect. A pyramid is a perfectly fitted triangular mountain of stones rising from a flat plain. Pyramids represent a reaching for the heights and a marker of an important location. Pyramids function as astronomy centers, initiation chambers and occasionally as tombs. From each of the pyramid's five points, energy is transmuted and accumulates in the geometric center. Here, decay of dead matter slows, and mummification occurs. Pyramids have the additional function to be used as almanacs, theodolites, compasses, geodetic markers and celestial observatories.

When humans began to construct artificial structures in the shape of pyramids, they used sacred geometry, which are numbers and measurements used in accordance with nature. The idea was to reflect the order of Heaven on Earth. Aesthetic awareness in relation to universal principles could alter states of consciousness, and enhance psychological and spiritual development. The most intellectually advanced ancient races of people—the Egyptians, Sumerians, Chinese, Maya and Tibetans—all were pyramid builders.

## Stone Alignments

Freestanding stone arrangements represent a profound understanding of the cosmos, especially the planet's relationship with the sun and moon. Stone circles were used as calendars to predict seasons, as planetariums to study the movement of stars, and as meeting places where tribes could gather and exchange information. The ability of these cultures to accurately predict the movements of the heavenly bodies such as the sun and moon surely gave them a sense of communion with the larger universe as well as, quite possibly, a sense of control. Although many have been lost, thousands of stone alignments remain worldwide, with the most famous being the medicine wheels of North America and the megalithic arrangements in Northern Europe.

Prehistoric people living in close harmony with the cycles of nature were highly sensitive to the earth's subtle influences. By identifying auspicious points of earth energy, early builders further enhanced the site with upright stones, mostly in a circular formation. It is possible that stone arrangements acted similar to acupuncture needles used to geomance the living planet. Modern research is investigating the possibility that standing stones can accumulate and transmit natural earth energies. Dowsers and scientific instruments, or sensitive people who can hone their perceptions, may detect such earth energy inside stone circles.

### Temples/Shrines/Churches

Temples, shrines and churches all share one common denominator—they were built to help people come closer to God. These structures are reminders that life and change are inherently constant. Visiting a building of our faith can help us recover our spiritual power and peace of mind. These buildings bring people together in an act of faith and love. No matter what denomination, sect or religion, the temples, shrines and churches of the world are devotional sanctuaries for anyone seeking divine inspiration.

Back in the day when the land was free of human development, there were obvious characteristics that humans perceived as special. Here, the first shrines were built, cities rose, and in the hallowed parts of early cities great temples and churches were erected. These "Sacred Precincts" were home to the priestly caste and the molders of civilization. In almost every case, the original center of an ancient city contained a temple, shrine or church denoting origin of the principality.

### Lost Cities

Some of the most interesting worldwide sacred sites are the lost cities no longer occupied by people. What makes them especially intriguing is the visitor's ability to experience a town as it was when the original inhabitants lived there. This gives the traveler a vicarious feel of a past culture, and in most cases, an opportunity to observe the religious center unmolested by modern growth. Best preserved examples of a lost city include: Pompeii, Italy; Hampi, India; Petra, Jordan; Persepolis, Iran; Machu Picchu, Peru; and the Forbidden City in Beijing, China. While spending time in a lost city, it is easy to transcend the consciousness of a past age, as well as perceive the religious priorities of a long-gone culture.

### Religious Centers

In this modern age, the defining aspect of a religious center is its pilgrimage value. All world religions and indigenous tribes encourage a pilgrimage somewhere. Primary destinations for the largest religions include: Christians pilgrimaging to Lourdes, France; Muslims to Mecca, Saudi Arabia; Hindus to the Ganges River, India; Buddhists to Mount Kailas, Tibet; and Jews to the Western Wall in Jerusalem, Israel. Early indigenous people primarily sought the wonders of nature for their spiritual journeys, such as Australian aboriginals venturing to Ayers Rock or native South Americans to Lake Titicaca.

Pilgrimages to holy places all share the same purpose —travelers seeking God, or seeking to find themselves. In some traditions, the destination is left deliberately ambiguous, whether the goal of the journey is actual or merely symbolic. Tibetan tradition relates the mythical Shambhala, which may have existed in ancient times or was an intentional metaphor for a state of consciousness.

## Masters and Natural Wonders

There is much we can learn from the shaman, holy men, indigenous people and supernatural influences in our lives. The earth magic rituals performed by esoteric practitioners continues to elude conventional scientists. Yet, apparitions continue to appear, and black magic happens. On a very subtle level, it is possible to perceive what the masters know about the underlying metaphysics of the planet. Those on a spiritual quest will want to hone every perception, heighten their every awareness and, most importantly, keep an open mind to anything that might happen at a sacred place.

The great monuments of antiquity retain their age-old mysterious wisdom in this accelerated modern age. While most sacred places in this book are bustling tourist and pilgrimage destinations, one can still find quiet moments at off-hours. The location, orientation, structure and function of a sacred place are based on timeless universal laws, which no tourist group can obstruct. Most human-made spiritual sites were constructed in an age when our ancestors lived in resonance with Mother Earth and could recognize subtle energy spots on the landscape. Footpaths became roads; stone circles became cathedrals; holy wells became cities. These universal principles of balance and harmony were never completely forgotten—they are still with us today.

Understanding mysterious people, places and things has its beginning with grounding ourselves and making a connection with the earth. Feel the planet's energy coming up from the ground through deep, conscious breaths. Some Native American people call this "Earth Breathing," and when done in a peaceful state, the result is a pleasant surge of vibration and a warm, tingling feeling all over. This places the person in a receptive state to deeply perceive the heartbeat of the planet and the primal energies that created these spiritual sites.

**Sacred places epitomize everything good about our collective humanity. Go to them for the right reasons.**

It is important to note that anyone visiting a sacred place should go with sincere intentions and no expectations. Having expectations can block what really needs to get through, and set up the traveler for disappointment. You can view a sacred site as an interesting pile of rocks or a place long venerated by our ancestors. You can see these locations as tourist traps or places where others commune with a higher force —no matter how many tourists are tramping about. With loving intentions, unseen forces are allowed into your being and healing can take place. If you believe a physical or mental ailment can be cured or alleviated at a power spot, just your openness to such an event is probably more important than the place itself.

## The past 20 years have brought record numbers of visitors to the world's sacred places.

Take a spiritual journey to the sites listed in this book. You are your own master capable of discerning each of these 108 sacred places individually. Go to them! Go with respect, reverence and a clear conscious. Some are very difficult to get to, some very easy. Some will inspire, others may disappoint. But without a doubt, no matter where you go, you will return a much more understanding and perhaps enlightened person. A simple travel mantra: "Open the mind, enrich the soul; Make world travel your ultimate goal." Seek and ye shall find!

## DEDICATION

This book is dedicated to the human race and our quest to facilitate a higher understanding amongst ourselves. May we learn to co-exist on this beautiful planet with all living creatures in harmony and respect.

## 12 Worldwide Sacred Sites and the Body Chakra Locations They Represent:

1.  *Table Mountain, South Africa represents the three-ring chakra existing beneath our feet.*
2.  *Uluru, formerly Ayer's Rock, Australia embodies the root chakra at the base of our spine.*
3.  *Kilauea Crater, Hawaii identifies our sacral chakra.*
4.  *Delphi, Greece defines our navel chakra.*
5.  *Mount Fuji, Japan symbolizes our solar plexus.*
6.  *The Tor in Glastonbury, England forms our heart chakra.*
7.  *Palenque, Mexico signifies our throat chakra.*
8.  *The Great Pyramid, Egypt is our third eye.*
9.  *Mount Denali, Alaska denotes our crown chakra.*
10. *Mount Shasta, California designates our three-ring chakra above our head.*
11. *Machu Picchu, Peru, South America indicates our Cosmic Portal at the topmost part of our aura.*
12. *Lake Titicaca, Peru and Bolivia specifies the aura above and surrounding an individual.*

# NORTH AFRICA

# AND THE MIDDLE EAST

**Let not a man glory in this, that he love his country; Let him glory in this, that he love his kind.** *—Persian proverb*

A S FAR BACK AS RECORDED TIME ALLOWS our ancestors observed, marked, and worshiped the heavens. Humans have long felt an instinctive need to display an interpretation of the interconnectedness that we share with our universe. Early Paleolithic paintings around the world depict humans in close connection with nature — all being part of the one. To further elevate an understanding of the cosmos, humans started building pyramids in Egypt and ziggurats in Sumer. These early stone structures were constructed in the "Cradle of Civilization" at the dawn of collective consciousness. Mesopotamia, the land between the Tigris and Euphrates Rivers, along with the fertile Nile River valley, is where humans first learned to farm and domesticate animals. Here began agriculture, permanent settlements, writing, and the concept of organized religion.

North Africa and the Middle East are locations of pilgrimage to many religious persuasions. The Holy Land of modern Israel is sacred to Christians, Jews, and Muslims alike. Here walked the very people who shaped Western religion. Homeland to such biblical heroes as Abraham, Moses, and Jesus, the Holy Land was residence to King Solomon, David, Mohammed, and many other luminaries. The crossroads of North

Africa and the Middle East have long been a melting pot of people, religion, and civilization. Perhaps the most enigmatic and mysterious country is Egypt—the land of Pharaohs and the Nile River, the mighty waterway that transposed ideas, pilgrims, and living gods for many millennia.

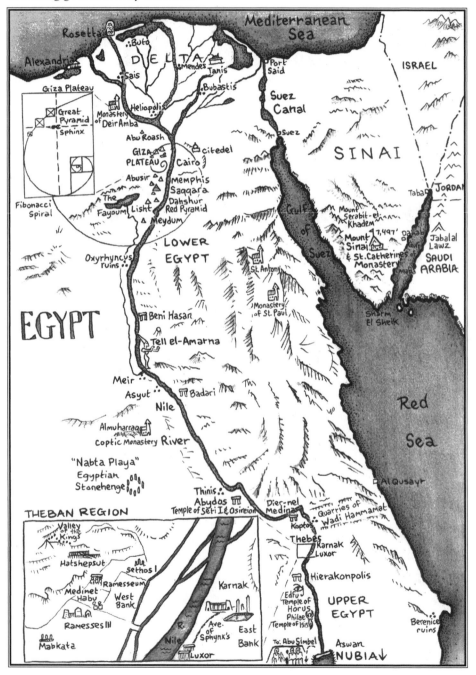

# EGYPT

E gypt is a land steeped in ancient history and is generally regarded as the birth-place of Western civilization. Egyptian monuments are some of the oldest edifices in the world and may represent the continued legacy of Atlantis. Most ancient Egyptian monuments are located on the western side of the Nile, signifying the land of the dead. Monuments on the east side of the Nile were for use of the living. Successive Egyptian pharaohs built massive stone structures dedicated to themselves and a pantheon of deities.

Ancient Egyptians worshiped many gods, both on earth and in the constellations. The sun god Ra was prominent in the daytime sky, while the star Sirius held greatest magnitude in the nighttime sky. A strong connection between ancient Egyptians and the heavenly bodies influenced the building of many monuments. In worship of Ra, the sloping pyramid sides represent spreading rays of the sun. During summer months, Sirius marked the flooding of the Nile and the beginning of the agricultural cycle. Unfortunately, the Nile no longer floods its banks. When the High Aswan Dam was constructed in 1966, several important monuments were flooded and the biology of the river was seriously altered. The dam now blocks silt and fresh water from replenishing the former flood zones, and as a result the fertile Nile delta is sinking into the Mediterranean and is in serious threat of becoming unfarmable. One important sacred site, Abu Simbel, built by Ramses II, was expertly relocated on the desert plateau above the newly formed Lake Nasser. While Abu Simbel is a fascinating monument to visit, its repositioning has altered the exact geographic location and thus cannot be considered a true sacred place any longer.

## Great Pyramid and the Sphinx

Towering 40 stories tall on northern Egypt's Giza Plateau is the Great Pyramid, supposedly 4,590 years old and thought to be a burial tomb for Pharaoh Cheops. This is a shortsighted theory, based on Arab writers of the Middle Ages and others from antiquity who associated the pyramid with the biblical narrative of the flood. These people believed ancient Egyptians had constructed it as a repository for their scientific knowledge and wisdom in anticipation of the disaster. At the base of the Giza Plateau rests the enigmatic Sphinx, another monument erroneously associated with a fourth dynasty pharaoh. Both monuments certainly provoke more questions than answers. Speculation and probing over the ages into who built the Great Pyramid and Sphinx has proven inconclusive.

Astonishing is the enormous Great Pyramid and its physical properties. The structure contains 2.5 million blocks, each weighing 1.6 tons (1,625 kg). The pyramid is level to one half of an inch over an area of 13.5 acres (5.4 hectares). There are enough blocks to build a one-meter-high wall around France, or 30 Empire State Buildings, or a one-meter wall from north to south across the United States. If a circle were drawn around the base of the pyramid it would cast a shadow at a different point on the circle on each of the 365 successive days, to determine a precise calendar year. The angle created by the side of the pyramid and the ground is equal to π (pi), or 3.14159, the critically important geometric concept supposedly discovered by the Greeks. The pyramid is located precisely on the 30th parallel, which is equidistant from the North Pole to the equator and serves as a standard guide for navigational and astronomical calculations.

The builders of the Great Pyramid knew of the cycle of the stars, their individual and collective influence on the earth and sun, their effect on human consciousness, and the fact that intelligent life was not limited to only our planet. With this as a precise marker on earth, a series of shafts within the Great Pyramid point to the prominent stars and constellations of Orion, Sirius, and Pleiades—points in the night sky believed to harbor intelligent life. In a sense, these windows can be viewed as part of an astronomical observatory. The Great Pyramid contains several passageways, various rooms, the Grand Gallery, and is equipped with air ducts. All chambers within the pyramid measure a constant temperature of 68° F (20° C), which is considered an optimum temperature for modern human living. Besides being an observatory, Edgar Cayce noted in one of his visions that "the Great Pyramid was built as a temple of initiation." This was no pharaoh's tomb as Egyptologists lead us to believe—it was a structure serving many advanced functions and encompassing multi-dimensional information. The Great Pyramid was specifically designed to bring ancient Egyptian students into an enlightenment-consciousness state after completing their twelve-year Eye of Horus studies. Some of the greatest names in history are said to have been initiated here, among them Hermes, Moses, Akhunaton, Pythagoras, Plato, and Jesus Christ. In addition, the Great Pyramid is believed to contain a hidden passage to another chamber, the Hall of Records, which contains the knowledge of earth past, present, and future.

In all its majestic glory, the Great Pyramid is the last remaining Wonder of the Ancient World and humankind's finest architectural achievement. Its very location represents a rare and powerful energy spot, one of only a few acupuncture points on the physical planet where major ley lines connect. The supreme monument of antiquity was constructed on a precise and very sacred piece of ground.

**What the position of the Great Pyramid represents is a profound understanding of the cosmos and the physical planet. This pyramid was constructed at the center of all landmasses on earth. Even more surprising, the Sphinx was built at this location thousands of years earlier.**

26

Whoever built the Great Pyramid knew the exact measurements of the physical planet. Looking at a flat map of the continents and the oceans, the pyramid is located precisely at the geographic center of the total planetary landmass. The Great Pyramid in Egypt is perfectly orientated with the four cardinal compass points of north, south, east, and west. The latitude of the Great Pyramid is exactly 30° north, one third of the distance from the equator to the pole. The north-south and east-west meridian lines, starting at the pyramid base, cover more land area than any other planetary longitudinal or latitude lines.

Today tourists are only allowed access through an artificial entrance passage to the Grand Gallery, which ultimately leads into the King's Chamber. Inside the King's Chamber are extremely hard granite blocks that are very difficult to cut, let alone polish, even by today's standards. The granite blocks are perfectly smooth over 19-feet lengths to within 1/100 of an inch! So exact were the cuts, that even today a thin razor blade cannot be inserted between them—and some of these blocks weigh more than 50 tons (45,350 kg)!

There is a tremendous gap in our understanding of the intelligence used to construct the Great Pyramid if we are to believe conventional Egyptologists. How could a people, supposedly only one step removed from the Stone Age, be in possession of mathematical and astronomical data that scientists of our age are only now beginning to fully understand? There appears to be much we still need to learn about this magnificent monument.

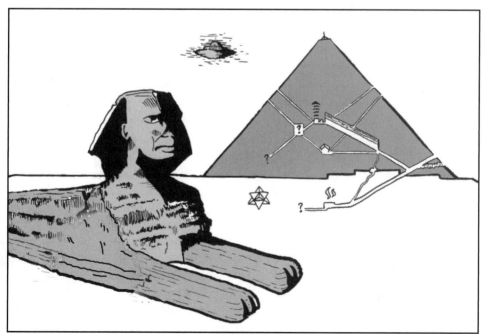

▲ More questions than answers remain about the true origins of the Great Pyramid and the Sphinx. Several chambers between both monuments have yet to be revealed.

The distinctive Sphinx features a human face wearing a Pharaoh-like headdress, combined with a long recumbent animal body. So contemptuous was its pagan beauty that a medieval Islamic dervish gave his troops the order to use the Sphinx's nose for target practice. The Sphinx has long been regarded by Egyptologists as representing Pharaoh Chephren, or so they guess. All agree it is extremely well crafted, depicts an animal with a human body and is carved directly from the bedrock of the plateau. Recent dating of weather markings on the underlying limestone level determines the Sphinx to be the oldest human made object on the face of the earth. The extensive weathering on the Sphinx, apparently caused by rainfall, is not found on the pyramids or any other monuments. Excessive wear patterns on the Sphinx, especially in the rear where gouges are up to 12 feet (3.6 m) deep, have been conclusively determined by geologists to be created by water. It is calculated that it would take at least 1,000 years of torrential rain to create this much water erosion, yet the Sahara Desert is a mere 9,000 years old.

Archaeologists and Egyptologists still argue vehemently that neither the Sphinx nor the Great Pyramids could possibly be anywhere over 5,000 years old. Or could they? Geology and archaeology now stand in direct contradiction. Siding with the geologists we can re-date the Sphinx to be at least 7,000 to 9,000 years old, and therefore predating the ancient Egyptians. If the geologists are correct an unknown people who had already attained an extremely high level of civilization and occupied the Nile Valley many centuries before the first pharaoh assumed power and carved the colossus on the Giza Plateau.

Advancements in petroleum industry probing devices now allow scientists to literally probe the insides of underground chambers. These underground sonar devices create artificial shock waves, or seismic pulses transmitted from the surface and analyzed for return echoes. Several independent teams have used seismographic devices to scan around the Giza Plateau, especially between the Great Pyramid and the Sphinx. Their findings are incredible. Several connected subterranean chambers have been detected, including two vertical tunnels under the Sphinx. The chambers are located at multiple levels and the deepest supposedly contains a large metallic disc. But perhaps the most significant chamber houses ancient records describing our Atlantean origins—physical evidence for the Hall of Records prophesied by Edgar Cayce. According to Cayce what exist below the Sphinx will inexorably change the course of history.

Why has this new information not been made public? Why is the world being deprived of perhaps the most important discovery of all time? It is because the Egyptian Antiquities Organization and various governmental powers will not allow this discovery to be known. It is because the authorities believe this discovery threatens to break down all conceptions of who we are on this planet, and it would reveal the true identity of a highly sophisticated civilization that constructed the monuments on the Giza Plateau. It is because a discovery like this would completely rewrite human history and subvert time-honored institutions, especially religion. Is evidence being covered-up and suppressed? So far denial and ridicule are the official responses, while those doing the independent research have been expelled from the country, and their equipment and findings confiscated.

Some proof of a "Nilegate" scandal occurred in 1993 when German robotics engineer Rudolf Gantenbrink maneuvered a small robot up the narrow southern shaft of the Queen's Chamber in the Great Pyramid. Millions of people viewed on television as the robot discovered a previously unknown chamber containing a limestone "door" with copper fittings. When Gantenbrink made plans in Germany to open the door with another sort of robot, he and his team of engineers were not allowed to return. In 2002 another robot drilled a hole in the door only to find another limestone slab blocking the passageway. Nothing more has been reported on the second mysterious door inside the Great Pyramid.

There is a saying that the truth cannot be stopped, only delayed. It is imperative that further, non-destructive investigation on the grounds beneath and surrounding the Sphinx be conducted immediately, and reported truthfully to the world. There can be no danger in understanding our true origins. What exists is the potential for light-speed advancements in consciousness once these records are revealed. There is nothing to be feared from re-writing our history books. We are who we are, and no governing body should have a monopoly on this information. The real riddle of the Sphinx is the collective memory of our antediluvian origins—a time capsule whose time has come to be opened.

### Getting to the Great Pyramid and the Sphinx

The Giza Plateau is 15 miles (24 km) due west from downtown Cairo, the capital of Egypt. Cairo is a modern city with a busy international airport. The Great Pyramid and the Sphinx are part of a larger complex of pyramids and tombs. One admission fee is charged for entrance to the Giza Plateau monuments, another fee is charged for entrance inside the pyramids. Be sure to see the sound and light show in front of the Sphinx every evening. In 2003 a massive 22-mile (35-km) wall was erected, completely surrounding the Giza complex and extending far out into the Libyan Desert. Some speculate the wall was built to hide archaeological activity, but the official explanation is to control tourist activity and to prevent terrorism.

## Power of the Giza Plateau

Although there are many other pyramids along the west side of the Nile, it is the three pyramids on the Giza Plateau that the world regards as the Great Pyramids, while Cheops (named after a supposed pharaoh) is quite simply The Great Pyramid. The next pyramid over to the southwest is attributed to Pharaoh Chephren.

It's nearly identical in size and shape, yet lacks the intricate inner workings of the Great Pyramid. The Chephren pyramid appears taller because it is on a higher level, but it is actually a few meters shorter than the Great Pyramid. An interesting aspect about the middle Chephren pyramid is that the top quarter retains a crown of the original casing stones. One can still get a feel of the eminently refined state all of these pyramids once held. The third pyramid, named after Pharaoh Mycerinus, was the last built and is much smaller in size than the other two. Several minor queens' pyramids flank the Cheops pyramid and the Mycerinus pyramid. Processional roads lead from the east to all three of the Great Pyramids.

The position of these three pyramids is very significant. They lay the foundation of a Fibonacci spiral and Earth Grid in which almost every sacred site in the world connects—mathematically coupled and delineated back to this single spot in northern Egypt. Recent discoveries in logarithmic spirals and planetary geomancy illustrate an Earth Grid, which has a definitive intersection at the right arm of the Sphinx. This area is known by geomancers as the solar cross and is considered the mother of all ley lines. The Giza Plateau is one of the most critically important energy fields on the planet.

## Tell el-Amarna

Midway down the Nile between the two ancient capitals, Memphis and Thebes, a rebel pharaoh started his own capital. The lost city of Tell el-Amarna was initiated solely by the pharaoh Akhunaton and his wife Queen Nefertiti. Amarna was selected as a virgin site during Akhunaton's reign towards the end of Dynasty 18 (1355 BCE), only to be abandoned shortly after completion. Although Akhunaton was pharaoh of Egypt for less than 18 years, in a short time he was able to change the course of religion. He was the first religious leader or head of state to institute monotheism, the idea of one true god. The sun was worshiped as a unity image—visualized as a solar disc—representing the only supreme god. To express his ideas, Akhunaton prompted the creation of a new expressive art form termed the "Amarna Style" after his capital. Akhunaton was born Amenhotep IV, but changed his name upon converting to monotheism. *Akhunaton* means "Horizon of the Sun." The living sun god he worshiped was named Aten, also known as Ra. The daily prayer to Ra reads as follows:

*Beautiful is your shining forth on the horizon,*
*O living Aten, beginning of life!*
*When you arise on the Eastern Horizon,*
*You will fill every land with your beauty.*
*You are bright and great and gleaming,*
*And are high above every land.*
*You are Ra, and you reach unto their end.*

Akhunaton was deemed a heretic for dismantling the pagan system, yet his beliefs and esoteric Eye of Horus school were so advanced, some believe he was an enlightened master. The Eye of Horus studies Akhunaton taught were of the "missing knowledge" used to produce Christ-conscious citizens. The 12-year course initiated nearly 300 people before Akhunaton was disposed. Although Egypt at the time had the most powerful military in the world, Akhunaton ordered his army not to fight unless first attacked. Not only was he a pacifist, he also assisted in the spiritual advancement of his subjects. In an age when pharaohs were considered living gods, Akhunaton lived up to his title by assisting his people in their quest to attain enlightenment.

### Akhunaton completely redefined Egyptian religion and artistic styles during his reign. Artwork of the Amarna Period expresses unity through worship of one supreme deity.

Egyptian art changed radically in the Amarna Period. The old benign portraiture style was replaced by realistic imagery. Although Akhunaton encouraged no change in the conceptual view of reality that Egyptian artists cherished, some idiosyncratic distortions were introduced, undoubtedly at his prompting, in the portrayal of himself, his queen Nefertiti, and their daughters. The subject matter deliberately depicted the family as having large and elongated heads, narrow torsos, and expansive waistlines. Akhunaton instructed the court sculptors to represent what they saw. Another characteristic of the Amarna Period was the innovative concept of representing space in two dimensions with overlapping figures. All artistic themes took on a new appearance, especially conventional images of the pharaoh.

Queen Nefreteti + King Akhunaton

▲ Tell el-Amarna was built as a sanctuary for the sun god Aten.

Akhunaton built the new capital at Tell el-Amarna for Aten, the sun god. After his reign it was completely dismantled, only to be unearthed some 3,100 years later by 19th century archaeologists. In building Tell el-Amarna, Akhunaton further broke tradition by situating the royal tombs on the east bank, whereas before they were always located on the western side of the Nile. The main buildings—temples, palaces, housing, and administrative quarters—were also on the east bank, stretching along the river for a distance of some eight miles (13 km).

In 1887, a peasant woman was digging in what was the center of the ancient city, and she stumbled upon a cache of some 300 clay tablets inscribed with the wedge-shaped cuneiform script. She had discovered the "House of Correspondence to the Pharaoh," effectively the diplomatic archives of the state records office. The tablets, now known as the "Amarna Letters," were written in Akkadian, the diplomatic language of the Middle East at the time. The letters reveal Egypt's relationship with vassals in the kingdom, and an equal relationship with other kingdoms, including "Urusalim," now known as Jerusalem. This discovery is another in a long list that shows Akhunaton to be one of Egypt's few peaceful and benevolent leaders. The entire city was completely deserted at the end of the Amarna Period, and being undisturbed, it has proven to be a fertile digging ground for archaeologists. Unfortunately, there is little to be seen today of the ancient city built by Akhunaton.

### Getting to Tell el-Amarna

With recent terrorist upheavals in Egypt and worldwide, tourism has dropped substantially throughout Egypt. The result of less tourism is cheaper room rates, more accessible public transportation, and no need for advance reservations to see the various sites. The best way to avoid attracting attention in Egypt is to arrive independently, and make travel arrangements as the need arises. A train departs Cairo twice daily for Luxor, and makes a stop at Tell el-Amarna.

## Thebes

The cyclical rhythms of nature—the annual flood of the Nile that made agriculture possible and the daily phases of the sun—became the basis for Egypt's worldview. The cycle of birth, death, and rebirth of both body and spirit led to elaborate religious rituals and artwork to ensure regeneration, including mummification, tomb burial, and grave furnishings. Some of the finest tombs in Egypt are located in the Valley of the Kings, where many famous pharaohs were buried, including Ramses II—the most prolific builder in Thebes. In 1922, the most spectacular find of the 20th century was discovered in the Valley of the Kings, when Howard Carter and Lord Carnarvon opened the sealed tomb of Pharaoh Tutankhamen. Along with priceless artifacts, a great deal was learned of the Egyptian view of afterlife, including a look at the invisible gods and goddesses in Egypt who controlled and ordered the natural world. They were depicted as human beings, but were often shown with animal attributes. After the death of Akhunaton, the priests of Karnak regained their ascendancy and persuaded his son-in-law Tutankhamen to reestablish the old religion at Thebes.

▲ Anubis was a common deity represented in Thebes.

**Thebes was the capital of Egypt and center of its religious life for many centuries.**

The ancient Egyptian name for Thebes was Waset, yet for reasons unknown it was given the name Thebai by the Greeks during their occupation, and the name stuck. Its geographical location near desert routes, far from the more volatile northern centers, made it an ideal region to re-locate the capital. During the 12th Dynasty in 2160 BCE, as the Egyptians were conquering surrounding territories, such as Nubia, Ethiopia, and Libya, Thebes replaced Memphis as the capital of the empire. The real power came to Thebes during the New Kingdom, when colossal building projects in the region reached its zenith.

The ceremonial avenue leading into the famous Karnak temple complex from Luxor was lined with statues of sphinx rams, possibly symbolizing the Age of Aries. The various temples at Karnak were the home of Amun, regarded as the most powerful of all Egyptian gods. The main Temple of Amun at Karnak, built during the late Thebes Empire, is the culmination of the Egyptians' passion for overpowering size and grandeur. The largest columns in the complex are 69 feet (20.7 m) high and 33 feet (9.9 m) in circumference. When initiates or priests would enter the massive complex, it became darker as the entrances became smaller and smaller the farther they went back. This effect was thought to bring the visitor closer to the presence of the gods. The Great Temple at Luxor was dedicated to Amun in his form as a fertility god, depicted with an erect sexual organ. During the annual flood a statue of Amun would be taken by boat up the Nile from Karnak to Luxor in a ritual celebration of the union with his wife Mut, the divine mother.

▲ Thebes contains some of the finest statuary in Egypt.

Across the Nile from modern Luxor are many impressive ruins. Perhaps the most celebrated is the funerary temple of Queen Hatshepsut, nestled below imposing cliffs near the Valley of the Kings. Constructed during the 18th Dynasty by an architect named Sen-Mut, it is a graceful departure from massiveness. The colonnades rise in three tiers to a sanctuary of solid rock. The worshipper is led to the small sanctuary through three large courts on ascending levels, linked by ramps along lengthy colonnades. This processional road is reminiscent of those at Giza, but with an impressive mountain rather than a pyramid as a backdrop.

## Getting to Thebes

Discovering the sacred sites of the upper Nile is one of the most profound pilgrimages on earth. All one has to do is take a convenient flight into Cairo, then follow the fertile Nile River valley south to the Sudanese border. In Luxor, it is easy to arrange local transportation to the Karnak Temple, or across the river to various mortuary temples. From Luxor, buses run regularly to Aswan (bus to Abu Simbel), and the Red Sea town of Al Qusayr (boat to Sinai Peninsula).

## Mount Sinai

Perhaps the most sacred mountain in the Middle East is Mount Sinai in northeastern Egypt. At the foot of the peak is the Greek Orthodox Monastery of Saint Catherine. Thousands of years preceding the monastery, according to the Bible, Moses and the Israelites wandered the Sinai desert for 40 years before settling in the Holy Land. It is atop Mount Sinai where Moses saw God in a burning bush, then received the Tablets of the Law containing the Ten Commandments, the most humane law being "Thou shalt not kill." Here the Israelites gathered with Moses to receive their laws directly from God, who "gave him the two tablets of the Tokens." Moses claimed the finger of God reached down from heaven and transcribed the two tablets. These tablets form a Covenant, which is the supreme cornerstone of Jewish history. The Covenant is based on the first five books of Jewish scriptures, called the Torah (in Greek, Pentateuch)—which is often translated "Law" but originally meant instruction by divine revelation. Mount Sinai is one of the few sites in North Africa revered almost equally by Christians, Jews, and Muslims alike. The prophet Mohammed once visited the Saint Catherine Monastery and blessed it, promising that Muslims would cherish it for all time.

> **Mount Sinai and Saint Catherine's Monastery have been the inspiration of Christian, Jewish, and Moslem pilgrimage for over 1,300 years. The Monastery is the oldest continuously used religious retreat on earth.**

The monastery was founded by Empress Helena, the mother of Constantine the Great, but was completed two centuries later by Emperor Justinian's architects in the sixth century CE. Continuing a Middle Age tradition, Saint Catherine's Monastery is the residence of a dozen Greek Orthodox monks. The monks live in complete silence and are hospitable only to males. Saint Catherine's Monastery houses a terrific collection of Byzantine art, along with the world's second largest collection of illuminated manuscripts. The books and icons in Saint Catherine's Monastery represent the oldest single collection in the Western world. Most of the treasures, books, and artwork can only be viewed by the monks and invited scholars. Saint Catherine monks claim to maintain a descendent of the original burning bush in a back courtyard.

The 7,497-foot (2,250-m) peak is an impressive site in the desolate Sinai Peninsula. Hiking to the summit of Mount Sinai is not difficult and takes most people about four hours of steady hill climbing. Most pilgrims opt to take the Steps of Repentance route, 3,000 steps carved into the rock face by a worshipful and very single-minded monk. A few visitors choose to spend the night atop the peak, but most wake at 2 a.m. in or near the monastery to reach the summit by daybreak. There are food and drink vendors at the top, as well as a little Greek Orthodox chapel. Several features mentioned in the Bible can be seen on the summit, including a small "cleft in the mountain" where Moses sheltered from the total glory of God.

### Getting to Mount Sinai and Saint Catherine's Monastery

Located in the rugged south of the Sinai Peninsula, Mount Sinai and Saint Catherine's Monastery are about 150 miles (240 km) north of the main Red Sea port city Sharm El Sheik. Also called Horeb or Jebel Musa, Mount Sinai rises from the lunar-like desert among nine other lofty peaks. Buses and taxis ply the routes daily from almost all Sinai cites, including: Dahab, Sharm El Sheik, Suez, and Taba on the border of Israel.

### EGYPTIAN TRAVEL ADVISORY

In November 1997, Islamist militants shot and killed 58 foreign tourists in front of the 3,500-year-old mortuary temple of Queen Hatshepsut near Luxor. This frightening event took place only a few months after a tour bus was bombed at the Cairo Museum when more than a dozen people were killed or maimed.

As Egypt's primary industry, tourism represents a fragmented economic hierarchy of have and have-nots. Resentment runs high among Egypt's poor who have no stake in this lucrative industry. The aim of the terrorist groups is to undermine the secular government by, quite literally, killing tourism. So far, they're achieving their goal.

Although tourism is still encouraged, travelers should take caution on their journey through Egypt. Travel in small numbers, avoid large tour groups and be on the constant lookout for any signs of danger. When these terrorists strike, they seek out the maximum number of tourists to attack at once. It is advisable to keep a very low profile in Egypt, even to the point of dressing yourself in local clothes.

# IRAN

The Islamic Republic of Iran adopted its modern name in 1935. Formally it was called Persia and named after the expansive empire that once stretched from the Red Sea and Turkey in the west, to the Caspian Sea and the Indus River in the east. The name "Persia" derives from the legendary "City of Parsa," a name inspired by the Greeks before Christ. The Persian people were originally a Medic tribe who settled on the eastern side of the Persian Gulf. They were Aryans and their language belonged to the eastern division of the Indo-European group.

Before the Persians, Iran hosted one of the earliest civilizations in recorded history. The Elamite civilization in southwest Iran is dated around 3,000 BCE, with a 1,000-year-older offshoot called Tepe Yahya found in southern Iran in the Soghum Valley. Stone tablets discovered at Tepe Yahya prove commerce was thriving in Iran 6,000 years ago. Much later, when Islam spread through Iran, the Imam Reza Shrine was erected at Mashad and became the holiest historic site to Iranian Muslims.

## Persepolis

The Islamic name is *Takhti Jamshid*, or the "Throne of Jamshid," designating a mythical king of Iran. The ancient name is "Parsa." Hellenistic Greeks under Alexander the Great coined the term "Parsa's City," or *Persepolis*. Once the grandest ceremonial capital of ancient Persia, Persepolis was built under Darius I, the greatest of the Persian kings. Described by Alexander's traveling historians as the richest city in Asia, it stood as an abiding monument to the absolute power of Darius I and successive rulers. A palace of epic proportions, Persepolis represented an enduring monument to the kings who ruled the empire from the mid-sixth century BCE, when Persia started to become extraordinarily wealthy.

▲ This carved finial was found at Persepolis.

Although prosperous, Persepolis was short lived. The downfall came in 330 BCE when Alexander the Great captured the city without resistance from the already shattered Persian army. After spending the winter quartered in the magnificent palace, the young Macedonian king held a drinking party to celebrate the arrival of the spring fighting season. During the festivities, Alexander made the fateful decision to burn down the entire city. He would later regret this decision, mostly because he wished the Persians to accept him as their own new king, not as an avenging invader. So vast were the riches won by Alexander at Persepolis, it required "10,000 pairs of mules and 5,000 camels" to carry away all the loot. Darius III was killed shortly thereafter, and the mighty Persian dynasty came to an abrupt and final end.

**Persepolis was built to celebrate Achaemenid glory —a testament to Persian dominance.**

During the reign of the multiple Darius rulers, Persepolis was the most renowned and greatest city of its time. Persepolis attracted scholars and dignitaries from all over the world. Impressive in size, the city's Apadana Audience Hall was one of the largest enclosures ever built. The city itself was conceived upon divine influence, after Darius' father Cyrus was converted to Zoroastrianism.

The site is marked by a large terrace with its east side leaning on *Kuhi Rahmet,* the "Mount of Grace." The other three sides are formed by a retaining wall. Varying in height on the west side are the magnificent double stairs leading to the top. Persepolis could only have been approached by the single grand stairway, adorned with relief sculptures depicting tribute-bearing subjects from all parts of the empire. On this terrace are the ruins of a number of colossal buildings, all constructed of dark-grey marble quarried from the adjacent mountain. The stones were laid without mortar, and many of them are still in place. Once inside, monumental architecture and a series of vast halls served to overwhelm the visitor. Especially striking are the huge pillars, of which several stand today. Many of the outlaying buildings were never finished. The remnants of Persepolis serve as a silent reminder to the utmost in ambitious vanity. For thousands of years it has attracted curious visitors, some on a spiritual quest, to see the stately ruins in a desolate location.

### Getting to Persepolis

Persepolis is located in the Iranian province of Fars, about 50 miles (80 km) northeast of the city of Shiraz. The ruins are located near the main road from Shiraz to Isfahan. Locals call Persepolis Takhti Jamshid. Behind the site are three massive sepulchers hewn out of a rocky hillside. The facades of these tombs, one of which is incomplete, are all richly ornamented with reliefs. People of most countries, including those of the United States, are restricted from travel in Iran. The hard-line Islamic rulers are being replaced by moderates, and the present "closed door" situation could change.

# IRAQ

Some 6,000 years ago, in a desert plain scorched by the sun and nourished by two mighty rivers, humankind first learned to write, use metals, and think about its human role on earth. In a flash of collective consciousness, the first true cities grew along the fertile banks of the Tigris and Euphrates Rivers, simultaneously in the valley of the River Nile, and on the flood plain of the Indus River. The ancient people of Sumer, or Mesopotamia, ushered in the dawn of civilization. Mesopotamia, "the land between rivers," is also considered part of the Fertile Crescent and its ancient boundaries almost perfectly parallel those of present-day Iraq. Within the thousand years between 3,500 and 2,500 BCE, the ancient peoples of Mesopotamia developed the prime elements of human culture: science and art, writing, and the exercise of reflective thought.

Civilization arguably arose with the invention of writing. The earliest known writing is inscribed on Sumerian clay tablets. A large majority of these tablets record mundane information, such as numerals in bookkeeping entries or illustrated land deeds. Other tablets are more esoteric, such as those describing the account of Enki, an

Anunnaki god, who tells the story of extraterrestrials coming to earth around 445,000 years ago from the supposed 12th planet in our Sun's orbit called Nibiru. Researcher Zecharia Sitchin interprets the Enki tablets as describing a time when giant extraterrestrials called the Anunnaki created the human race through genetic manipulation to assist their mining of earth's gold resources. Visitation or not, ancient Sumerians were prolific writers and illustrators. Predating Sumerian writing are the Mesopotamian seals. Similar in style to the Indus seals, the personal seals of Sumerian city dwellers depict mythological animals, important events, and religious themes. Sumerian seals were used to indicate endorsement or ownership by pressing the carved image into clay.

## Ur and Uruk

The high civilization of Mesopotamia emerged concurrently with the blooming of Indus culture and Egypt under Pharaoh rule. Unlike Mesopotamia, the Nile in Egypt is a narrow fertile strip protected by harsh desert environments. The Tigris and Euphrates consist of a wide shallow trough with few natural defenses. For such reasons, Mesopotamia was much harder to unite under one ruler, and thus city-states such as Ur and Uruk emerged with separate figureheads. As civilization in Sumer evolved, the connection between heaven and humanity became the art/science known as astrology.

Among the first ancient cities of Mesopotamia rose the sacred towers called ziggurats. High on these pyramid-like towers, the astrologer-priests paid tribute to the monotheistic deity Marduk. These holy men of Mesopotamia also developed a mathematical method of dividing up the night sky by graphically marking the stars and visualizing geometric shapes and recognizable symbols. History records the Sumerians as the first to exactly predict when each new season for planting and harvesting would arrive.

The Sumerians emerged sometime before 4,000 BCE and spoke a tongue unrelated to any other language, yet contact with Egyptian and Indus River civilizations has been proven. Indus seals have been found in Mesopotamia and resemble Sumerian writing in cuneiform (wedge-shaped) characters on clay tablets. The city of Ur once contained some of the most richly endowed tombs, similar to Egyptian tombs, in the shape of vaulted chambers below ground. But the greatest similarity to Egypt is the Sumerian ziggurat, a stepped pyramid that took an immense effort to build and served as a religious landmark. The layout of the Sumerian cities revolved around a vast architectural complex of several buildings connecting to a central temple. The sacred precincts included smaller shrines alongside workshops, storehouses, and quarters for the scribes.

## The city center of both Ur and Uruk was dominated by a sacred enclosure containing temples and a huge ziggurat.

▲ The goddess Lilith was a protector of Uruk and all of Mesopotamia.

On a raised platform in each city-state stood a temple complex devoted to a local god. The ziggurats in each complex reached the heights of true humanmade mountains constructed of reinforced solid brick masonry. The ziggurat of Uruk included a ramp and stairs to the upper platform. On top of the platform was a sanctuary called the "White Temple" because of its whitewashed exterior facade. It is believed that priests made observations and sacrifices from atop the Uruk ziggurat. The ziggurat at Ur, built by King Urnammu, originally had three levels and would have dominated the Sumerian landscape. Little is left of the upper two levels, but the bottom level, some 50 feet (15 m) high, has been restored and allows the visitor an understanding of ziggurat layout. Another 4,000-year-old ziggurat near Ur is the reported birthplace of Abraham, a key figure in both the Koran and Bible. It is from the city of Ur that Abraham migrates to the Promised Land of Israel under command from God.

The best-known resident of Uruk was Gilgamesh, a royal traveler similar to the Buddha who set out from his luxuriant kingdom on a quest for eternal life. The *Epic of Gilgamesh* describes his many adventures, including an encounter with the Sumerian Noah, the only person alive who had survived a legendary flood long before his time. The tale mentions the Sanctuary of Eanna surrounded by gardens and orchards inside the famous city walls of Uruk. Gilgamesh was a demi-god and folk hero to the urban residents of his era, foreshadowing both the biblical story of Noah, and the Homeric wanderings of Odysseus and Hercules. The tale was first written down in Sumerian, then in Akkadian, Hittite, and eventually into almost all the ancient languages of the Near East.

### Getting to Ur and Uruk

The Sumerian city of Uruk survives near the Iraqi town of Warka, also called Erech in the Bible. The ruins of Ur are 10 miles (16 km) southwest of Nasiriya, a city that saw much fighting and resistance in the second Gulf War. Ur is located inside a military installation and special permits are necessary. Most nationalities are restricted from travel inside Iraq, but if entry were possible, both Uruk and Ur would be best served by bus from the southern Iraqi city Basra. A train from Basra to Baghdad also stops at the towns near the archaeological sites.

## Babylon

The temples of Mesopotamian soared above the flat river valley, rising tier upon tier to the sanctuaries that crowned their parapets. As centuries passed, their walls grew even higher, culminating in the colossal neo-Babylonian ziggurat of Nebuchadnezzar and the biblical Tower of Babel. Many scholars believe the soaring architecture inspired other priests to worship in "high places." None would rival Babylon.

No other city has existed in the human imagination longer than Babylon. This Mesopotamian city is rich in folklore and history from pre-biblical times. Babylon was the legendary home to the Tower of Babel, the forced captivity of the Jews, and the Hanging Gardens—one of the Seven Wonders of the Ancient World. Over many centuries two rival populations, the Assyrians and the Babylonians, battled for supremacy in Mesopotamia. Eventually the Assyrian Empire would be eclipsed by the kings of Babylon, whose sovereignty also waxed and waned over the centuries. Legends of a great cataclysm or flood come from Babylonian sources. Evidence for these earth changes exist at the port city of Ur, which today lies buried in sand far from any coastal shore.

Babylon went from a small town to a bustling city-state around 1900 BCE. A hundred years later, the famous lawgiver Hammurabi made it the capital of his imperial kingdom and elevated the city's god, Marduk, to national god status. Hammurabi's most memorable achievement was his law code, justly famous as the earliest uniform written laws and insightfully humane and rational in conception. The series of minutely detailed laws are believed to be the first law codes in the world, predating the Ten Commandments by nearly 1,000 years. Hammurabi's success as a ruler established the city as a political center for the nation of Babylonia. Over the centuries new dynasties ruled the city including the Assyrians, but it wasn't until King Nebuchadnezzar (604-562 BCE) completely remodeled the city and erected his massive palace, the Hanging Gardens, an improved ziggurat, and the Temple of Marduk, that Babylon reached its zenith. It was at this time that the Babylonians captured Jerusalem, destroyed the temple, and took the Jews into exile. Babylon has passed into Western tradition as a symbol of oppression and iniquity, and its fate of destruction has served to remind all secular authority of the abusive nature of power.

**Assyrian Winged Beast**
Babylon, IRAQ

## The Hanging Gardens of Babylon, the Tower of Babel and the Ishtar Gate are legendary reminders of the ancient world's most famous metropolis.

Enclosed within massive walls, the inner city of neo-Babylon housed the city's royal and sacred buildings, and served as the center of Nebuchadnezzar's empire. Most of the monumental buildings lined a major avenue called the Processional Way, which stretched southward from the lofty Ishtar Gate directly to the inner city. Nearly a half-mile (1 km) farther south along the Processional Way are two adjacent plazas containing the city ziggurat and the Temple of Marduk. The ziggurat was characteristically Mesopotamian and is presumed to be the prototype for the Tower of Babel. The Temple dedicated to Marduk, whom the Greeks called Bel, also contained shrines devoted to other gods. Greek historians of the day reported that the worship of Marduk required more than two tons of imported frankincense each year, while the statue and other aspects of the Marduk cult consumed more than 20 tons (18,140 kg) of gold.

▲ The worship of Marduk was a primary duty to all priests of Babylon.

Babylon must have seemed like an earthly paradise to all who paid a visit. The Hanging Gardens were built by Nebuchadnezzar for one of his wives, daughter of the King of Medes, who, unaccustomed to the hot sun and dust of Babylon, longed for the green hills of her childhood. The original Tower of Babel was reported to have been taller than the Great Pyramid in Egypt, and built at a time when there was a common language among all people. Babylon is where Alexander the Great died in 323 BCE of a fever, just one week shy of his 33rd birthday. The cause of death remains a matter of controversy because some researchers believe he was poisoned. Others say he died from complications stemming from an insect bite, contaminated water, or a wound gone septic.

### Getting to Babylon

The ruins of Babylon reside along the banks of the Euphrates River, six miles (10 km) north from the modern town of Al-Hillah. The site is 55 miles (90 km) due south of the Iraqi capital, Baghdad.

### IRAQ TRAVEL ADVISORY

In March 2003, coalition forces led by the United States executed a concerted ground and air attack on Iraq. This was a follow-up to the first Gulf War in which Saddam Hussein managed to retain his Iraqi dictatorship. During both wars, bombs and gunfire damaged archaeological sites, especially in southern Iraq.

People of most Western countries, including those of the United States, are restricted from travel in Iraq. There is anti-American and anti-British sentiment in Iraq for the harm done to the buildings and its people. If one can get in, it is advisable to keep a very low profile in Iraq, even to the point of dressing in local clothes.

# ISRAEL

I srael is a land of contrasts and contradictions. It is an ancient land of enormous historical significance yet remains a divided and embattled country. It is one of the most hotly disputed territories on earth yet is considered one of the most sacred. The Holy Land contains spiritual sites to three major world religions: Judaism, Christianity, and Islam. The age-old conflict between Arab and Jew, East and West, Israeli and Palestinian, remain as intense as ever, despite several recent peace treaties aimed at diffusing tensions. Everlastingly steeped in history of biblical proportions, travel through Israel is like a walk through time. Names like Bethlehem, Jericho, Jerusalem, Masada, and Nazareth seem rather odd on modern highway signs. But there they are, along with international religious tourists seeking out the sacred destinations of their faith.

## Jericho and the Dead Sea Caves

In a dry and desolate region in the Judaean desert of Israel lay some of the most important archaeological sites in the world. The town of Jericho is the earliest known continuously inhabited settlement on earth, and is a treasure-trove of artifacts. Close to Jericho are a series of caverns, known as the Dead Sea Caves, which produced some remarkable ancient documents. This region north and west of the Dead Sea was significant because over many centuries the Judaean desert was a safe haven for all kinds of religious zealots, political refugees, and prophets. This sparsely populated area and inhospitable environment provided an atmosphere conducive for religious experience. Furthermore, the rough terrain allowed dissidents who required anonymity to remain elusive to the authorities.

The ancient Jericho ruins lay more than a mile (2 km) south of the modern settlement of Jericho, together regarded as the world's oldest inhabited village. According to the Bible, it is here where Joshua "blew his horn, and the walls fell down." Through the centuries Jericho has been razed many times, and on each occasion rebuilt on top of the rubble. Archaeologists have uncovered evidence of at least 21 previous civilizations. Digging from the ancient Jericho rubble mound can be like opening a time capsule. An impressive find was the remains of a Hasmonean (Jewish religious group) Palace that contained Hellenistic elements from Greek influence, combined with Jewish practices, including ritual baths for the High Priests so they could maintain personal purity in line with the law of Moses. The current Jericho rubble mound at its highest point is 45 feet (13.5 m) above the road.

A Roman Legion determined to quash the First Revolt of the Jews captured Jericho around 68 CE. Jerusalem was next, then Qumran on the Dead Sea where the village priests scrambled to hide their sacred texts in nearby caves. Fearing the Romans

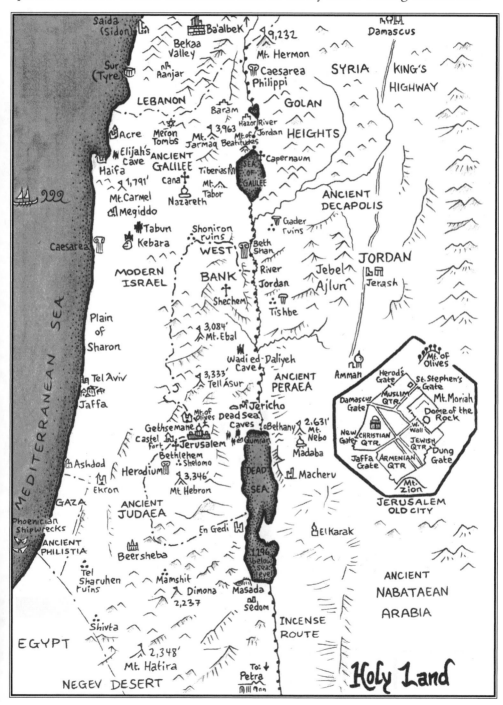

would destroy the last remaining copies of the Bible, this small group of ancient Israelites hid hundreds of parchment scrolls in the caves within the shear desert cliffs. The texts, now known as the Dead Sea Scrolls, almost certainly represent the beliefs and practices of the Essenes—one of several Jewish religious groups existing at the time.

**The unearthing of 11,000-year-old skulls at Jericho now predate the earliest civilizations of Mesopotamia, making this site one of the oldest settlements on earth. Discovered close to Jericho, the Dead Sea Scrolls are described as the most important archaeological find of the 20th century.**

Just after World War II, a young Arab shepherd climbed into a Judaean cave and stumbled upon the first of the Dead Sea Scrolls. In all, there were eleven caves and nearly 800 manuscripts discovered between 1947 and 1956. Half of all recovered texts were duplicates written in three languages: Hebrew, Aramaic, and Greek. Taking duplication into account, about 400 texts are distinct compositions. Carbon dating shows that the scrolls were written between the last two or three centuries BCE and the first century CE, written in ink on the hairy side of leather pieces and sewn together with flaxen threads.

The Dead Sea Scrolls are believed to have come from the monastery of the Essenes in the town of Khirbet Qumran. The Essenes of Qumran were a strict religious sect of pacifist Jews who did not maintain contact with the Temple in Jerusalem. Instead, this secretive sect of all males followed their own interpretation of the Torah (Law of Moses) and lived in communal seclusion. It is believed that John the Baptist, and possibly Jesus, spent time with the Essenes, but did not espouse their beliefs. The scrolls mention nothing of Jesus or John the Baptist, yet taken together with Essene belief show similar parallels with Judaism. Scholars divide the Dead Sea Scroll content into three categories: writings already known before their discovery; original compositions purposely omitted from Jewish and Christian Bibles; and the "Sectarian Dead Sea Scrolls" which consist of a mixture of poetic and legal works, as well as pieces of Bible interpretation and narrative. The Sectarian texts describe the various sects, or groups of people during their time. In short, the Dead Sea Scrolls confirm the history and most of the events described in the first five books of the Bible's Old Testament.

### Getting to Jericho and the Dead Sea Caves

Jericho, also called Ariha, is located in Palestine and may be closed to travel from Israel, depending on current relations between the two volatile nations. The Dead Sea Caves are easily accessible as a day trip from Jerusalem. The Arab and Egged public buses stop along the road at Qumran, also called Khirbet. It is a hot climb up to the caves, so bring plenty of drinking water. If the border is open, regular bus departures leave from Jerusalem daily and drop passengers off in the modern town of Jericho, which lies about 10 miles (16 km) from the Dead Sea. After passing the Dead Sea—the lowest point on earth at 1,266 feet (386 m) below sea level—the bus continues on to Tiberias in the north.

## Jerusalem

The old walled city of Jerusalem is the most hotly contested archaeological site in the world. This sacred city is home to three of the oldest and most influential religions in the world: Judaism, Christianity, and Islam—all of whom have an interest in preserving their heritage. Jerusalem displays tremendous contrast between ancient and modern and has a multicultural, multiethnic population. The ancient city is surrounded by walls and has four quarters: Jewish, Christian, Armenian, and Muslim. When exactly Jerusalem came into existence, is reason for debate. Some researchers believe the town did not exist in the time of David because of scant evidence. Yet, there are letters from the Egyptian Pharaoh Akhunaton in the 14th century BCE that refer to the town of "Urusalim." Making matters more complicated for archaeologists is the Temple Mount atop ancient Mount Moriah. Atop the Temple Mount, once known as the City of David, is the oldest inhabited part of the city and cannot be excavated. All these clues suggest that Jerusalem is as old as the Bible suggests.

Based on biblical accounts, the traditional view of Jerusalem implies that at the time of David (1,000 BCE) Jerusalem was a small, well-fortified village occupied by the Canaanite Jebusites and the center of an independent city-state. According to biblical stories in Samuel, Kings and Chronicles, this small town was captured by King David, who expelled the Jebusites and transformed Jerusalem into the capital of the United Monarchy of Israel. David's son and successor, King Solomon, enlarged the town and built several palaces and a grandiose temple. King Solomon's temple was the First Temple for the Jews. The Bible describes Jerusalem as a beautiful city during King Solomon's rule —the capital of a large and wealthy empire.

Moses was next on the scene, leading a band of Jews out of Egypt to the Promised Land. From the Great Pyramid, Moses supposedly carried out the Ark of the Covenant along with the bones of Joseph (famous for his multi-color coat), and eventually deposited the items in the Jewish Holy of Holies, or King Solomon's

▲ The Islamic Noble Sanctuary atop the Temple Mount in Jerusalem.

Temple. The plans and drawings are so complete that King Solomon's Temple could be rebuilt today if there was enough money and craftsmen. Little doubt remains that in 586 BCE the Babylonians devastated Jerusalem and destroyed the First Temple. The Jews were taken into exile in Babylon, not to return to Jerusalem until many years later. The Western Wall (formerly called the Wailing Wall) is sacred to the Jews as being the site of the First Temple built by King Solomon. The blocks on the Western Wall (the *Kotel* in Hebrew) were actually constructed by Herod the Great in 20 BCE, yet the Second Temple was destroyed by the Romans in 70 CE after the First Revolt by the Jews. Judaism's holiest site, whose only exposed remnant is the Western Wall, is a 10-minute walk from the Stations of the Cross where Jesus is said to have walked to his crucifixion.

▲ The Old City of Jerusalem is surrounded by high walls.

Atop the Western Wall is the Temple Mount, upon which stands the Dome of the Rock, the third holiest mosque in Islam. The Dome is the center of *Haram esh-Sharif*, which means "The Noble Sanctuary" in Arabic. The shimmering gold Dome of the Rock is one of the oldest Islamic buildings in the world, dating back to the seventh century. The octagonal walls are covered inside and out in brilliant blue, surrounded with large Arabic quotations from the Koran, the Islamic holy book. The Sacred Rock inside the Dome of the Rock is where Abraham was supposed to have offered his son Isaac to God, and where Mohammed is said to have ascended to heaven on his horse, Borek. Below the Temple Mount are numerous secret chambers and caves, one of which supposedly held the sacred Ark of the Covenant.

**Despite all the times it has been sacked by invaders, the name Jerusalem ironically means "City of Peace." Jerusalem is the heart of the Holy Land and is a sacred city to Jews, Muslims, Christians, and the Ba'hai faith.**

Christians believe Jerusalem was the site of Jesus Christ's last days as a living prophet and son of God. At the age of 33, Jesus was convicted by the Romans for heresy and sent to his death by crucifixion. Christian pilgrims can follow the Via Dolorosa, the traditional route followed by Jesus as he carried his cross to the Calvary. The faithful follow along the sacred trail to the 14 Stations of the Cross where Jesus was put on trial, was crucified, where his resurrection took place, and where he rose to heaven. The Christian Quarter of the Old City centers around the Church of the Holy Sepulchre, which is generally agreed to be the place where Jesus was crucified, buried and resurrected. Thus, the three great Western monotheistic religions are interwoven into the fabric of the city, each revering and making pilgrimage to its various holy sites.

### Getting to Jerusalem

Jerusalem is a major city and capital of Israel and easily reached by train or bus from all parts of the country. Most international visitors arrive via the Ben Gurion Airport in Tel Aviv, less than an hour drive to Jerusalem. Highway No. 1 connects Tel Aviv and Jerusalem, passing the historic Castel Crusader fortress before entering Jerusalem. The New City of Jerusalem is a crossroads for the Egged and Arab bus networks, making the city a convenient base for exploring the rest of Israel.

# Masada

In a barren desert with few resources, the Masada mesa contains the ruins of a prosperous city that fell to the Romans. The site has long been regarded as a symbol for Jewish perseverance through adversity. Masada is best known as a zealot outpost and last refuge to Jewish rebels after a revolt against Rome. In 66 CE, about 1,000 rebels recaptured Masada and Jerusalem from the Romans in a skirmish called the First Revolt. Rome struck back fiercely and quashed the rebellion in 70 CE, destroying the temple in Jerusalem and then advancing on other Judean cities of resistance. Masada became the last Jewish stronghold three years later. With the fortress as their base, the rebels waged guerrilla warfare against the occupying Romans for several years. When the rebels realized in 74 CE that there was little hope of either winning or holding out against the Roman army, they chose to kill themselves rather than surrender and become wretched slaves. When defeat was inevitable, the 967 men, women, and children of Masada decided to die by their own swords rather than submit to Roman slavery. Only seven women and children survived by hiding in a cave.

The only reason Masada held up so long against the superior Roman army, according to the Roman historian Josephus, is because of its strategic natural surroundings. Rising 1,400 feet (420 m) above the Dead Sea, this desert fortress was easily defended from the mesa top against a much stronger army because there was no easy entrance. It wasn't until the imperial Roman army built an enormous land bridge across a natural spur that they could penetrate the walls. By the time the Romans entered the city, they were surprised to find no resistance and all but a very few already dead. When Josephus discusses Masada he describes the Jewish rebels as the "Sicarii." The Romans were quite impressed with the determination of their enemy.

**Masada is used today as a symbol for all those who cherish freedom. The modern State of Israel declares an oath: "Masada shall not fall again."**

Towering above the surrounding desert on the western coast of the Dead Sea, Masada is the most dramatic archaeological site in Israel in both location and its role in Jewish history. Besides being the last holdout of Jewish rebels against the Roman Empire, Masada had been a storehouse of ancient texts and artifacts predating the Roman occupation. Recently uncovered hidden documents, much like the Dead Sea Scrolls found near Qumran, reveal much about life in biblical times. The texts, uncovered by Masada excavators between 1963 and 1965, describe much of the same subject matter as the Dead Sea Scrolls, yet were produced by a different religious sect and are distinct for that reason. Originally Masada was built as a royal palace for Jewish Kings, including Herod the Great, who died in 4 BCE. Herod's throne was passed on to his three sons who divided the empire. The one son in charge of Judea, which included Masada, was overthrown by Rome, who then appointed Pontius Pilate for overseeing the region. Pontius Pilate was responsible for sentencing and executing Jesus. Most of the ruins of Masada are from Herod's luxurious palace, which commands a spectacular view of the surrounding desert.

### Getting to Masada

Masada is about 60 miles (97 km) south of Jerusalem and is a two-hour bus ride along the west shore of the Dead Sea. Buses access Masada from most Israeli cities and stop at the Visitor's Center at the base of the mesa where there is a pleasant youth hostel. Visitors can hike a moderate trail or take a cable car up to the plateau. The best times to view the ancient city and surrounding area is at sunrise and sunset. From the beginning of April until the end of October there is a Masada Sound and Light Show held on Tuesdays and Thursdays.

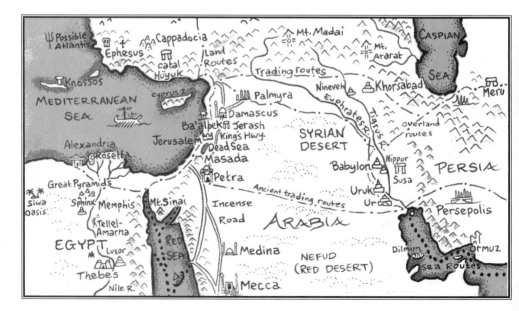

# JORDAN

At the dawn of civilization the nation known today as Jordan was a critical cross-roads for traders, travelers, and armies. Its strategic location was highly prized, resulting in outsiders from the Romans, to Crusading Christians, and finally to Islamic leaders taking a turn at governing. Early on, when Abraham departed Egypt, the Jordan Valley was a fixed and vital settlement. Centuries' later, in 1,280 BCE, the Israelites, led by Moses, also left Egypt on their famous exodus. Denied access along the King's Highway (then, a nation called Edom), Moses and his band spent the next 40 years in and around the harsh Jordanian desert before reaching the Promised Land.

## Petra

The main trading route through Jordan, called the Incense Road in Greco-Roman times, was a major exchange of Middle Eastern wealth. The route was a critical connection between Egypt, the Saudi Peninsula, and the Syrian Desert to the north. The principle crossroad in antiquity was a successful trading city called Petra. Carved into a rose-red canyon by the ancient Nabataeans in the third century BCE, Petra is an archaeological treasure-trove from the glamorous age of caravan travel. The Nabataeans commanded the trade route from Damascus to Arabia, and became spectacularly prosperous through the passing of silk, frankincense, spice, and slave caravans.

As the wealthy capital of the Nabataeans, Petra attracted artist and invader alike. The finest stone workers of the age added their skills in creating Petra. The city was strategically set in a rocky gorge, entered only by a narrow and easily defended pass through barren hills. Inside the fortifications, the Nabataeans carved their elaborate buildings and tombs directly out of the solid rock. For centuries the city prospered without being successfully invaded. However, just before the birth of Christ, the Romans captured the city and added their own style of art and architecture. Eventually new land routes and sea traffic made Petra's position obsolete, and the city was abandoned and forgotten for over 1,000 years. It was rediscovered in 1812 by a Swiss explorer named Johann Burckhardt who gained access by disguising himself as an Arab. He had heard rumors of a fantastic city hidden in a valley behind the Wadi Musa (Valley of Moses), and bribed a Bedouin to take him there. The central city was not uncovered and thoroughly explored until 1958.

**Temples, courts, dwellings and tombs were carved right out of the colorful sandstone cliffs. The Bible refers to Petra as "a rose-red city half as old as time."**

Most of the temples and tombs that have survived at Petra were hewn into the rock-face from top to bottom. There are several hundred of them, ranging in size from tiny

▲ The so-called "Treasury Building" in Petra was actually carved out of the living stone as a tomb for wealthy nobles, and perhaps also used as a temple.

to massive. In the hills surrounding Petra are a number of sanctuaries known as the "high places." Many feature large altars of sacrifice and carved stones depicting the royal animal deity named Dushara, and the common people's deity called Al-Uzza. These sanctuaries feature niches for lamps and benches where little understood rituals took place. Virtually everything at Petra was carved directly out of the living rock. In places, the different layers of stone give the appearance of silk or marble. The soft sandstone can easily be chipped away and crumbled in the hand. Fortunately, Jordan has virtually no rain, otherwise the monuments would have crumbled away long ago.

Today, Petra is the number one attraction in Jordan, even though it is far from any major city. Getting to Petra is half the fun because the surrounding landscape, such as Wadi Rum, is absolutely breathtaking. Entering the incredibly narrow mile-long (2 km) gorge called the Siq has all the awe-inspiring qualities of an Indiana Jones movie. The first building encountered is the elegantly sculptured *Khazneh* (Treasury), considered Petra's finest ruin. A little farther on the city proper has palaces, temples, tombs, storerooms, stables, and even some freestanding buildings. Exceptional views of the landscape and more ruins can be gained by climbing up to the monastery, Crusader Fort, Umm al-Biyrar, and the high places of sacrifice. Each of these climbs requires at least a half-day, so plan to spend a few days or even a week at Petra.

## Getting to Petra

People intending to spend more than a day at the ruins usually stay in the village of Wadi Musa, two miles (3 km) uphill from the site entrance. Bus tours and service taxis frequently travel the route from the Jordan capital Amman to Wadi Musa. Most of the tours are round-trip, returning tourists to their hotels in Amman on the same day. Tour groups also leave from Elat, Israel, or Aqaba, Jordan, and arrive back the same day.

# LEBANON

**B**efore the seemingly endless civil war that engulfed the nation in the 1980's and 1990's, Lebanon was once a major tourist destination and quite a wealthy country. The capital city Beirut was considered the Paris of the Middle East before fighting broke out between Muslim and Christian countrymen in the mid-70's. Lebanon has since rebounded, but it is still considered unsafe for travel by people of the United States and some European countries. Although a small country, Lebanon is packed with historical and religious sites. Most popular are the many fine Crusader castles, particularly the one at Sidon. The impressive ruins at Byblos are quite famous, likely spawning the derivative word "Bible."

## Ba'albek

Snuggled deep within the scenic Beqa'a Valley is an age-old acropolis devoted to, at different times, a wide variety of gods and goddesses. It was originally dedicated to Semitic divinities: El; Ba'al; and his goddess partner Astarte, whose cult involved prostitution and sacred orgies. Next came the Greek temples of Zeus, Aphrodite, and Hermes. The Romans built right on top of the Greek locations but changed the deity names to Jupiter, Venus, and Mercury. Biblical sources attribute the founding of Ba'albek to Cain after his banishment by Jehovah. The three Roman temples are the only to survive largely intact, and the Venus monument is regarded the most complete Roman temple in the world.

In times of antiquity, large numbers of pilgrims came from Mesopotamia and the Nile Valley to visit the legendary Ba'al–Astarte complex and its oracle. The Bible mentions Ba'albek in the Book of Kings. Underneath the temple complex is a vast network of underground tunnels, which were likely intended to provide shelter for the multitudes of pilgrims. Ancient Arab writings tell

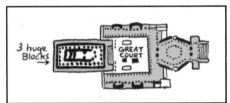

▲ An overview of the entire temple complex, including the location of the Trilithon Blocks.

that the Temples of Ba'al–Astarte were constructed a short time after the Great Flood. According to legend, the structures were built at the order of the renowned King Nimrod and a "tribe of giants."

The acropolis of Ba'albek, with its massive temples and imposing ruins, is one of the most enigmatic sites in the world. The Roman sanctuaries were located upon earlier Greek temples, and those were built upon much older Semitic ruins. While the Roman and Greek architectural wonders do not pose archaeological problems, the earlier Semitic ruins certainly do. Most confounding is the enclosure wall called the Trilithon, composed of three hewn blocks of stone each weighing more than 750 tons (680,000 kg)!

## The Trilithon Blocks at Ba'albek are the largest cut and fitted stones in the world.

▲ The Roman ruins dominate Ba'albek.

The Trilithon wall is an amazing feat of construction. The colossal blocks of stone were raised 22 feet (6.6 m) above slightly smaller blocks. There is no crane in the modern world that can lift even half the weight of these Trilithon stones. Furthermore, not even a knife blade can be inserted between these gigantic blocks because they are so expertly fitted together. Another stone called *Hadjar el Gouble,* Arabic for "Stone of the South," is in a nearby quarry and is even larger than the Trilithon stones. The Stone of the South is 13 by 13 feet (4 m) and nearly 70 feet (21 m) long, and is estimated to weigh at least 1,000 tons (907,000 kg)! It is the largest hewn stone in the world.

Although Ba'albek contains a large amount of Roman ruins, it is very unlikely the Romans or the Greeks constructed the Trilithon, but merely 'piggybacked' on an already sacred site as is common worldwide. The Greeks called the site "Heliopolis," which means "Sun Temple" or "Sun City," yet this prehistoric Sun Temple was built on the ruins of a much older Semitic structure. The massive platform was constructed by an ancient race of highly sophisticated builders, who, it has been suggested, employed a sort of sound harmonics to render the stones weightless in order to set them into place.

### Getting to Ba'albek

Ba'albek is located 44 miles (71 km) northeast of Beirut. The small town of the same name near the ruins of Ba'albek has a population of about 10,000, and contains amenities for the traveler, including lodging and food. Until internal turmoil settles down in Lebanon, the ruins of Ba'albek are considered inaccessible. At present the traveler risks kidnapping or death by venturing into Lebanon.

# SAUDI ARABIA

H istorically, Saudi Arabia was part of the ancient frankincense caravan route that carried slaves and culture from the Horn of Africa and Yemen into the Middle East and beyond. The present government of Saudi Arabia is an autocratic monarchy ruled by a single king. The country comprises most of the Arabian Peninsula, which is largely barren desert and one of the hottest places on earth. The kingdom is so dry that it does not contain a single river or permanent lake. However, Saudi Arabia is an oil-rich country, and as such is very wealthy and expensive to travel within.

## Mecca and Medina

In the early 600's CE, when the soon-to-be-prophet Mohammed lived in Mecca as a trader, the city was a small but crowded village of about 3,000 people. Mecca resides in a forbiddingly dry and sandy valley surrounded by a double range of desolate and treeless hills. The only thing that made life possible here was the well of Zamzam in the town square. Also in the middle of town was the Kaba, a boxlike shrine that contains a sacred black meteorite. The Kaba in the heart of Mecca would become the holiest place in the world to followers of the new Islamic religion. Today the Grand Mosque in Mecca attracts untold millions to behold the sacred Kaba, and be present in the city where Mohammed received his revelations from God. According to Mohammed's command, all Muslim prayers worldwide must be directed toward Mecca. It is estimated that one billion Muslim faithfuls turn towards the Grand Mosque in prayer five times daily.

Mohammed moved his ministry to Medina soon after his revelations began in 610 CE. The principle revelations were conveyed to Mohammed through the archangel Gabriel. These visions continued with him up until his death in Medina in 632. By that time, Islam had swept aside all other religions on the Arabian Peninsula. In a century after the Prophet's death, the Arabs ruled a vast empire stretching from Spain to India and north into Russia. Medina became the new administrative center for the expanding Muslim empire. As the adopted capital and city where Allah's word spread through Mohammed, Medina is second only to Mecca as a pilgrimage city. Mohammed is buried in Medina's Mosque of the Prophet.

**Mecca and nearby Medina are the most visited pilgrimage sites in the world, and the ultimate goal for one billion believers in Islam.**

At the time of the Hajj pilgrimage, which occurs once a year by the lunar calendar, as many as 4 million gather for a period of about a week. In this phenomenal event, Muslims of every race, country, and social status meet in one place with the sole purpose to worship God, ask for forgiveness, and bond with their brethren. During Hajj the rich and poor cannot be distinguished. All wear the same long robes called *ihram*. All Muslims who are physically and financially able must attempt at least one Hajj in their lifetimes. By doing so, Muslims complete their faith, all the while praying and repenting for past sins. The pilgrims circle the Kaba, drink from the miraculous well of Zamzam, pray in white tents on the Plain of Mina, then return to the Kaba for one incredible moment when thousands of devotees touch their forehead to the ground in awe of Allah, then shout "Allah-Hu Akbar" in unison. This chant, meaning "Allah is greater than anything," reverberates throughout Mecca and can be heard from miles away. At the end of the pilgrimage, Muslims celebrate the Eid al Udha, or the Festival of Sacrifice, which pays homage to Abraham's willingness to sacrifice his son. To symbolize the Eid, Muslims around the world sacrifice an animal, distributing the meat to poor people and family members in thanks for the coming blessings of the year.

▲ Islamic faithfuls circle the ultra-holy *Kaba*, located at the heart of the Grand Mosque in Mecca.

The rituals of Hajj date back to the prophet Abraham, considered the father of all three major Western religions — Judaism, Christianity, and Islam. Abraham migrated from Mesopotamia to Mecca, where he reconstructed the *Kaba*, meaning the House of God. Almost every act performed during the Hajj relates analogously to the prophetic history of Abraham and his wife Hagar during their time in Mecca. On the Plains of Arafat pilgrims gather small stones to throw at three pillars, symbols of the three devils who tempted Abraham. It was Abraham and his son Ishmael who first circled the Kaba seven times and began to preach a pilgrimage of salvation. Thus, the Hajj is known as the pilgrimage of purification, following a tradition Abraham started thousands of years ago.

### Getting to Mecca and Medina

The two holiest sites of Islam—Mecca and Medina—are strictly off-limits to non-Muslims. Steep fines are imposed on those arriving at the Mecca and Medina checkpoints without the proper paperwork. All pilgrims coming to the Kingdom must have special visas declaring their religious status in Arabic. Medina is located 275 miles (445 km) north of Mecca. Tourist visas are not available for travel in Saudi Arabia, and visas of other sorts are difficult to obtain. Pilgrims wishing to visit Saudi Arabia's holy cities must arrange a visitor's visa from someone already in the country who can verify the visitor's faith.

# TUNISIA

The long and tantalizing story of this North African country starts with the first wandering tribes. Hardly changed throughout the ages are the nomadic Berbers, a people one generation removed from Neolithic times. The Berbers were the first white settlers in North Africa, migrating from the Middle East as early as 7,000 BCE. Like the precursors of civilization in Mesopotamia, these tribesmen were herders of sheep and tillers of the soil. The name Berber is derived from the Greek word for "barbarian," yet it was these people who survived wave after wave of invading forces and managed to retain their customs of old.

# Carthage

Perhaps the most famous inhabitants of Tunisia were the Punic people of ancient Carthage. The city of Carthage was founded in 813 BCE by the seafaring Phoenicians, a Semitic-speaking people who had long inhabited several cities along the coast of modern Lebanon. They became a rising sea power in the ancient world, and many centuries later would clash with the Romans over control of the sea-lanes and colonies of the Western Mediterranean. So brutal was Rome's conquest after the Punic Wars that the Roman army salted the ground so the Carthaginians could never return to their capital. Before, during, and after their wars with Rome, Phoenician traders traversed all parts of the Mediterranean and ventured into the Atlantic. They were the first explorers to sail around the whole of Africa, and quite possibly to North and South America. The Phoenicians' overwhelming cultural achievement was the development of an alphabet, which they passed on to the Greeks sometime in the eighth century BCE. This Phoenician alphabet later evolved into the alphabet we use today.

Two places in the ancient Punic city of Carthage were considered particularly sacred: the Byrsa Hill and the Tophet. The Byrsa Hill overlooks the all-important Punic harbors, as does the Tophet, which was used for human sacrifices. The most elegant temple in Carthage was the Temple of Eshmoun, destroyed with all other Punic monuments on the Byrsa Hill by the conquering Romans. Byrsa Hill was completely remodeled with new structures during the Roman era. Crusaders in 1270 CE added a Christian cathedral and a chapel to Byrsa Hill.

> ### Carthage's Byrsa Hill has long been, and continues to be, an intellectual and religious center—an ongoing testament to its importance.

The Tophet, on the other hand, contained darker energies. The term *Tophet* is known in the Bible as a location of human sacrifice, and here they were performed. Children up to four years old were offered to the supreme deities Baal Hammon and Tanit in exchange for favor in wars, crop yields, or for good health. Tombstones of sacrificed Punic children still occupy the Tophet, including inscriptions bearing magical signs to bring good luck and ward off evil spirits. An enticingly similar human sacrificial stone is located in Chicago, Illinois where enterprising Phoenician copper merchants likely erected a Punic temple. For more information on the "Waubansee Stone," see *Sacred Places North America: 108 Destinations* by Brad Olsen.

The majority of ruins in and around modern Tunis, and elsewhere in Tunisia, are largely Roman. Tunis remained a vital Roman port for many centuries. Relics of ancient Carthage in modern Tunis are the Tophet necropolis, the Antonine Baths (mostly Roman), and portions of Byrsa Hill. Other Punic ruins in Tunisia include: a second century BCE mausoleum at Dougga, a whole excavated city called Kerkouane, as well as excellent Punic relics in the Bardo and Carthage museums.

## *Getting to Carthage*

Ancient Carthage is modern Tunis today, the capital of Tunisia. Flights and ferryboats, most originating from Europe, arrive daily in Tunis. A popular Mediterranean ferry route originates in Sicily, stops in Malta, and carries on to Tunis. Local Tunis buses and taxis access the many sacred sites of ancient Carthage.

# THE FAR EAST

If there is light in the soul,
There will be beauty in the person.
If there is beauty in the person,
There will be harmony in the house.
If there is harmony in the house,
There will be order in the nation.
If there is order in the nation,
There will be peace in the world.
—*Chinese proverb*

THE DRAGON IS A POWERFUL SYMBOL OF THE FAR EAST—one that has been ignorantly banished for centuries as a symbol of evil. Spiritual bureaucracies have endowed this symbol with fear lest it become an innate force for individual identity. The truth, so often disguised in polarity consciousness, is the exact opposite. Ancient Chinese philosophers such as Lao Tzu thought the dragon to be omnipresent and omnipotent—visible in the writhing roots and branches of a tree, a shaft of sunlight in a droplet of water, the craggy rocks of a mountain peak, or the guardian of individuals. To many in the Far East the dragon is Gaia and worshiped as a living aspect of nature. Notable sacred Chinese mountains include the Dragon Jade Snow Mountain, Mount Emei Shan and Yellow Mountain. The dragon lives in these mountains as well as mundane aspects of our lives.

# CHINA AND ITS GREAT WALL

Perhaps the most famous of all Chinese dragons is the Great Wall of China. Nicknamed the "Long Stone Serpent," the wall stretches from Korea, around the Yellow Sea, across the northernmost curve of the Huang River, and all the way out to the far reaches of the Gobi Desert. It extends more than 1,500 miles (2,400 km) in length. It is the world's longest defensive wall, traversing a succession of hilltops across the northern boundaries of the "Middle Kingdom." Construction began in 214 BCE and was extended and maintained for many centuries afterward. The Great Wall was built of stone and brick, filled in with dirt, and watchtowers were added at intervals of about two arrow-shots apart. The Great Wall's most notable distinction is that it is the only human-made object on earth visible from outer space. The cosmic serpent.

China has a long history of opening and shutting its doors to the rest of the world. The Great Wall was erected to keep out the enemy, and, in the last century, the Communists swept into power and expelled all the "Foreign Devils," while usurping minority peoples, such as those from Tibet. As China steams forward at breakneck economic speed, it has opened its doors once again to foreign explorers. Like Marco Polo and countless other Westerners who traveled the Silk Road to the Far East, modern explorers can venture into China for one of the most unique travel experiences on the planet. Filled to the brim with history and humans, the Middle Kingdom is a unique and mystifying travel experience.

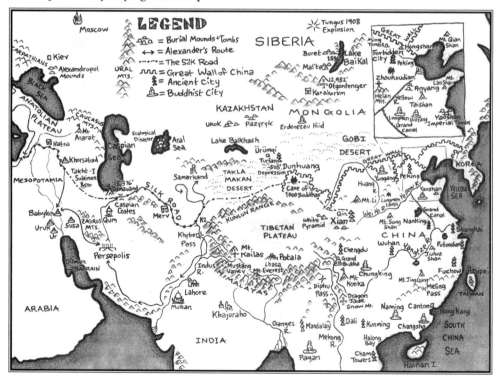

## The Silk Road

For many centuries the Silk Road was the main artery between cultures of the East and West. Extending for more than 5,000 miles (8,000 km), from the Mediterranean Sea to the far reaches of East Asia, its purpose was trade, namely silk, yet its transmission of ideas, religions and treasures made it famous as a route of consciousness. Along this route, Alexander the Great marched on his historic journey to the East, and in the same way, the Chinese approached Western civilization. In just one century, when the Mongols unified the entire Silk Road, a young Italian named Marco Polo passed along this road on his way to join the court of Kublai Khan. He recorded his journeys and brought back tales of its splendor to an astonished Western world.

### The Silk Road is the world's oldest continuously used trade route, connecting China with the Mediterranean.

Without a major sailing fleet for trade, China's primary link with the outside world was the ancient Silk Road. Leaving China, the land route headed south of the Great Wall, with its series of linked forts, and then westward along the northern edge of the Tibetan Plateau. Once the Great Wall ended near Dunhuang, caravans heading west were, in a sense, leaving civilization behind and heading into the great unknown. Dozens of monasteries, desert settlements and sacred caves lined the route, but once into the Gobi Desert to Afghanistan and Persia, travel was difficult and full of bandits. The route crossed harsh, waterless terrain over high desert regions. A southern branch originated in India and became the route over which Buddhism was brought into the Far East. Chinese trading caravans would opt to group together for added security. Silk was the primary item carried along the route because, at the time, only the Chinese knew the technique of extracting silk from silk worms. Because the fabric was in such high demand, the Chinese would in turn import valuable metals, precious stones, jade from Central Asia and pearls from Arabia.

The Silk Road begins and ends where human civilization initially started. In the west was Mesopotamia between the Tigris and Euphrates Rivers, Egypt along the Nile, and various city-states near the eastern Mediterranean Sea. The Far Eastern terminus is located in the home of Chinese culture—where the Yellow River makes its great northward loop, and the Wei River, its main tributary, continues straight west. The age-old city of Xian was the traditional termination point of the Silk Road in China, but sub-routes continued on to eastern China, as well as Vietnam.

From the fertile valleys of eastern China emerged many innovations. Chinese inventions include paper money, the printing press, acupuncture, herbal medicine, the magnetic compass, gunpowder, the decimal system, *T'ai Chi*, various forms of self-defense, and the *feng shui* art of correct planning. A method of divining prophesies comes from

▲ The Great Wall roughly parallels the Silk Road in western China.

the world's oldest oracle, the *I Ching* or "Chinese Book of Changes." These tools of Chinese consciousness slowly and steadily made their way along the Silk Road into world civilization, where they remain today.

### Traveling along the Silk Road

Even though trade on the Silk Road was largely finished in 1368 CE, when the Ming Dynasty shut off China from the rest of the world, portions of it remained as vital trading routes for the newly emerged Muslim states in the Middle East. Today, Iran and Afghanistan prevent travelers from taking the traditional routes through the high desert. Sometimes permission is granted, but the route is still quite volatile and dangerous. Along with warfare and hostile political movements, travelers are also advised to watch out for avalanches and highway robbery. And whether aboard a camel or a Land Rover, the contemporary traveler must be aware of the lack of supplies along the road on the high desert plateaus.

## Xian

The ancient city of Xian lies in the protected Wei River Valley, one of the oldest and most important archaeological sites in China. Impressive tomb excavations in the area include Paleolithic and Neolithic sites. Excavated near Xian are the ruins of a Neolithic settlement more than 6,000 years old. This settlement, called the Banpo village, is one of the best-preserved late-Stone Age sites in China. Xian was the original capital of the Han Dynasty (202 BCE–220 CE), and by the Tang Dynasty (618–917 CE) had become one of the most prosperous cities in the world. The wealth and influence Xian enjoyed was largely due to its strategic location on the main trade route between East and West. As a former entrance to the legendary Silk Road, the city is a veritable treasure trove of priceless objects from the Qin, Tang and Ming dynasties. Xian was a major Far Eastern center of commerce for more than 2,500 years. Attesting to its further importance, workers drilling a well in 1974 accidentally discovered a replica of an army of lifesize terra cotta soldiers, horses and wagons. They are all arranged in battle formation, and carry real swords, spears and crossbows. So far, 8,000 figures have been unearthed and archaeologists are still counting. To protect the holy silence of his tomb, Emperor Qin Shi Huangdi (259-210 BCE) ordered his royal sculptors to duplicate the exact likeness of his top soldiers and bury the statues near his tomb. Emperor Qin also gave the original work order for the Great Wall to be built. His undisclosed tomb has yet to be excavated and is said to contain fabulous treasures.

## Xian is regarded as the cradle of Chinese civilization. It was the capital city of Imperial China through eleven dynasties and a time span of 1,080 years.

About 40 miles (65 km) south and west of Xian are the 16 pyramids at Shensi. The largest of the 16 pyramids, the "White Pyramid," or "Great Pyramid of China" is more than twice the height of the Great Pyramid in Egypt, and is just over twice the base perimeter, giving it twice the mass. The White Pyramid was built with the exact same angle of elevation, the same four sides, and compass orientations as the Egyptian Great Pyramid. The U.S. Air Force originally captured the 16 pyramids on film during surveillance of China during World War II. The pyramids loosely encircle the ancient walled city of Xian, where very old settlements and the terra cotta soldiers have been uncovered. For unknown reasons, the White Pyramid is in a highly restricted military zone and few people have ever seen it. The Chinese government even denies its very existence! One of the World War II pilots who first sighted it described it as "shimmering white ... with a large piece of precious gem-like material as its capstone." The colossal size of the White Pyramid, estimated at 1,000 feet (300 m) in height, makes it by far the largest pyramid in the world. It is likely that the Great Pyramid of China is located at a key intersection point of ley lines, which form part of an ancient network of pyramids worldwide built to tap the earth's natural energies. The White Pyramid and others in the surrounding valleys may have been arranged to mirror the shapes of certain constellations in the night sky. All the pyramids are extremely old; even the oldest known records call them ancient.

### Getting to Xian

Today, Xian enjoys an excellent reputation as one of China's premiere tourist attractions. The Qing Dynasty walls still surround the city center. As the capital of Shaanxi Province, Xian continues to be an influential locale and is serviced by many national and international flights, central train routes and bus lines from all over the country. Unfortunately, the White Pyramid is off-limits on a top-secret military base.

▲ Pagoda towers scatter across central China.

# Cave of a Thousand Buddhas

Just inside the Great Wall of China along the ancient Silk Road is one of the most remarkable Chinese sacred sites of antiquity. Located in the Gobi Desert town of Dunhuang, this site is a hive of more than 460 grottoes of varying sizes, carved directly into the soft sandstone cliffs. Devout Buddhist monks inhabited the caves a long time ago, starting in 366 CE when a lone monk started carving the first of many caves. Other monks followed and they carved a honeycomb pattern of chambers, interconnected by ladders and walkways. The caves contain some of the finest Buddhist sculptures and wall paintings in all of China. Many of the caves carved from the cliff-face contain multiple levels connected by wooden balconies. The most notable cave is a mile-wide temple called the "Cave of a Thousand Buddhas."

Dunhuang flourished as a center of Buddhist culture for many centuries. While other towns along the Silk Road were also graced with similar cave clusters, including massive temples and relief statues of the Buddha over 100 feet (30 m) tall, what made Dunhuang extra special was the legend of a lost library. The rumors of an ancient archive kept inside the Cave of a Thousand Buddhas had apparently been forgotten for almost 1,000 years. These ancient texts were supposedly stored in a sealed room guarded by a lone, self-appointed monk. Rumors of this lost library became fact in the late winter of 1907 when Anglo-Hungarian explorer Marc Aurel Stein trekked 3,000 miles (4,830 km) along the Silk Road to Dunhuang. Stein convinced the lone monk to open the storeroom and what he discovered surely surpassed all expectations. A hoard of Buddhist manuscripts, paintings, books and other writing were discovered in the hidden room. The multi-lingual manuscripts, including an undecipherable script, remained in excellent condition after 800 years, preserved in a pristine state by the dry desert air.

### The Cave of a Thousand Buddhas was the most important repository of ancient Buddhist and Chinese texts to survive.

The most significant finds at the Cave of a Thousand Buddhas were ancient Chinese governmental records, along with irreplaceable translations and transcriptions of early Buddhist texts. Some of the earliest texts date from the fifth century CE and their origin can be traced all the way back to India. The most significant discovery was the world's oldest known printed text, a copy of the Buddhist *Diamond Sutra*, a work dated 868 CE —well over five centuries before Gutenberg printed his first Bible in Europe. The majority of books, many over a thousand years old, record the former days of greatness when China was among the most vital empires in the world. Imperialist Great Britain sent Sir Aurel Stein to acquire the manuscripts. Stein and French scholar Paul Pelliot secured a majority of the texts for a pittance from Abbot Wang, a caretaker in dire need of funds to restore the caves. Most of these works today are part of the Stein Collection in London's British Museum.

## Getting to the Cave of a Thousand Buddhas

The Cave of a Thousand Buddhas is located just outside the town of Dunhuang, also spelled "Tunhuang." Early morning buses leave daily for the caves, which close in the early afternoon. Regular flights to Dunhuang from Lanzhou via Jiuqian are available. The overland bus or train ride to this remote province is grueling travel, but rewarding in many ways. Besides being off the beaten track, the caves are dramatically situated in the Flaming Hills. Not too far from the caves is the Turfan Depression, an inhospitable basin that sinks 505 feet (200 m) below sea level. Most travelers opt to visit the caves on their way to the interesting desert town of Turpan, some 440 miles (720 km) away.

# The Forbidden City

The original location for a Forbidden City was established sometime in the 11th century during the Song Dynasty. When Genghis Khan and his Mongol army stormed into northern China around 1210 CE, they would have recognized an earlier royal compound. Although nothing remains of the first settlement, it is believed the Mongols established their own imperial court on the exact location of the older royal city. Genghis Khan's grandson Kublai Khan united China in 1276, and so began the Yuan Dynasty. The Mongols were the first to establish the northern capital of Da Du (*Khanbaliq*), later renamed Peking, a place close to their Mongolian homeland. It was during the reign of Kublai Khan when the Venetian traveler Marco Polo made his epic journey along the Silk Road and returned to Italy with a glowing account of the Mongol capital. The indigenous and numerically dominant Ming Dynasty eventually drove the Mongols from China. After the Mongol capital Da Du was destroyed, the Ming emperor moved his capital to Nanjing, only to return to Peking a few decades later. Chinese culture flourished during the Ming Dynasty (1368-1644) and the new capital experienced a spectacular building boom.

Starting from scratch, the Ming emperor Yong Le planned out the entire city of Peking in a fashion of squares and rectangles. The imperial city Yong Le created has a dream-like air, with a functionality seen in very few large cities. But the crowning achievement was a perfectly symmetrical city within the scope of a much larger city. The center of the metropolis was the emperor's own Forbidden City. Legend shrouds the story of how Ming emperor Yong Le came to plan his imperial city. One version relates a mysterious astrologer, possibly Tibetan, appearing shortly after Yong Le was crowned emperor. This stranger handed him a sealed package containing the complete plans for an as-yet constructed imperial city. Another story tells of how, as a young child, his Buddhist teacher instilled theory and concept of imperial city design unto him. This teacher remained a trusted advisor to the emperor for many years, and said the city design ideas came to him from his dreams. One way or another, Yong Le was a determined emperor who designed a massive city on a strict north-south, east-west basis. At its center was the Forbidden City — a geometric microcosm of a larger whole.

**The Ming design was that of two walled cities: one in the north, which was square, and the other in the south, which was rectangular. The Forbidden City incorporated symmetry and harmony from the larger city as auspicious residence for the Son of Heaven.**

Down to the minutest detail, the Forbidden City was designed to be in perfect symmetry with itself. If created correctly, the Chinese believed their palaces would confer health and good fortune upon all who entered. This is the art of *feng shui*, or correct planning, where the proper alignment of buildings and interior objects, within their natural setting, will contribute to auspicious happenings. Instruction as to proper alignment was a crucial ingredient in the plans mysteriously given to the emperor. Everything, whether large or small, had to replicate itself harmonically. From the great Qian Gate on the outskirts of the city connected to the Imperial Way, the emperor's processional route, which led directly to his throne room in the heart of his private sanctuary.

The focus of the Forbidden City is directed upon three great halls in the city's largest courtyard. Each is built on three interconnected terraces of gleaming white marble. Each terrace is surrounded by white marble balusters beautifully sculpted with dragons and other mythical creatures. The first hall, the *Tai He Dian*, or Hall of

▲ A mythical guardian beast protects the inner precincts of the Forbidden City. Another statue just like it is not far away. Everything is represented in pairs or symmetry.

Supreme Harmony, was used as a reception hall for important state events. The second hall was called the *Zhong He Dian*, or Hall of Perfect Harmony. It was the smallest of the three and was used as a preparation room for the emperor. The third hall was named *Bao He Dian*, or Hall of the Preservation of Harmony. This was the emperor's audience hall, where he received dignitaries from other provinces and rulers from dependent countries. Scholars, generals, traders and other notables came to present their tribute to the emperor in hopes of receiving his imperial blessings.

During the Ming and Qing dynasties the Forbidden City was closed to all, apart from the emperor's court and invited dignitaries. Rumors of its mystique and intrigue slowly percolated to the West, but it wasn't until 1600 CE that a group of Jesuits arrived at the city gates and was allowed entrance. Subsequently, traders, diplomats and missionaries from Holland, Britain and Russia came back with amazing stories, just as Marco Polo had done 300 years earlier. Soon the floodgates were open, and the European powers were forcibly setting up shop in various parts of China. Internal turmoil was inevitable, and the conclusion of Imperial China happened within the confines of the Forbidden City. The last emperor and the millennium-old dynasty system were forever lost to China after the Revolution of 1911.

### Getting to the Forbidden City

The Forbidden City is in the middle of modern Beijing (Peking), China's capital city. No longer off-limits (the penalty was swift execution), the Forbidden City, now called the Palace Museum, is today open to the masses. Directly across from the Forbidden City are Mao's tomb and the infamous Tiananmen Square, where hundreds of students were massacred in June, 1989. Beijing is a destination easily reached by the expansive Chinese train system. Beijing is also serviced by a plethora of airline flights, both domestic and international. There is a good subway system in the city of Beijing, which has a station near Tiananmen Square.

# TIBET

S ince time immemorial, Tibet was a theocratic country ruled solely by one chosen man, the Dalai Lama. His Holiness the Dalai Lama was initially chosen by the wise men of Tibet when he was a mere infant. Tibetan Buddhists believe the Dalai Lama is a living god, the reincarnation of the bodhisattva Avalokiteshvara, the bodhisattva of compassion. Tibetan ancient society, ruled by a recognized master, desired no "progress" from the outside world, including travelers, nor any of its focus upon material items. Tibetans simply wished to be left alone to ponder the teachings of Buddha, and develop extraordinary human abilities in order to overcome limitations of the flesh. After Communism swept the Chinese mainland in 1949, their next expansion was into Tibet. Soon after, the 14th incarnation of the Dalai Lama was shamefully forced to flee his country for India. As of this writing the Dalai Lama remains in exile, but travels extensively promoting world peace and freedom for his country. He is ever optimistic, proclaiming, "Wherever one feels at home with peace and tranquility, it is there that he finds his homeland. Wherever I go I find my Tibet."

The Tibetan capital city Lhasa was once known as "The Forbidden City," that is, before the Chinese takeover. In former days, foreigners were rigidly denied entrance into the city. Lhasa was the holy city of Lama Buddhism, and thus could not be tarnished by the souls of alien faith. This is not the case under Chinese rule today, as the Lhasa monasteries are open as tourist attractions. Highlights include a trek into the Yarlung Valley, regarded as the cradle of Tibetan civilization; a visit to the Valley of the Kings, including burial mounds of ancient lamas; a visit to the Jokhang Temple in Lhasa, one of Tibet's most famous temples; or travel to Samye, Tibet's first monastery.

Once self-governed by very tall "monk police," Tibetan crime was greatly reduced through intimidation. Apart from being a generally happy and peaceful people, all Tibetans followed these seven sensible laws:

1. Return good for good.
2. Do not fight with gentle people.
3. Read the Scriptures and understand them.
4. Help your neighbors.
5. The law is hard on the rich to teach them understanding and equity.
6. The law is gentle on the poor to teach them compassion.
7. Pay your debts promptly.

## Potala

Atop a holy mountain in the middle of a fertile plain rises the majestic Potala Palace. The imposing golden-roofed palace overlooks Lhasa, the capital city of Tibet. Before the Chinese takeover the Potala had been the most sacred monastery in all of Tibet. Now the whole complex is a state-run museum. The position of the Potala dominates the cityscape of Lhasa and can be seen for many miles in all directions. The Potala is a massive 13-story grouping of interconnected buildings constructed upon a prehistoric volcano mound 420 feet (126 m) tall. In 1642, the fifth Dalai Lama, Lobsang Gyatso, built the present monastery-temple on the *Marpori* (Red Mountain). There are 1,000 rooms in the Potala containing altars, chapels, statues and wall paintings. In the center of the Potala is the Red Palace, which was once the Dalai Lama's private quarters and is now a museum exhibit. The top floor was reserved as the Dalai Lama's exclusive residence, as none should be higher. The White Palace on either side of the Red Palace once contained the dimly lit offices and apartments of his administration. Pilgrims from all over Tibet continue to make their way to the Potala, the place of their beloved leader and seat of immense wisdom. The present buildings are only about 400 years old, but they are built upon ancient palaces and fortifications from time unknown.

## Built in the country called "the Roof of the World," the Potala is venerated as the living heart of Tibet. It is the focus of all Tibetan thoughts, prayers and hopes.

Very early Tibetan legend speaks of a former glorious civilization on earth when all people had telepathic abilities. Regardless of local language, this highly advanced race of humans could convey their thoughts telepathically, travel in the astral, see by clairvoyance and levitate themselves or heavy objects. People in this age, before the so-called "Fall of Man," were people with an amazing ability to utilize their "light bodies" at will. One version of the Fall of Man describing people abusing these occult powers and using them for self-interest, rather than the development of humankind as a whole. The universal capacity of telepathy was lost (represented in the Bible as the Tower of Babel), and humans were thrust back into dense third-dimensional bodies. While Tibetan Lamas never forgot these ancient human abilities, they kept to themselves in isolated development throughout the ages. It was not until the recent Chinese occupancy that these remarkable human abilities became known to the Western world, and then only gradually.

Although no one is allowed entry, it is reported that deep inside the Potala mountain there is a labyrinth of hidden caves and corridors. This subterranean system of passageways is dominated by a huge cave with several passages radiating from it, including one that ends at a sacred lake. The lake contains several islands that were once used for initiating lamas. The lake flows into an underground river, which empties into the River Tsang-po some 40 miles (65 km) away. The subterranean chambers under the Potala are said to contain all the jewels and treasures of Tibet, along with a gigantic golden statue of the Buddha. One of the most curious underground rooms is the Temple of Secret Wisdom, containing bodies of a giant race of people unknown to modern archaeologists. The mountain and caves are believed to have

▲ The Potala Palace is the most sacred building in all of Tibet.

originated before the planet's last polar shift, a time when Tibet was a country at sea level. The plates shifted, new continents formed and Tibet rose as the Himalayas thrust the northern land skyward. Successive monasteries were built and rebuilt upon the same mountain, that very same mountain which is a treasure-trove of secret passageways and ancient esoteric knowledge from the very early days!

For many centuries in the Current Era the Potala was a destination of countless pilgrimages. Most pilgrims would travel on foot for months at a time to complete this one-time journey to the Tibetan "Holy of Holies." These people would come from all parts of Tibet to see the home of the "Inmost One," as Tibetans call the Dalai Lama. Pilgrims would flock around the main road leading up to the Potala in hopes of gaining a glimpse of the Dalai Lama, and thus be blessed in this lifetime. All pilgrims would then make the six-mile (10-km) circuit around the foot of the Potala.

Before Chinese occupancy, the Potala was a self-contained township and sacred residence of the Inmost One. The Dalai Lama was Supreme Head of church and state, and had the final say in all matters. He was always appointed to the post upon birth, when other high lamas would follow astrological signs and search the countryside for the re-born child of the same spirit. The child was identified by its aura and was subject to many "memory" examinations. One such examination was to take various objects from the Dalai Lama's past life and mix them up with other similar objects. If the young child could identify his old possessions, it was yet another sign that he was the next Dalai Lama. At a young age the Dalai Lama would be taken to the Potala where he would rule Tibet until his death, and subsequent re-birth. One obvious trait of the Dalai Lama is his universal love and compassion for not only the people of Tibet, but for all of humankind.

### Getting to the Potala

The mountain of buildings comprising the Potala Palace faces the center of Lhasa City. Tours of the Potala are given daily (except Sunday) by local Tibetan guides. Lhasa is the regional capital of China's huge Xizang (Tibetan) Autonomous Region. At a high mountain altitude of 13,120 feet (4,000 m), the Potala is to be visited only by people in good health. The climate can be harsh, so try to time visits for the summer and autumn. The most common route to Lhasa is by air, via Chengdu in Sichuan province. From several western Chinese cities there is a bus or train connection to Lhasa. Overland routes from Nepal, India, and Pakistan are open, but may close with little notice, namely if internal protests arise in Lhasa. If all is calm, the Nepalese route from Katmandu can be the quickest overland approach, yet is still a rough ride.

## Mount Kailas

Religion and spirituality pervade the high desert area surrounding Mount Kailas. Tibetan Buddhism, also known as Lamaism, is the chief religion and philosophy of the region. To the ultra-ancient Bön Po—the native Tibetan religion pre-dating Buddhism—Kailas is the spot where their founder alighted from heaven. Kailas is the mountain home to many gods, including Lord Shiva and his consort Parvati, both prominent Hindu deities. In Buddhist tradition Kailas is the home to Samvara, a wrathful manifestation of Sakyamuni. To Tibetan Buddhists, Kailas is considered the "Navel of the World." The mountain has four sheer walls that align almost perfectly with the four cardinal compass points of north, south, east, and west. Mount Kailas is 22,028 feet (6,608 m) above sea level, soaring over the remote western Tibetan Plateau, already elevated at 15,500 feet (4,650 m) high. The mountain has never been climbed and is one of the tallest mountains in the Himalayas. The sacred peak is situated far away from any life, in a sort of lunar landscape.

Circling the lingam-shaped mountain is a pilgrimage route known as the *kora*, a 32-mile (52-km) path that circles the mountain. Prostrating themselves on the ground along the way, pilgrims have come to Kailas for thousands of years to behold this profoundly spiritual place. Most pilgrims come specifically to walk the *kora*. The biggest challenge of the trek is crossing the Dolma La Pass at 18,300 feet (5,490 m). Stupas, icons and prayer flags from several faiths adorn the *kora* on the outer slopes of Kailas, especially atop the Hill of Salvation. Both Hindus and Buddhists consider a pilgrimage to Mount Kailas as the highest point of a spiritual life. Kailas represents Asia's most sacred mountain to millions of faithful adherents of several religions. To all of them, one circuit is believed to be enough to erase a life-

▲ Mount Kailas is a sacred mountain in Tibet revered by millions of Asian people.

time of sin, while 108 circuits is said to ensure enlightenment. Adding to the lore of its life-enhancing properties Mount Kailas is the source of four great rivers: the Karnali (Ganges), the Indus, the Sutlej and the Brahmaputra. All four rivers flow down from the lofty heights of Kailas like a giant swastika-shaped mandala extending thousands of miles into the Indian seas. Many spiritual seekers believe that Mount Kailas represents the crown chakra of the earth. At the base of the mountain are two lakes, one shaped like the moon and one like the sun. From the solar lake flow the four rivers in four directions.

**To the Hindus, Buddhists, Jains and adherents of the ancient Tibetan pre-Buddhist sect called Bön Po, Mount Kailas is the dwelling place of the gods, a location where the eternal and temporal meet.**

Festivals abound year-round at Mount Kailas. Perhaps the most prominent celebration is the spring full-moon festival honoring Buddha's birthday, enlightenment, and death. Drumming through the night, Khumba monks chant and dance under the silver glow of the moon, joined by those from other religious persuasions. For the Hindus, Mount Kailas is the home of Shiva, who lives there in paradise and is worshiped on the eve of every new moon. For the Jains, Kailas is the place where their founder and first saint, Rishabanatha, attained spiritual enlightenment. As all faiths merge into one while under the white domed power of Kailas, an ongoing drama of renunciation and revelation continues as it has for thousands of years. The 11th century Tibetan saint Milarepa spoke of this peak: "The prophecy of the Buddha says, most truly, that this snow mountain is the navel of the world, a place where the snow mountains dance."

Mount Kailas is one of the most traveled pilgrimage routes for Hindus, Buddhists and hearty travelers of all nations. Several well-trodden routes coming from all directions are well known by native Tibetans and relocated Chinese people. The sacred peak is known alternatively as the holy "Mount Sumeru" or "Meru." Tibetans call the mountain *Kang Rimpoche*, meaning "precious jewel of the glacial snows." From afar, the snow formations on the top of the mountain resemble a palace, complete with icy domes and turrets. Pilgrims wishing to walk the *kora* route around the mountain must travel on foot over high and desolate terrain for five days. Altitude sickness is more a rule than an exception. Prepare for extremely cold weather and a lack of necessities, including limited food and fresh water.

### Getting to Mount Kailas

The impressive Mount Kailas is located in the far western reaches of Tibet, near the borders of both Nepal and India. The area is one of the most desolate and barren places in the world. Several bumpy roads access Kailas. The most viable way is the northern route from Lhasa across the Chang Tang plateau. Another northern route extends over the Tibetan plateau from Pakistan. Traveling through the Himalayas, it is now possible to trek from the Nepalese border to Mount Kailas. Driving routes from India and Nepal have shortened travel time to within a week, but the roads are very bumpy and uncertain. Check localized travel information before setting off on any trek.

# JAPAN

Shintoism is the original indigenous religion of Japan, predating the introduction of Buddhism by several centuries. The origins of Shintoism come from the southern island of Kyushu, where the first expression of nature worship centered upon the spirits, or *kami*, which dwelled inside the mountains, trees, rocks, springs, and other

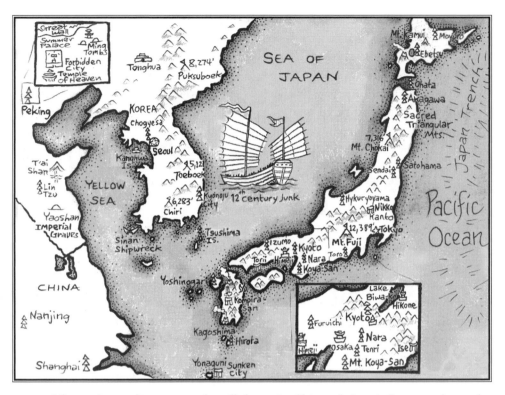

natural forms. It stands to reason that all the major Shinto shrines in Japan are located in regions of great natural beauty. The Shinto religion still preserves its original form of animism, which is not so much about idol worship, but rather an expanded relationship between the universe, the earth, all human beings and all living organisms. In essence, Shintoism is a holy expression of Gaia consciousness. Buddhism was introduced to Japan through Chinese and Korean priests from the sixth to eighth centuries CE. With them they brought the arts, skills, language, philosophy and science, all of which were eagerly assimilated. Architecture of that earliest Buddhist era is preserved in the ancient pilgrimage city of Nara. For many centuries the country lived in complete isolation, until 1868 when U.S. Commodore Perry forced the borders open and Japan entered the modern age.

## Mount Koya-san

Many Buddhist monastery complexes are scattered across Japan, but few match the lore and respect of Koya-san. A massive cemetery bordered by 120 temples of the Shingon School of Esoteric Buddhism nestle on a raised tableland covered with thick forests. Over 7,000 monastic inhabitants live in the sprawling temple city. The temple area around Mount Koya-san is largely regarded as the holiest of all monasteries in Japan, and the heart of Esoteric Buddhism. Koya-san was founded in a vision by the great Buddhist saint Kukai, known posthumously as Kobo Daishi. Japanese folklore radiates with praise and affection for Kobo Daishi, the wandering priest who had an enormous impact on the culture of early Japan. Out of reverence and curiosity, more than one million Japanese pilgrims per year flock to the Okuno-in, the mausoleum of Japan's most famous traveling mystic.

### The mountaintop temple complex Koya-san is a major center of Esoteric Buddhism, built at the request of an enlightened Japanese master.

In the year 816 CE, tradition speaks of Kobo Daishi being awaken from a deep meditative trance by a hunter and two dogs staring at him. The two dogs, one black and one white, accompanied the hunter, who was really a forest god there to guide the young master. The three beings had materialized in order to show Kobo Daishi a sacred spot where he should construct the first temple of a prophesied religious community. Soon the hidden glen on the slopes of Mount Koya-san was a bustling monastic complex of the Shingon sect of Buddhism. Two years before founding the monastery, Kobo Daishi traveled to China, studied Esoteric Buddhism and introduced the Shingon sect upon his return. For much of his life he traveled throughout Japan practicing humanitarianism, sometimes posing as a poor beggar, other times as a wise sage or teacher of calligraphy or language. As a priest, Kobo Daishi would bestow miracles in the form of a spring well or bountiful orchard upon worthy village communities. His teachings are legendary in all parts of Japan, but Mount Koya-san was his home and it was here he passed away as an elderly man. However, the followers of Kobo Daishi do not believe he is actually dead, but in a deep meditative pose awaiting the Future Buddha (Maitreya, or last Bodhisattva), at which time Kobo Daishi will awake and they both will assist in the enlightenment of humankind. The Okuno-in mausoleum is situated above a sprawling cemetery within a sacred cedar grove where thousands of previously influential Japanese have their ashes interred near their master.

Pilgrims to Mount Koya-san over the centuries have included emperors, nobles, generals and common people, all climbing to the top of the mountain to pay

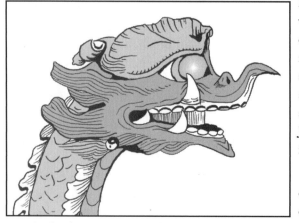
▲ The dragon is a powerful symbol represented throughout Japan.

their respects to Kobo Daishi. Women, unfortunately, were barred from entering the sacred grounds of Koya-san until 1872. Today, the monastery complex is a thriving religious community of 7,000 devotees gleefully welcoming the multitude of visitors. Its reputation, along with 50 temples that provide overnight accommodation, make Mount Koya-san a popular year-round spiritual destination. The city is divided into two precincts: the Garan (Sacred Precinct) in the west, and the Okuno-in Temple, with its vast 2-mile (3.6-km) long cemetery, to the east. As the headquarters of the Shingon School, it presides over nearly 4,000 temples nationwide and numbers 10 million adherents.

### Getting to Mount Koya-san

Mount Koya-san is located in the northern region of Wakayama Prefecture, 465 miles (750 km) west of Tokyo and 124 miles (200 km) southeast of Osaka. Local trains depart from Osaka's Namba Station every half-hour for Gokurakubashi station at the base of Mount Koya-san. The trip from Osaka takes about three hours each way. Japan Railway connects Gokurakubashi station with the city of Wakayama. Private and public buses make the journey from all over the Kii Peninsula. A cable car provides frequent connection between the base and the mountaintop community, or strong hikers can make the trek. Book your temple lodgings (*shukubo*) at the tourist office near the cable car station.

## Mount Fuji

Rising 12,389 feet (3,776 m) as a near perfect conical volcano, Mount Fuji (Fujiyama) is visible from downtown Tokyo on the increasingly rare clear day. As citizens in the Land of the Rising Sun, the Japanese are quite fond of their symbolic mountain. In the climbing months of July and August, thousands of pilgrims scale this inactive volcano in hopes of catching a flaming morning sunrise. Huts along the way and at the top provide shelter, as well as a little Japanese kitsch. At the summit you can send a postcard from the world's highest post office or enjoy a soft drink from the world's highest vending machine. Most pilgrims purchase a souvenir walking stick at the bottom and have it branded at each station along the way. Like worshippers of sacred mountains worldwide, pilgrims ascending Mount Fuji are seeking the realm of the gods. There is a difference, however, because Fujiyama is not only the realm of the gods, but a god itself.

Shinto adherents in Japan revere Mount Fuji above all other natural sites in Japan. For Shintoists, the mountain is virtually the incarnation of Gaia spirit. The Fuji-ko sect, who maintain several Shinto shrines around the base of Fuji and even inside the crater, believe the mountain is a holy being with a soul. The Shinto goddess Sengen-Sama, also nicknamed Konohana Sakuya Hime, resides within the mountain. Her nickname translates: "causing the blossom to bloom brightly" —a reference to the cherry and plum trees that blossom every spring in stark contrast to the snow-clad peak. A shrine to her at the top of the peak remains buried in snow until the trekking season begins. An annual fire festival is dedicated to Sengen-Sama at the end of the climbing season.

### Mount Fuji is the highest and most celebrated mountain in Japan. The Japanese word for the summit is *zenjo,* meaning "perfect concentration."

Fujiyama is especially revered because it is a dormant volcano that "never died." Japanese mythology asserts the mountain was created in a single night by the ancient gods. Geologists assert it was formed 600,000 years ago during the Pleistocene era. Originally considered sacrilegious to climb, over 40,000 annual pilgrims flock to its summit each summer. The first known pilgrimage route to its summit was established in the 14th century. The peak of Mount Fuji is the first place to see the light of every new day, hence the popular nickname for Japan as "the Land of the Rising Sun." But don't expect a mystical experience unless sharing the summit with up to 2,000 other hikers isn't a problem. Climbers have complained that the jam-packed trails often demystify the experience, especially if the weather is foul.

Encircling the northern base of Mount Fuji are five lakes—Yamanaka, Kawaguchi, Saiko, Shoji and Motosu—collectively known as the Five Fuji Lakes. The lakes certainly add mystique and charm to Mount Fuji, and contribute to the common belief that Fuji is one of the most beautiful mountains in the world. The surrounding countryside is, for some strange reason, the most popular place for Japanese citizens to commit suicide. Mount Fuji is covered with snow in the winter, and even in the summer the snow never completely disappears from the summit. Skiing and skating are enjoyed in the Fuji area during the winter. A major dragon line, or ley line, intersects Mount Fuji and is the source of great seismic activity. Dragon lines, or *chiryu,* are derived from a Chinese origin and correspond with the fundamental polarity of yin and yang. Many myths describe Mount Fuji as being a dormant monster with the capability to awaken and wreak great havoc. The gods of lore once scooped out Lake Biwa-ko, Japan's largest lake, and formed

▲ Medieval bridges are still used on Honshu Island.

the cone mountain. Mount Fuji's last eruption in 1707 covered Tokyo and the surrounding region in a thick blanket of ash, which subsequently sent the country into a severe famine. All in Japan know to beware of the sleeping giant that has never died.

### Climbing Mount Fuji

Mount Fuji and the Fuji Five Lakes are part of the Fuji-Hakone-Izu National Park located southwest of Tokyo. The mountain is a three-hour drive or train ride from central Tokyo, and some 30 miles (48 km) from Miyanoshita in Hakone. The mountain can be easily reached by JR express trains from Tokyo's Shinjuku station. There are five trails leading up the mountain from Kawaguchiko, Fuji-Yoshida, Lake Shoji, Gotemba and Fujinomiya. Kawaguchiko and Gotemba are the most popular routes. From Kawaguchiko it is possible to take a bus up to the 8,286-foot (2,514-m) level on the slopes on Mount Fuji and make the climb to the top in five-and-a-half hours. Most climbers choose to stay the evening in one of the many warming huts and reach the summit by sunrise. The official climbing season is from July 1 to August 31, but the ideal time is mid-July to August 20. Appropriate, warm clothing should be taken for the ascent, including a light raincoat. Brave winter mountaineers climb Fuji on New Year's Eve to see the first sunrise, called *goraiko*.

# Kyoto

Despite modernization, Kyoto lives on as the spiritual home of the Japanese people. As Japan's fifth-largest city, Kyoto is blessed with far more religious buildings than any other Japanese city. Towering skyscrapers juxtapose next to medieval castles, palaces, temples, shrines and beautiful gardens throughout the city. Elegant timber buildings —both religious and domestic—cluster within the urban environment as a walk down any narrow street will reveal. Because of its historic importance Kyoto was spared the destructive firebombs of World War II, unlike neighboring cities in the Kansai region. There are hundreds of Shinto shrines and well over a thousand Buddhist temples preserved in Kyoto, many of them officially designated as national treasures or housing national treasures.

## Kyoto is considered the repository of ancient Japanese culture.

Kyoto was the political seat of power to emperor and shogun alike. In most dynasties the emperor was controlled by the shogun military elite, a succession of powerful families who exercised absolute control from medieval times until 1868. Among Kyoto's many famous landmarks is the old Imperial Palace, which for more than a millennium, from 794 CE to 1868, was the capital of Japan and home to the omnipotent emperor. Though simply designed and decorated, the palace has a rich history. The city and palace came alive during the lavish ceremonies when emperors were

**▲ Kiyomizudera Temple is an elegant timber building overlooking the city of Kyoto.**

enthroned. The emperor was historically the spiritual leader and the most respected individual in Japan. The present Imperial Palace dates from 1855, rebuilt after the previous buildings were destroyed by fire. The present complex was reconstructed exactly the same as before, thus preserving their national heritage. In sharp contrast with the rather bland Imperial Palace is the elaborately decorated Nijo Castle. Built in 1603 by Tokugawa Ieyasu, it contains priceless paintings and decorations. A unique feature of the castle is a specially constructed floor near the inner apartment of the shogun. The floor emits a high, sighing sound when stepped upon to ward off anyone approaching, or "anti-assassination whispers." The exquisite landscape inside the Nijo Castle walls is especially renowned.

Nationally regarded sacred temples abound in Kyoto. Two of the city's most photographed buildings are the *Kinkakuji*, or Golden Pavilion, and the *Ginkakuji*, or Silver Pavilion. These two famous structures were originally the residence of local shogun, but they have since been converted into Buddhist temples. Almost as popular as the two metallic-covered buildings themselves are the gardens attached. Nearly every structure of note in Kyoto, including the Imperial Palace and Nijo Castle, features a lovely garden, and Kyoto gardens are famous throughout the country. Perhaps the most renowned garden is attached to the Ryoanji Temple, a landscape that contains no trees or plants. It achieves its design by the artistic placement of rocks and stones on a field of white sand. Another garden, totally different in concept, is attached to the Heian Shrine, one of the most important buildings in Kyoto. Built in 1895 to commemorate the 1,100th anniversary of the city, the shrine is patterned after the first Imperial Palace and the buildings are brightly colored and decorated. The charming garden at Heian Shrine is noted for its cherry trees and irises. Most Japanese people consider the cherry tree to be the most beautiful tree in the country, and every spring there are gala cherry tree blossom parties, especially near the holy Heian Shrine.

## Getting to Kyoto

Kyoto is a modern metropolitan city easily accessed by train or roadway from other major cities in Japan. Most travelers who fly into the country to visit Kyoto arrive in nearby Osaka Airport, which is only an hour subway ride from downtown Kyoto. The ancient city of Kyoto is a world-renowned artist and traveler mecca. A popular walkway on the eastern side of the city is called the Path of Philosophy.

# Nara

Most of Japan's original Buddhist buildings reside in Nara, a city celebrated for ushering in the new faith from East Asia. Starting in the sixth century, Buddhism arrived from China via Korea in a period known as the "era of the imitation of China." Planned cites like Nara and Kyoto were laid out, emperors were relegated living god status, and the philosophy that encouraged all to quest for spiritual enlightenment swept the island nation. Buddhism blended well with the indigenous Shintoism because both faiths emphasized the sacredness of all living things. Though largely distinguished by the cluster of Buddhist buildings and shrines, Nara also contains Shinto sacred sites, including the renowned Great Shrine of Kasuga.

Founded at a time when a strong imperial government and the Buddhist philosophy started overwhelming Japan, Nara quickly became a city of enormous centralized power. Nara was the original Japanese capital for Buddhist emperors from 710 to 784 CE, and also acted as the headquarters of Buddhism well into the eighth century. The city plan was devised by Emperor Tenchi, who resided 11 miles (18 km) from Nara at the Horyuji monastery. Nara was founded on virgin land deemed auspicious by the emperor. The city was laid out on a Chinese-style grid plan much like the Forbidden City in Peking, China. This planned city incorporated palaces, administrative buildings, markets, Buddhist monasteries, granaries and pagodas in a capital worthy of its powerful emperor. The central structure at Horyuji is the oldest existing temple in Japan, as well as the world's oldest wooden building. Founded in the year 607 CE, the Horyuji temple contains many priceless works of art. But Nara's time as the capital city was short-lived. Its final downfall came in 794 CE from a peasant revolt when the emperor was forced to move the capital to nearby Kyoto where it remained for over a thousand years.

**Nara played a vital role in the early development of Japanese civilization by way of religion, industry, literature, crafts and the arts.**

Around the year 735 CE, a deadly smallpox epidemic swept through Japan. When it reached Nara it claimed many members of the aristocracy and imperial court. To calm the wrath of angry heavenly powers, emperor Shomu announced plans to erect an enormous image of the "Universal Buddha." The statue supposedly curbed the epidemic and elevated the power of the emperor over his newly unified country. In its final form, the statue rose 53 feet (16 m) in height and contained more than a million pounds of bronze, along with several hundred pounds of the purest gold. The building where the Buddha statue resides is equally impressive. Its name is the Todaiji, and it extends 284 feet (85 m) in length and reaches a height of 152 feet (46 m). It is regarded as the largest wooden building in the world. In a ceremony of intense devotion, 10,000 priests consecrated the colossal statue in 752 CE. The

Horyuji Monastery
Nara, JAPAN

occasion of unveiling the statue marked Japan's coming-of-age among Asian civilizations. The Great Buddha statue gave official status to a religion that had originated in India, spread to China, and come to Japan by way of Korea. Even today it remains the largest metallurgic image of Buddha in the world.

### Getting to Nara

Being a major tourist destination as well as a modern city, Nara is easily reached by train or bus from all parts of Japan. Like Kyoto, the ancient buildings of Nara intermingle closely with modern buildings. Unlike other Japanese cities, Nara has preserved the natural setting near the city center, especially the hills surrounding the ancient city, which are studded with interesting trails. Thousands of tame deer prefer the city streets of Nara to the hills, largely because the throngs of tourists feed them regularly.

# RUSSIAN SIBERIA

The history of the indigenous peoples of Siberia is largely unwritten. For many thousands of years they were nomadic hunters who followed reindeer herds and the seasons. This region is not all permafrost, as summer temperatures can sometimes rise to 105 degrees Fahrenheit (40 $^\circ$C). Most of the indigenous tribes have vanished or assimilated into Russian culture, but some still exist and retain their ancient ways of life. The entire area of Siberia has a population of approximately 30 million people, of whom 90 percent are Slavs from Russia or the Ukraine.

## Lake Baikal

The word "shaman" comes from the language of the Tungus reindeer herders of the Lake Baikal region in Siberian Russia. Although the roots of shamanism go back 50,000 years to early Stone Age times, the term can be applied to all indigenous healing practices worldwide. The Tungus people of Siberia believe a shaman is a person of either sex who can master the spirits in this material world. The Tungus shaman can introduce spirits into their own bodies and use their power over other spirits, especially in the interest of helping members of the tribe. The Tungus people travel periodically to Lake Baikal for healing, spiritual renewal and vision quest. The lake is the center of the universe in Tungus cosmology.

Surrounded by mountains on either side, Lake Baikal is situated between two fault lines in the Baikal Rift System. The mountains of the Baikal Range and the faults in the Eurasian Plate have created a major rift in Siberia where Lake Baikal resides. The lake is a massive 12,162 square miles (31,500 sq. km) in size, and an amazing 5,316 feet (1,620 m) deep. Lake Baikal is by far the deepest lake in the world. A stone dropped in the deepest part of Lake Baikal will drop more than a mile before hitting bottom. The second deepest lake is Tanganyika in Africa, another freshwater lake along a deep fault line. Lake Baikal contains more water than all five of the North American Great Lakes combined. The lake is host to over 3,000 plant and animal species, with 2,000 species being totally unique to Baikal. Among the indigenous species are the epishura, a bacteria-eating crustacean, and the nerpa, a freshwater seal.

**Lake Baikal has been a sacred place to nomadic wanderers and hunters for thousands of years. Its sheer size and incredible depth strike awe into locals and visitors alike.**

The classic "Venus" figurines so prominent across Europe are unknown in prehistoric Siberia, although female statuettes have been recovered at the Mal'ta and Buret gravesites near Lake Baikal. These statuettes are especially interesting because they depict well-insulated clothing, including headgear, which must have been essential for survival in Ice Age Siberia. Also recovered from these graves are animal figurines, including ducks, swans and other waterfowl. A child burial at Mal'ta revealed sophisticated ornamentation in the form of a complex necklace, and the child was sprinkled with red ochre and charcoal.

At 7:17 a.m. local time on June 30, 1908, a massive explosion occurred in the Tungus area of central Siberia. The Tungus is a desolate forested plateau near the Tunguska River, 500 miles (800 km) northwest of Lake Baikal. Few witnesses survived, but those who did reported seeing a giant fireball entering the earth's atmosphere and exploding before impact, blasting all trees down within a 20-mile (32-km) radius. As recently as the 1960s, the charred tree trunks, many of them with bark torn off, could still be seen from the air. Since the physical evidence of the Tungus explosion is equally mysterious (no impact crater, intense heat, high levels of radioactivity on the ground) theories vary widely: Anti-matter particles or a black hole from outer space? An atomic blast from a crippled alien spacecraft? Most likely it was a giant meteorite exploding in mid-air from heat generated by its entry into the atmosphere.

The largest supply of fresh water on the Eurasian continent is close to being polluted beyond reversal. For the last four decades a Russian pulp and paper mill in Baikalsk has pumped over 140,000 tons (127,000,000 kg) of dioxin-laced waste into the pristine lake. Additionally, farm waste, pesticides, silt, sulfur and chlorine from the industrialized Selenge River spill into Lake Baikal. As a result, many fish and mollusk species, the nerpa seals, and the epishura are becoming endangered. If the Selenge Delta on Baikal's south shore isn't detoxified immediately the lake could become irrevocably polluted by 2012. Incidentally, it could be the lucrative tourism industry that reverses the pollution trend because the locals see the high stake in losing their precious natural resource. The incentive of visiting a polluted Lake Baikal is greatly diminished.

### Getting to Lake Baikal

The Trans-Siberian Railroad, the 5,973 miles (9,617 km) of track connecting St. Petersburg with the Russian Pacific seaport of Vladivostok, skirts the southern shore of Lake Baikal. The Trans-Siberian Railroad also extends south to Beijing, China. Both railway lines pass through the lakeside city Irkutsk, regarded as the artistic center of Siberia. The Russian airway Aeroflot and a few Chinese Airline (CAAC) flights access Irkutsk.

# INDIA

# AND THE SUB-CONTINENT

Look to this day, for it is life, the very life of life.
In its brief course lie all the realities and verities of existence;
the bliss of growth, the splendor of action, the glory of power.
—*Sanskrit proverb*

O NE OF THE EARLIEST CHAPTERS IN THE EPIC OF HUMANKIND unfolded in the Sub-Continent of South Asia. Among the first civilizations to emerge from the Stone Age was a string of cities along the Indus River valley more than 4,500 years ago in what is today Pakistan. Mohenjo-daro and other Indus city-states were highly sophisticated settlements, with established trade routes extending all the way to Mesopotamia and Egypt. Indus cities were skillfully planned, and a highly organized agriculture system was founded and supplemented by active commerce. Invading forces over the centuries ended the Indus culture, yet introduced many new ones, including Islam. The last occupying force was the British Empire, which left behind its language, system of government and a well-developed infrastructure. For the modern traveler this means ease of communication and reliable transportation within India and the Sub-Continent.

Several major religions were founded in ancient India. Hinduism is the world's oldest religion, founded more than 5,000 years ago in the Himalayan foothills. As Hinduism spread throughout the Sub-Continent it assimilated tribal religions which

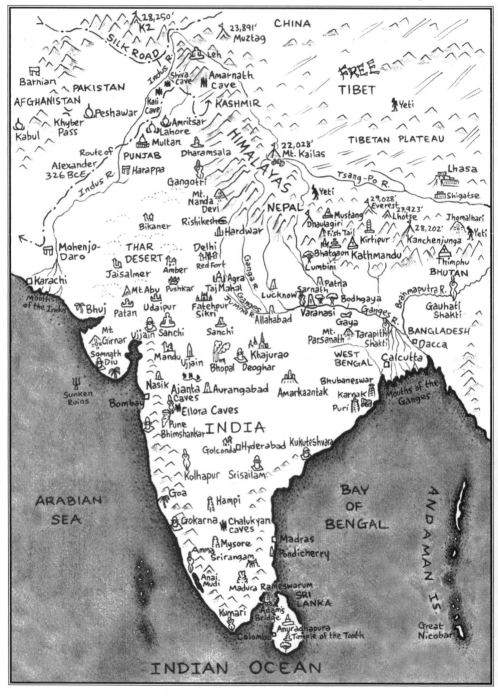

were characterized by a pantheon of gods and goddesses. Gautama Buddha, a Nepalese prince who renounced his wealth to seek inner truth, introduced Buddhism. Other minor religions still in practice include Sikhism, Jainism and Zoroastrianism. The Indian Sub-Continent offers a patchwork of diversity derived from various influences over the centuries. Those seeking earthly sexual delights continue to be instructed by the *Kama Sutra*, while the pious nature of Muslims lives on in the many mosques across the land. Religion, philosophy, and a rich heritage are just a few gems awaiting the spiritual traveler.

# BHUTAN

Bhutan —called by its people *Druk Yul*, meaning "the Land of the Thunder Dragon"—is home to a remarkable variety of climates and ecosystems. Several sacred mountains grace the western border of Bhutan, and none have ever been climbed. The highest unclimbed peaks in the world are all in Bhutan and will remain unclimbed according to Bhutanese law. Trekkers can hike through wild virgin forests to the 13,000-foot (3,900-m) base camp of Jumolhari and sit in the shadow of the 28,000-foot (8,400-m) peak that has only been climbed once. Nearby, Gangkar Punsum at 24,700 feet (7,529 m) is one of the world's highest unclimbed peaks.

## The Himalayas

The small Himalayan kingdom of Bhutan is landlocked between the world's two most heavily populated nations—China to the north and India to the south. Long shut off from the decadent influences of the outside world, Bhutan is reluctantly emerging from a medieval Buddhist society into the Modern Age. A central government policy emphasizes "Gross National Happiness" for the people instead of economic growth. There are no franchise outlets, no modern highways, no multinational corporations, but satellite television is slowly making its way into the tiny kingdom.

Located partly in Bhutan, the towering peaks of the Himalayas have awed and inspired spiritual seekers since time immemorial. Many Eastern classic books of wisdom refer to the Himalayas as the abode of the gods and home to the immortals. These descriptions do not stem merely from the majesty and grandeur of the natural surroundings, but allude to a special environment where communion with the divine is believed possible through contemplation and meditation. Both Buddhist and Hindu alike consider the soaring mountain range as the "Center of the World." The mythical mountains fasten together the underworld, the earth, and the heavens above. The Himalayas are not only the world's tallest peaks but also the only mountains on the planet that continue to grow. From thrusting tectonic plates the Himalayas continue to inch higher each year, while all other mountain ranges drop in elevation due to erosion.

**The Himalayas have attracted spiritual seekers since humans first came into consciousness. There is a discernible aura about these mountains, something readily detectable.**

▲ Small Himalayan hamlets scatter across Bhutan.

Although Bhutan is strictly a Buddhist nation today, in times past the people were of the Hindu faith. Elements of both religions pervade in the high mountainous regions. The Himalayas in Hindu mythology have always been the abode of Lord Shiva—destroyer and renovator of all things. The snowy mountain peaks are his pearly white teeth, the micro-climates of the lower slopes are his living body, while the rivers flowing downward represent his long, matted dreadlocks. Alive in this towering mountain world are a host of other deities; most notable is Shiva's consort Parvati, whose name literally means "of the mountains." Parvati is the daughter of King Himalaya, as well as an aspect of the supreme goddess Jaganmatri, who is "Divine Mother of the World." The Buddha was born in the fifth century BCE in Lumbini, Nepal. A prince who renounced the world, the Buddha taught that all people, regardless of caste, gender or other circumstance, could overcome the suffering of life. The Buddha spoke of the middle road as he traveled throughout the Sub-Continent, a path which is neither too extreme. He also spoke of moderation, detachment from material items, a freedom from desires, as well as the need to be kind to all living creatures. Through moral actions and the accumulation of merit (*karma*), a Buddhist devotee can achieve an end to the constant birth-and-rebirth cycle.

Since the late 1800s, there have been literally hundreds of sightings of the Yeti, or Abominable Snowman, all across the Himalayas. Legend says these man-beasts are incredibly strong, live in caves high in the mountains, have enormous feet, and avoid humans at all cost. Many sightings of the Yeti are near the Nepalese sacred mountain of Gauri Shankar, which the government says is forbidden to climb. Another sacred mountain, Kanchenjunga on the Nepal, Sikkim and Bhutan border, is also a region of many Yeti sightings. Kanchenjunga is the third highest mountain in the world and the Arun River runs just west of it. This is an area of high Yeti incidence, where they are sometimes called the "Kanchenjunga Demons." Whatever the Yeti might be, or if they even exist, their legend simply adds to the mystique of the Himalayas.

### Getting to the Bhutan Himalayas

The Buddhist Kingdom of Bhutan lies along the lofty ridges of the eastern Himalayas. Within an area of 28,520 square miles (46,000 sq. km), Bhutan is comparable to the largely mountainous Switzerland in both size and topography. Only 6,000 foreign visitors are allowed into Bhutan per year and all must be registered on designated, state run tours. Most visitors arrive by airplane in the capital Thimphu and set off on mountain adventures from there.

# INDIA

There is something about India that is both ancient and very spiritual. It is easily detected the moment you arrive: holy men wandering the streets, ubiquitous temples devoted to a multitude of gods, and an ancient way of life hardly blemished by the Modern Age. Most people of India are reverent and gentile by the very nature of Hinduism. Although 83 percent of Indians are Hindu, India is home to other creeds including Islam, Sikhism, Christianity, Jainism, Buddhism and Zoroastrianism. Religion is very powerful in India and rules the lives of everyday people through action and thought. The most visible and unique aspect of religious India is the millions of cows roaming free in the cities and countryside. Bovines are considered sacred animals —incarnations of Hindu Indians —so they are not to be killed and eaten.

**However pious India may seem to the spiritual seeker, it still has its share of serious problems.**

India is plagued by one of the fastest growing and largest populations on the globe. Millions of people are malnourished and living in desperate poverty. The environment is in shambles and appears to be headed toward complete eco-breakdown. Despite these major problems, India has a long spiritual history and usually ranks high on most travelers' favorite destination list. Out in the remote mountains, deserts, jungles or beach regions, a visitor will discover an ancient land steeped in religious diversity. For thousands of years, India has been sacked and invaded by foreign forces. The Persians, Greeks, Moguls, Muslims, Turks and finally, the Europeans, all had a go of it. Because the British were the latest and most prolific colonizers, India has an extensive railroad system and the English language is widely spoken.

## The River Ganges

The flowing potency of the River Ganges is Mother Earth to millions of Hindus. She is commonly referred to as "Ganga Ma" or "Mother Ganga." The Ganges is an extremely sacred river, a highly revered and physically dynamic life force to the Hindu faith. Millions throughout India make a pilgrimage every year. Over the centuries, countless yogis have left countless blessings along her banks. Some spiritual seekers have noted a discernible aura encompassing the river as they envision the flowing water as a living deity. Through intense devotion, the river becomes perceptible as a wholly static or geometric design. The Ganges becomes a fractal representation of a larger cosmic order.

The fantastical origin of the river is a glacial cave high up in the mountains—the home of almighty gods. Amid the eternal snows and silences of these lofty Himalayan heights the River Ganges slowly makes her long, 1,550-mile (2,495-km) journey to the Bay of Bengal, affecting millions of souls along the way. Hindu gods find their refuge at her many Himalayan origins. River Ganges rises from the feet of Brahma, while *Ganga Ma Cal*, the water that flows out from the top of Lord Shiva's head, is his direct manifestation of the river's dynamic energy flow. Hindus believe it is through the hair of Shiva, or "King of Yogis," that the River Ganges flows from heaven to the world.

### An often-heard Ganges River purification chant praises Shiva: *"Jai Shiva Shankara, Hara Hara Ganga!"*

Thousands of temples adorn the shores of the Ganges, and every day bells ring to call the devout to worship and bathe at the nearest Ganga temple. Hindus believe that washing the body in the River Ganges removes karmic blocks and cleanses past sins. To a new disciple, a Hindu would say, "Have faith, jump in and let yourself be engulfed by her warm embrace! Don't mind the garbage—it is merely an indication of Mother Earth's presently polluted state." Somehow, despite widespread pollution, scientific tests on water purity remain inexplicably high around the many Ganges' bathing centers.

Many bathing and burial ghats grace the shores of the Ganges, with the highest concentration in the holy city of Varanasi (Benares). Varanasi is India's holiest, and perhaps oldest, city. The Hindus believe the departing souls of those who recently died and are cremated along the shores of the River Ganges will be transported immediately to paradise. Varanasi is a destination to which every devout Hindu attempts to make at least one pilgrimage, especially upon death. A slow boat trip on the River Ganges at dawn, past 1,500 Varanasi temples, shrines, palaces, burning

▲ Bathers along the many river ghats feeding the Ganges. ghats and bathing ghats

where thousands of pilgrims come daily to wash away their sins, is one of the greatest spiritual sights in the world.

Rishikesh is a famous town along the Ganges, the name literally translated as "village of seers." Anyone who goes there knows Rishikesh is blessed with a sacred vibration. For centuries it has attracted saints, sadhus and all those wishing to become *rishis*, or seers. So important are the seers, there is even an eye hospital in the town for those needing improvement on their physical eyesight! A multitude of temples graces the east side of the city, where dozens of ashrams are present. Rishikesh is located in the Himalayan foothills, close to where the River Ganges emerges from the mountains.

The riverside city of Sarnath is where Buddha preached his first sermon about the middle way after having attained enlightenment. Travelers may view ruins of the old city and such spiritual sites such as the old Dhamek Stupa (a little Chinese Temple) and the Mulagandhkuti Vihara, which is a magnificent Buddhist temple with murals depicting the life of Buddha. Also in Sarnath is an Asoka Pillar with a lion capital, which has been adapted as the state emblem of the Republic of India. Sarnath is located only 6 miles north (10 km) of Varanasi.

## Khajuraho and the Kandarya Mahadeva Temple

The Khajuraho complex in north central India is one of the best-preserved collections of temples in the country. Only about 20 of the original 85 temples are left standing, but together they represent some of the finest examples of devotional art from the Chandella period. Today, Khajuraho is best known for the difficulty of getting there, as well as the ornate sculptures decorating various temples. The sculptures depict everyday activities such as plowing the fields, big banquets, the playing of musical instruments and traditional dancing. But the most popular scenes are those depicting tantric sexual positions—just about every position and posture imaginable. Khajuraho has been described as the *Kama Sutra* in stone, with more than some truth.

▲ Couples flirt in a carving from Khajuraho.

**Integrated in the Khajuraho sculptures can be found an illuminated glimpse of Jain and Brahmin life. Those who carved these sculptures expressed their fondness for living, especially their favorite sexual positions.**

Dominating the complex is the 11th century Kandarya Mahadeva temple dedicated to the Hindu god Shiva. In

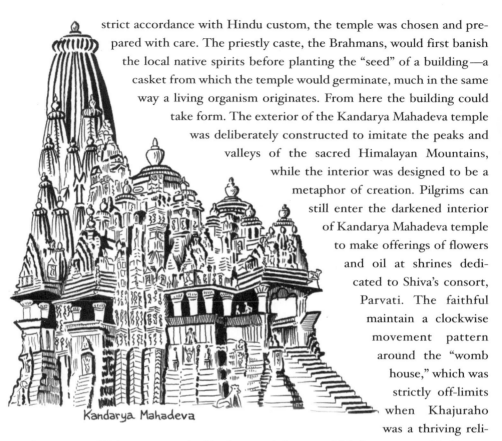

strict accordance with Hindu custom, the temple was chosen and prepared with care. The priestly caste, the Brahmans, would first banish the local native spirits before planting the "seed" of a building—a casket from which the temple would germinate, much in the same way a living organism originates. From here the building could take form. The exterior of the Kandarya Mahadeva temple was deliberately constructed to imitate the peaks and valleys of the sacred Himalayan Mountains, while the interior was designed to be a metaphor of creation. Pilgrims can still enter the darkened interior of Kandarya Mahadeva temple to make offerings of flowers and oil at shrines dedicated to Shiva's consort, Parvati. The faithful maintain a clockwise movement pattern around the "womb house," which was strictly off-limits when Khajuraho was a thriving reli-

Kandarya Mahadeva

gious center. Visitors can see inside the womb house, which houses a marble lingam—a symbol for Shiva, potency and the universal life force. Even in the near-darkness it is possible to make out the intricately carved erotic statues, positioned prominently near the womb house. Hindus regard the sexual act as a symbol of unity in the cosmos, a manifestation of creation, thus making Khajuraho one of the most sacred sites in India.

### Getting to Khajuraho

Transportation to Khajuraho has typically been very difficult, except by chartered aircraft or direct bus tour. The sheer popularity of the site is opening up new possibilities, however it is still a long way from anywhere. The town of Satna is the nearest railroad stop coming from the Bombay/Varanasi/Calcutta route. From Satna, it is a four-hour bus ride to the ruins. Another train stop on the Agra/Bombay route is Jhansi, where there are regular buses (six hours one-way) to Khajuraho.

## India's Sacred Caves and Lost Cities

As one of the oldest inhabited areas on earth, India is a land rich with archaeological ruins, especially abandoned cities and caves. Once-mighty Hindu dynasties, Islamic sultans, and various religious sects left behind stupendous stone-cut cities and monasteries. Some of the ruins were deserted in the past few hundred years while others, like the Ajanta Caves, were abandoned for 2,000 years. Imagine the surprise of the British army officer who, in 1819, accidentally stumbled upon the Ajanta complex while hunting a panther!

The most famous cave complexes are Ellora and Ajanta in the state of Maharashtra located in central India. The Kailas Cave at Ellora is a huge, monolithic temple sculpted from the top down, right out of the living bedrock. Ellora possesses carved figures of gods, men and beasts in Michelangelo-esque realism and proportions. Nearby, Ajanta is the site of more than 20 Buddhist monasteries with five massive cathedrals. Everything in Ajanta is rock excavated, with all the ceilings supported by massive fresco-painted pillars. The rock-cut Buddhist monasteries of Ajanta are set in a remote river glen interconnected by a series of walkways. The exquisite sculptures of Ajanta are enriched by an unsurpassed display of painted walls and ceilings. Both Ellora and Ajanta are best reached from the city Aurangabad.

## Amazing are the colossal proportions of India's lost cities and intricately sculptured sacred caves.

Fatehpur Sikri is a vast sandstone lost city located near Agra. Built by Akbar the Great in 1570, it acted as the Mogul capital for 16 years. Yet in 1586, it was suddenly and mysteriously abandoned by Akbar—leaving behind the grandiose palaces, fortifications and mosques to antiquity. Lack of a steady water supply is the likely reason Fatehpur Sikri was intentionally deserted. Akbar's magnificent city is today a perfectly preserved example of art and architecture from India's colorful Islamic age. The main building in the city, the Jami Masjid, is said to be modeled after the Grand Mosque at Mecca. With Islamic zeal, Akbar the Great at first violently persecuted the Hindus he had conquered. "As I grew in knowledge," Akbar stated later in life, "I

▲ The lost city of Fatehpur Sikri is a labyrinth of courtyards, passageways, and ornately carved buildings in an excellent state of preservation.

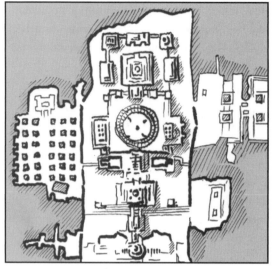

▲ An overview of the Kailasa Temple at Ellora.

was overwhelmed with shame. "Miracles occur in the temples of every creed." Fatehpur Sikri is 25 miles (40 km) west of Agra, and is a perfect day-trip after visiting the Taj Mahal.

The ultimate lost city of India is called Hampi, the "City of Victory" located the state of Karnataka. Built during the Vijayanagar period, Hampi was a resplendent capital until 1565, when the dynasty came to an abrupt end. The Mohammadan Sultans of the north conspired to defeat the Vijayanagar kings and swooped down to sack their capital. So brutal was the Sultan invasion, few survived, and the city was left to ruin and abandonment. It is in this deserted state that we find Hampi today, a wonderful assortment of ruins scattered around a surrealistic landscape of boulders. Most fascinating are all the palaces and temples, including the stone chariot in the Vittala Temple, the Hampi Bazaar and the Purandara Desara Mandapa temple complex along the Tungabhadra River. Buses run frequently from the railroad town of Hospet to nearby Hampi.

## KUMBHA MELA

With more than 2 million gods in the pantheon of Hindu religion, it is believed that Indians have more festivals than any other culture. The most significant religious festival in India is the *Kumbha Mela,* held in rotating-year cycles for many millenniums. Devout Hindus gather by the millions to meet thousands of swamis, sadhus, yogis and ascetics of all kinds. Many of the holy men who attend the *melas* are hermits who never leave their secluded haunts, except to attend this religious fair and bestow their blessings on worldly men and women. *Kumbha Mela* is held every third year, successively, in Hardwar, Allahabad, Nasik and Ujjain, and returning to Hardwar "Doorway to God" to complete a 12-year cycle. Each city holds a half (*Ardha*) *Kumbha* in the sixth year after its *Kumbha;* thus *Kumbha* and *Ardha Kumbha* are held, in different sacred cities, every three years.

The first foreign account of the *Kumbha Mela* was made in 644 CE when the Chinese traveler Hieuen Tsiang visited a vast gathering in Allahabad, a holy city at the confluence of three sacred rivers. He recorded the presence of Harsha, the king of northern India, who bestowed his entire wealth on the pilgrims and monks attending the

*Kumbha Mela*. When Tsiang departed for China, he refused Harsha's parting gifts of gold and jewels, but carried away 657 religious manuscripts, which he deemed of far greater value. These manuscripts may have been partially recovered in China's Cave of a Thousand Buddhas.

## Holy Cities of India

Sprawling cities scatter throughout India, yet some are pilgrimage destinations or hold other distinctions that relegate them as being sacred cities. Many of the holy cities in India continue to support a sizable population and large commercial districts. In the southernmost part of Karnataka is the fascinating city of Mysore. Like Hampi, the architecture and sculpture of Mysore achieved its highest perfection under Hindu kings in the 11th to 15th centuries. Unlike Hampi, Mysore today is a bustling city. Surrounding modern Mysore are some of India's finest monuments. The temple at Belur is unsurpassed in the world for minute detail and exuberant imagery from this period. Mysore is easily reached by train, bus or airplane service.

On an island in the Palk Straits, near the southern tip of India, is a sacred city called Rameswaram. The main temple in the city, the huge Ramanathaswamy Temple, is among the most highly venerated Hindu temples in the country, and is considered one of the finest examples of south India architecture. This major pilgrimage center is tied into Rama legends and the story of the Ramayana. Rameswaram is 414 miles (666 km) from Madras, and is connected to the mainland by railway and bridge.

### The holy cities of India continue to attract untold millions of pious devotees every year.

The holy city of Puri is home to the famed Temple of Jagannath, which is one of the titles of Krishna, who is the eighth avatar of Vishnu. The deity Jagannath is called "Lord of the World." The famed Jagannath Shrine on Blue Hill is the only Hindu temple in India where caste barriers have never existed. Multitudes of pious Hindus, representative of every province in India, arrive daily on their pilgrimage to this very sacred site. Non-Hindus are not permitted access into the Temple of Jagannath. The entrance area outside the temple, however, is quite lively and well worth a look. Those non-Hindus refused access into the temple may pay a nominal fee to climb atop a nearby rooftop for a view inside the Jagannath Shrine. Puri is located in the state of Orissa and is easily reached by train or bus.

▲ Large temples dominate the skyline in many Indian cities.

91

▲ A bridge in Rishikesh crossing the Ganges River.

Another major Hindu pilgrimage center is the Vishnupad Temple in the city of Gaya. The temple does not allow non-Hindus to view a footprint of Vishnu, which is the object of desire to countless Hindu pilgrims. Seven miles (11 km) to the east of Gaya, which is the Hindus' second holiest city after Varanasi, is Bodhgaya, where Buddha attained enlightenment under the Bodhi tree. The present tree is said to be a direct descendent of the original tree beneath which the Buddha sat. Of course, the original Bodhi tree died long ago, but many generations of saplings were preserved in Sri Lanka and then transplanted back to Gaya. Bodhgaya and the Mahabodhi Temple remain a major pilgrimage destination and a very sacred place to all Buddhists.

The sacred city of Amritsar is very close to the Pakistan border in the volatile state of Punjab. This holy city to the Sikhs is home to the Golden Temple, considered one of India's Seven Wonders. The Golden Temple contains the "Granth Sahib," the Sikh holy book. The temple is made of inlaid marble walls set inside an artificial lake called the Pool of Immortality. The waters around the central island are thought to be "life enhancing," and *amrit* means "elixir of life." In the garden Guru-ka-Bagh, the Baba Atal Tower has frescoes depicting the life of the founder of the Sikhs, Guru Nanak. The Sikh religious sect is an offshoot of the Hindu religion. Male Sikh devotees do not cut their beards and have long hair coiled beneath their turbans. Ram Das, the fourth Sikh Guru, founded the Golden Temple in 1577. Sikh religion became a bridge between the Muslim religion and the Hindu religion. Around the time Indira Gandhi was assassinated in 1984 by her Sikh guards, Amritsar was a closed city, due to social strife. It is open again, and easily reached by train or bus.

## Taj Mahal

The grandiose Taj Mahal was created out of love and devotion to a spouse. Built by the Mogul king Shah Jehan as a monument to his beloved wife, Mumtaz Mahal, the Taj Mahal remains one of the most recognizable monuments in the world. The love story goes like this: Shah Jehan married the beautiful Mumtaz when she was quite young, and Mumtaz passed away prematurely after bearing several children. So heartbroken, Shah Jehan undertook the building of a burial space of epic proportions. So grand was his love, Shah Jehan hired only the finest craftsmen available anywhere in the known world. Shah Jehan and his cherished Mumtaz are buried side-by-side in a subterranean chamber underneath the Taj. Together at last, this passionate king is forever at rest with his cherished wife.

## Built in devotion for a deceased wife, the Taj Mahal remains the pinnacle of Mogul design and architecture.

Construction began in earnest after Shah Jehan ascended the throne in 1628 CE, comprising more than a thousand men employed full-time for 22 years. Shah Jehan himself gave precise directions to the craftsmen, who decorated the highly polished marble walls with semi-precious stones inside intricate lace carvings. Huge Arabic quotations from the *Koran* surround the interiors. Shah Jehan was rumored to have wanted to build an identical black marble Taj across the river for himself, but was placed under house arrest in the Agra Fort by his son, Aurangzeb, instead. Shah Jehan died in 1665, alone and in exile. His only consolation was a view from his room of the Taj Mahal.

The Taj Mahal is probably the most celebrated, and certainly one of the most beautiful buildings in the world. Visitors approach the Taj through the West Gate, which stands an impressive 100 feet (30 m) high and leads to the lovely 42-acre (17-hectare) courtyard. A paved promenade on either side of two long canal-pools and a center pool, edged by dark green cypress trees, leads to the mausoleum. The oblong reflecting pools in front of the Taj

▲ The author poses in front of the Taj Mahal.

contribute to its pristine beauty. The Taj Mahal stands on two platforms—one red sandstone, one marble—and has four minarets, each 162 feet (49 m) high.

The city of Agra where the Taj resides was once called the Rome of Hindustan. It was the seat of the Moguls in India who ruled their Mohammedan Empire out of Agra. Almost as spectacular as the Taj Mahal itself is the Agra Fort, which consists of a labyrinth of passages, ornate palaces and imposing fortifications located along the banks of the sacred Jumna River. About a mile away and within perfect view from the Agra Fort is the majestic Taj Mahal. Unfortunately, Agra has become an industrial and polluted city as of late. The acidic morning dew from industrial smoke is destroying the intricate marble on both of these priceless structures. The Taj Mahal is in danger of collapsing in the next few decades if the pollution is not reversed.

### Getting to the Taj Mahal

The Taj Mahal resides on the southern bank of the Jumna River in the city of Agra. The city of the Taj is 130 miles (200 km) southeast of India's capital, New Delhi.

Everyone in Agra knows where the Taj Mahal is, and first-time visitors are encouraged to walk along the Jumna River to discover it for themselves. Several train and bus stations serve Agra.

# NEPAL

I ndia and most of the Sub-Continent are situated south of the towering Himalayan mountain range, one of the most awesome sights in the world. Nepal rises from steamy jungles to foothill valleys, all the way up to soaring peaks. On the border between Nepal and Tibet looms the world's tallest peak, the 29,029-foot (8,709 m) Mount Everest, commonly called the "Roof of the World." The lofty Hindu kingdom of Nepal, tucked away in the shadow of the Himalayas, only opened its doors to the outside world in the mid-20th century. Now adventurous travelers can see for themselves this tiny Shangri-La, whose trademarks are majestic mountains, the Yeti or Abominable Snowman, breathtaking vistas, and the legendary endurance of its Sherpa porters.

## Kathmandu Valley

Two major world religions began in Nepal. On the lower slopes of the highest mountains in the world sprang Hinduism and Buddhism, along with other minor belief systems. Thousands of holy men from all over the Sub-Continent make pilgrimages to the sacred Kathmandu Valley every year. Gautama Buddha was born in southern Nepal in 560 BCE, and as a young man he often visited the Kathmandu Valley where there are now several Buddhist shrines, temples, and other holy places. The pagoda was developed in Nepal as a representation of a peak before the image spread throughout the Orient. High in the mountains in various manifestations lives the immortal Babaji, a Christ-like being of pure light. It is reported that Babaji will occasionally meet visitors, but only if they are coming to him with pure intention.

Kathmandu is a timeless city, a place where the modern and the ancient blend harmoniously. Holy men and monks wander the streets, giving the city a quasi-mystical guru atmosphere. Kathmandu is a charming medieval

Bodnath Stupa

city, graced with many square oriental pagodas, little shrines and temples at every turn, the constant ringing of bells, the smell of incense, garlands of flowers on statues, and the sound of unceasing prayers being recited. Indeed, Kathmandu is a sacred and mystical place. The heart and soul of the city is Durbar Square. The square, also called the Hanuman-Dhoka, is home to an intriguing assemblage of temples and palaces. Many of the Hindu buildings near the square contain erotic wood carvings on the walls, which legend says protect the buildings from the destructive Goddess of Storms. Supposedly, Mother Nature is rather prudish, and thus refrains from striking Durbar Square with her thunderbolts. Near the square stands the House of the Living Goddess (Kumari Devi), where a young female and her entourage reside. Before reaching puberty, the chosen girl is worshiped as a living deity. Upon puberty she is replaced and thus returns to human status. The goddess is taken through the city on a special carriage during the Indra Jatra Festival, celebrated in September.

**The Kathmandu Valley has long been a pilgrimage center for Hindus and Buddhists. It is home to many temples, palaces, shrines, stupas and a living goddess.**

The elliptical-shaped Kathmandu Valley is sprinkled with many spiritual sites. Throughout the history of Nepal the valley has been the cultural and political core of the nation. Surrounded by the most revered mountains in the world, it was almost a given that the valley would develop a complex sacred topography. Nepali legend relates the tale of the Kathmandu Valley once being covered in water by the Lake of Snakes. One day a demigod named Manjusri was meditating on a mountain overlooking the lake when he suddenly decided to free the lake. Taking his great sword, he cut the mountain in half and the lake emptied into the plains of India, taking all the snakes with it. As such, the river drainage at Gorge of Chovar on the southwest end of the valley is an important pilgrimage destination. Perhaps the most famous site in the valley is the Boddinath Stupa, the highest stupa in the world. The characteristic eyes of the "All-Seeing" on the stupa remind everyone of the "enlightened ones" who are ever-present, yet invisible. Prayer flags surrounding the stupa send continuous prayers Heavenward. Boddinath is residence to Tibetan refugees, Buddhist monks and a Tibetan lama as its chief custodian.

Of Kathmandu Valley's more than 2,500 shrines and temples, only a few remain purely Buddhist or purely Hindu. In the distant past, a blending of faiths led to a strange intermixing of the two major religions, which continue to co-exist peacefully in Nepal. Just outside Kathmandu is the riverside Pashupatinath temple complex where Shiva, also called "Lord of the Beasts," is worshiped. Hindus revere the Bagmati River as a source of the sacred Ganges, and thousands come daily to cleanse themselves of past karma. The holiest Buddhist shrine in the valley (also sacred to

▲ Dubar Square in the old section of Kathmandu is one of the finest city squares in Asia.

Hindus) is Swayambhunath, or the Bowl of Buddha, and is occupied by a vociferous pack of monkeys. The Bowl of Buddha hill and lofty sanctuary are said to lie along two powerful ley lines, and reputedly dates back to Buddha's visit of Kathmandu. Buddhists faithfully flock to the hill every day to walk around the base, turn prayer wheels and prostrate themselves to earn merit from such devotional practices.

## Getting to Kathmandu and the Himalayas

Kathmandu is the capital city of the Kingdom of Nepal, and is easily accessed by international flights or by bus. The land route connecting China may or may not be open, depending on the current political situation in Tibet. Several bus companies from India run buses across the border several times per day. All major bus routes within Nepal connect with Kathmandu in some way. One-month visas to Nepal are available upon entry.

The best way to experience the splendor of the Himalayas is to walk many days among them. Trekking in Nepal is an age-old religious custom, as well as a practical mode of transportation. Walking with a group of friends is an exhilarating experience, yet being alone with nature and the elements can be equally satisfying. The austere surroundings awaken spiritual consciousness. The three most popular treks in Nepal are Annapurna Circuit, Everest Base Camp and Annapurna Sanctuary. Excellent day hikes also exist outside Kathmandu and Pokhara. Bus routes access most of the popular trailheads. Camping and trekking supplies are easily obtained in Kathmandu or Pokhara.

# PAKISTAN

The country of Pakistan only came into existence in 1947, but the area is home to one of the oldest civilizations in recorded history. Around the third millennium BCE or earlier ancient cities started sprouting up along the Indus River valley, revealing a genius for big-city planning. These cities were eventually transformed by repeated waves of invaders, and the religious culture changed many times over in Pakistan's long and varied history. Sacred sites in Pakistan are mostly Muslim mosques because Islam has been the chief religion for many centuries. Most Islamic sacred sites are located in the Middle East, primarily Mecca in Saudi Arabia, in which direction devout Muslims face to pray five times daily.

Looking closely at the fabric of Pakistan, one discovers its diverse origins. Across the north is the old Grand Trunk Road, which intersects Lahore, a beautiful city from the Mogul Empire. Similarly, the swashbuckling Pathans left behind their capital, Peshawar. But the real gems lie in the far north of the country, where the Himalayas begin to rise in dramatic fashion, crowned by K2, the world's second highest mountain. Skirting the mountains is the old Silk Road and an open land route into China's Xinjiang Province.

## Mohenjo-daro

Along the fertile banks of the Indus River began one of the first traceable civilizations, thriving at approximately the same time early cities were developing in Mesopotamia and Egypt. The Indus people of this age organized a powerfully commercial and highly advanced society. Their genius for city planning remains unrivaled in ancient times. To date, almost 1,000 Indus cities and sites have been discovered in what is today Pakistan and western India. The best-preserved and most important settlement is Mohenjo-daro, a sacred city that contains the earliest traces of Hinduism.

Mohenjo-daro was a settlement of great importance. It was a wealthy city whose merchants plied the waterways and fertile valleys along the mighty Indus River. Mohenjo-daro shared capital status with its sister city Harappa 400 miles (645 km) up river, another centrally planned city also constructed entirely of baked bricks. Mohenjo-daro's riverfront position established it as a major trading center and agricultural outpost. The massive granary in the hub of the city denotes the region's economic activity. Near the granary is the Citadel mount, a huge pyramidal mound whose top was cleared away in the second century CE to make room for a Buddhist shrine. Also in the Citadel area is the religious and ceremonial center know as the Great Bath.

**Mohenjo-daro is regarded as the world's first
planned city—square in outline and laid out
along the lines of a right-angle grid.**

Religion in Mohenjo-daro centered around a large pool known as the Great Bath. The Great Bath was used for ritual cleansings, a practice that remains an integral part of the modern Hindu faith. In Mohenjo-daro, pilgrims and high-ranking governmental officials would arrive for a priest's blessing and a soak in the sacred waters of the community bath. Surrounding the 8-foot (2.4-m) deep swimming pool is a pillared veranda, and above the baths lived the city administrators and the priests who enjoyed private baths of their own. Mohenjo-daro and other Indus cities were networked with a centrally planned drainage system that ran under the streets of the city. The most striking sculpture unearthed at Mohenjo-daro is that of a richly dressed priest, a man who likely held sway over the people and conducted the sacred bathing rituals.

▲ An Indus priest sculpture found at Mohenjo-daro.

Clues about the religion and civilization are found in the enigmatic Indus seals. Similar in nature to Mesopotamian seals, the Indus seals were square rather than round. Indus seals have been discovered on the island of Bahrain in the Persian Gulf, proving that eastern contact was made with the other great civilizations to the west. The seals, which may have been used to identify a person or signify religious status, were carved on small pieces of soft stone. An undeciphered text usually runs along the top of the seal, along with a relief carving of an animal, mythical creature, goddess, sacred tree, seated god or several human figures co-mingling with animals. Amazingly, this Indus script is similar to the undeciphered text found on Easter Island in the South Pacific. One Indus seal has been identified as a three-headed meditating god in the likeness of Shiva, one of the supreme deities of Hinduism. Other religious seals represent the pipal, or fig tree, which is still sacred today to Hindus as well as Buddhists.

The Indus people used the wheel, had a system of writing and counting, were prolific farmers, and developed tools and weapons out of bronze. But what happened to these skillful and advanced people? Along the topmost street level of Mohenjo-daro, meaning "Mound of the Dead," were uncovered skeletons of men, women and children, many holding hands and sprawling in the streets, as if some horrible doom had taken place. Surprisingly, the bones do not show severe sword or ax cuts, but high levels of radiation! These skeletons are among the most radioactive ever found, on par with those who died at Hiroshima and Nagasaki. Soviet scholars found one skeleton that had a radioactive level 50 times greater than normal. Furthermore, fused lumps called "black stones" were found at the site. They appear to be clay vessels melted together in extreme heat. Harappa (another Indus city which shows high levels of radiation) and Mohenjo-daro are said to be two of the seven Rishi cities of the Rama Empire, according to ancient Indian epics. Could these be the same Rama cities attacked by a highly advanced Atlantean culture of lore? Substantiating the mystery of Mohenjo-daro is a recently discovered Harrappan civilization city deep beneath the sea near India's western state of Gujarat. Acoustic images from the seabed reveal the presence of symmetrical built-up structures. A block of wood with deep fissures from the site has been recently carbon dated to around 7,595 BCE, dating this city as one of the oldest ever found.

### Getting to Mohenjo-daro

Over the centuries the Indus River has shifted its course many times and today the ruins of Mohenjo-daro are two miles (3.5 km) away from the current riverbank. Trains from either Karachi or Lahore access this remote location. Departing from Larkana train station, hire a taxi or auto-rickshaw to take you to the site. Private tour buses also travel direct to Mohenjo-daro from major Pakistani cities, but are more expensive. There is a small museum at the site with a good collection of the various finds.

# SRI LANKA

In lore of old, Sri Lanka was called Serendipity, or simply Lanka. The first aboriginal "Yaksha" people to occupy the island were considered uncivilized and demonic. Through the centuries, successive waves of new cultures from India made their way to this beautiful mountain island. The most lasting legacy is Theravada Buddhism, still practiced on the island 2,300 years after it was introduced. Sri Lanka is the world's oldest Buddhist nation. As a result, Buddhist sacred sites and ancient legend pervade the island. Some of the earliest references of Sri Lanka appear in the Indian epic *Ramayana*. In the drama there is a demonic Yaksha ruler named Ravana, King of Lanka, who aggressively craves the beautiful Sita, Queen-mother of India. Ravana abducts her and most of the epic describes how the hero, Rama, conquers much of the island in the process of rescuing his wife. The most endearing part of the tale is Rama's relationship to Hanuman, a faithful monkey-god who helps Rama liberate Sita in a heroic rescue. Hanuman is a very popular god in India today, personifying loyalty, courage and strength. Most of the *Ramayana* epic is believed to have taken place in and around Sri Lanka's ancient sacred cities.

## Anuradhapura

The religious city of Anuradhapura was established around a cutting from the "tree of enlightenment," the Buddha's Bodhi tree, imported to Sri Lanka in the third century BCE by Sanghamitta, the founder of an order of Buddhist nuns. Anuradhapura was one of the original settlements of the Sinhala clansmen, who were considered the original non-demonic inhabitants of Lanka. The Sinhala were the first race to establish a permanent agriculture-based civilization on the island. By the time Buddhism

▲ Most Hindu and Buddhist temples in South Asia contain 108 prayer wheels around their base.

arrived in 247 BCE, via the son of Emperor Asoka and an entourage of monks, Anuradhapura was already a bustling city. This auspicious pilgrimage effectively opened the door to Buddhism, which quickly spread throughout the island, with Anuradhapura developing as its philosophical capital.

Anuradhapura remained the political capital of Sri Lanka for more than 1,000 years, starting from the fifth century BCE when it was founded. Later Buddhist monuments and royal palaces date from the time of Christ. Several large irrigation reservoirs near the city attest to the advanced state of ancient Lankan engineering ingenuity. The city was much more refined and advanced than many others in neighboring India. Anuradhapura, a Ceylonese political and religious capital that flourished for 1,300 years, was abandoned after an invasion in 993. Hidden away in dense jungle for many years, the splendid site, with its palaces, monasteries and monuments, is now accessible once again.

## Nine colossal public buildings were erected in Anuradhapura, along with an enormous reservoir and hundreds of temples.

The ancient historical capital is situated on tranquil miles of parkland amid plentiful ruins. According to the *Mahavansa*, the Sinhala Buddhist chronicle, the city was a model of precise planning. Among Anuradhapura's most notable ruins are the Thuparama Dagaba built in the third century BCE, Ruvanveliseya from the second century BCE, the 7-story Lovamahapaya (also known as the Brazen Place), the Jetawana Dagaba and the recently excavated precincts of the Abhayagiri Dagaba. Perhaps the most popular attraction is the Sri Maha Bodhi tree, which is the oldest historically documented tree in the world. Many pilgrims come to celebrate here in May, during the festival time in honor of Buddha's birthday and Enlightenment Day.

### Getting to Anuradhapura

Airline flights arrive daily in the capital city Colombo from most major Indian cities. Ferryboats also connect Sri Lanka with India. Anuradhapura is 128 miles (205 km) northeast from Colombo. From Colombo public buses, taxis and guided bus tours ply the main highway bisecting Sri Lanka. The ancient city of Anuradhapura is located along the main highway, almost halfway between Colombo and Jaffna to the north.

## *SRI LANKA TRAVEL ADVISORY*

The teardrop-shaped island off the southeastern tip of India has seen an insurgency of terrorism in the last two decades. An ongoing struggle for independence by minority Hindus (known as Tamil rebels) has engulfed Sri Lanka in a hostile guerrilla civil war. The tit-for-tat terrorist skirmishes reached an all-time low in January 1998 when three suicide bombers crashed a truck through the gates of Sri Lanka's holiest Buddhist temple, killing themselves and eight others. The attack was on the Temple of the Tooth in Kandy, where a tooth from the Buddha is enshrined. Although the tooth was not harmed, the blast ripped through the temple's roof and outer facade.

Travelers visiting Sri Lanka are warned to take the utmost caution when visiting the island's sacred sites and urged not to engage in any political discussions. Although tourists have not been targeted, it is strongly advised to travel with extreme caution. The Tamil rebels have launched dozens of bombings since the civil war began in the 1980s and in all, more than 51,000 people have died in the violence. A cease-fire was negotiated in 2001 between the government of Sri Lanka and the rebel army, the Liberation Tigers. So far, a shaky peace reigns in Sri Lanka.

# SOUTHEAST ASIA

*If you really want peace on earth, create peace in your heart, in your being. That is the right place to begin with —and then spread, radiate peace and love. —Dhammapata*

THE FASCINATING SAGA OF RELIGIOUS DEVELOPMENT in Southeast Asia spans several centuries and more than a few cultural influences. Ancestor worship and animism, the belief that natural phenomena and inanimate objects possess spirits, prevailed in both mainland and peninsular Southeast Asia prior to the arrival of Hinduism and Buddhism in the first millennium. Even today, ancestors and spirits are worshiped within their natural setting and in sculptural form. Because indigenous traditions intermingled with Hinduism and Buddhism, native beliefs assimilated into mainstream Hindu and Buddhist practice. The polytheistic nature of Hinduism allowed great diversity of practice and worship, with Vishnu, Shiva, Durga and Ganesha figuring most prominently in Southeast Asia. From its inception, Buddhism was a proselytizing faith that spread throughout India and the Himalayas, and later across central Asia and to China, Japan, Korea and Southeast Asia. Wherever Buddhism emerged it developed different schools and complex philosophical systems. Buddhist sculptures were created to decorate temples and serve as primary objects of devotion. By the 15th century CE, Islam had established itself throughout much of insular Southeast Asia. Islam is based on the faith and practice of religion set forth in the Koran; the oneness of god, Allah; and the primacy of the prophet Mohammed. In the 16th century and later, Spanish Christian missionaries converted most of the population of the northern Philippines to Catholicism.

# BURMA (MYANMAR)

The art and architecture of Burma, much like that of Thailand, was largely produced in the service of Theravada Buddhism. The faith was introduced to both countries from India in the fifth century CE. The practice of accumulating merit (karma) through donations to religious establishments resulted in the construction of large ceremonial temples and monasteries all over Burma, especially along the Irawaddy River. Since its inception to the present day, Buddhism remains the spiritual heart of Burma. Scattered across the country are countless testaments to the faith. Some of the spiritual sites are located in populated cities, others are found in deserted regions. In the center of Rangoon the capital city is the Dagon Pagoda, containing ancient relics of Gautama Buddha, including a 320-foot (96-m) golden bell imbedded with precious stones. A day trip away from Rangoon is Pegu, site of a 180-foot (54-m) sprawling statue of a reclining Buddha. In Mandalay, near Mandalay Hill, is the Kyauk Dawgyi Pagoda, which contains an enormous image of the Buddha carved from a single block of marble. Nearby, the Kuthodan Pagoda contains 729 white marble tablets that preserve ancient Buddhist text and scripture.

## Pagan

The Burmese people migrated from southeastern China in the ninth century and founded the city of Pagan on the banks of the Irawaddy River. While expanding their political power, they endowed religious institutions and constructed stupas, making Pagan a fantastical "City of Temples." At its peak (1056 to 1200 CE), Pagan, formerly named Aramaddanapura, had more than 10,000 Buddhist structures. Today, over 2,000 temples and stupas remain to make up the 16 square miles (26 sq. km) of ancient Pagan. The historic city remains mostly deserted under the beating hot sun of central Burma. Some temples have decayed into nothing more than gravel hills, while others are beautifully preserved, each containing impressive statues of the Buddha.

### Pagan is considered the Buddhist cradle of Burmese civilization.

Stone images of the Buddha adorn the interior of most Pagan temples and tell fascinating stories. To be found encircling the exterior of most Buddha statues are glazed terra-cotta plaques representing the previous lives (*iatakas*) and the historical life of the Buddha. Many of the statues in the lower niches show the stages from birth to Nirvana of the Bodhisattva. Also present in many Pagan temples are representative Buddha footprints on pedestals, perhaps indicating a previous pilgrimage to Burma. Largely regarded as the most impressive Pagan monument is the Ananda Temple, literally "divine love" in Sanskrit. Founded in 1091 CE, Ananda is best known for its monumental size (17 stories!) and the abundant images of the Buddha it contains. Ananda and its sister temple Thatbyinnyu are both over 800 years old and graced with 30-foot (9-m) gilded Buddhas with their hands in different positions, representing the attainment of nirvana. Inside Ananda is a maze of corridors fashioned with inset statues of the Buddha and plaques inscribed in Mon script. The catacomb-like structure contains a wide variety of colossal and small statues of the Buddha. Another feature is a stone block in the center of Ananda with four sides facing directly north, south, east and west. Four standing statues of the Buddha stare out at the four cardinal compass points in blissful meditation.

For 50 consecutive kings Pagan served as the primary cultural and political center of Burma. The dynasty ended abruptly with the invasion of the Mongolians in 1287 CE. The oppressive Kublai Khan and his Mongol army sacked the city and began dismantling some of the buildings for military purposes. After the Mongol invasion, the empire fragmented into rival states and the capital continued to move as each king sought to establish his own kingdom. This started the long period of decay at Pagan that is still in progress today.

### Getting to Pagan

Pagan lies northwest of Rangoon on the east bank of the Irawaddy River. There are daily flights to the nearby airport at Nyaung-U, and from Mandalay. Buses and taxis ply these routes daily. Burma is just opening up to foreign visitors after many years of governmental repression and extreme poverty. For the first time in decades it is permitted to travel freely within Burma. Tread lightly.

# CAMBODIA

D uring the Dark Ages in Europe, Cambodia was emerging as a major power in Southeast Asia. The once-mighty Angkor empire, which 800 years ago stretched into what is now Vietnam, Laos, Thailand and the Malay Peninsula, was ruled by a succession of strong-armed kings. Before the Angkor kings, the first Cambodian civilization was the third century CE kingdom of Funan, which began as a successful trading post called Chenla southeast of the present-day capital Phnom Penh. Funan acted as a buffer between India and China, two mighty empires that greatly influenced the development of Cambodia. Pilgrims and traders traveling the land and sea routes between India and China brought new religious and architectural ideas to Cambodia, eagerly adapted by the Khmer rulers. These early kingdoms of Funan and Angkor paid tribute to China while adopting many elements of India culture, including its style of dress, eating habits, Sanskrit writing system and the Hindu religion.

Modern politics and internal conflict have ensured that we are familiar with the ancient name Khmer. In old times, Khmer was the name of the people who built the temples of Angkor. In the late 20th century it was the Khmer Rouge, a band of guerrillas who wreaked havoc in the jungles near the Thailand border. The Khmer Rouge, led by Pol Pot, were responsible for killing more than a million fellow Cambodians during their reign of terror from 1975 to 1979. Stark reminders of genocide, re-education camps and the infamous "killing fields" are apparent on any visit to Cambodia.

## Temples of Angkor

The sprawling complex of Angkor was first founded by King Jayavarman II, who proclaimed himself the "universal monarch" during his reign from 802 to 850 CE. It was this powerful ruler who consolidated his kingdom and initiated large building projects for his new capital. Although few of his original buildings survive, it was Jayavarman II who put the unique stamp on Khmer religion and renamed the country "Kambuja," an early version of "Kampuchea," or "Cambodia."

In what is regarded as the world's largest temple complex, successive kings added their own monuments in and around Angkor. Covering more than 135 square miles (220 sq. km), Angkor is a patchwork of sandstone temples, chapels, causeways, terraces and reservoirs. Adorning the temple walls are thousands of carvings depicting

▲ The Magnificent Angkor Wat in northwestern Cambodia.

battles between gods, sensual dancing women, royal processions with kings riding elephants, and many scenes from classical Hindu mythology. Basically, each complex was built for and commemorates the god-king who commissioned its construction. Each temple complex of Angkor acted as the king's capital during his lifetime—then his tomb upon death.

**Possibly the largest collection of religious edifices ever built, nearly every temple at Angkor is a labyrinth of corridors and interconnected buildings featuring elaborate carvings and sculptures. Angkor literally means "Capital City" or "Holy City."**

The most magnificent and best preserved of all Angkor temples is Angkor Wat, constructed by King Suryavarman II at the height of the Khmer Empire in the early 12th century. This massive "temple-mountain" is dedicated to the god Vishnu, regarded by Hindus as "the protector." Five huge beehive-like towers dominate the skyline at Angkor Wat, while the long causeways and wide pools give the visitor a sense of freedom in space. Angkor Wat is considered the best example of Khmer architecture at its most refined state. Composing a half-square mile (200 hectares), Angkor Wat uses its massive proportions to astonish any visitor. Similar to large-scale monuments in Egypt, there is a long approach to the temple, an imposing entry foyer, followed by a center temple rising pyramid-like on three superimposed terraces. Angkor Wat is a complex of great drama, utilizing various courtyards, towers, a large moat and various ancillary buildings. The four towers on each corner and the middle tower replicate a mountain-like appearance, which most experts believe to

▲ 108 Cambodian king statues grace a causeway leading to an Angkor temple.

represent Mount Kailas — the center of the universe to both Hindus and Buddhists (see page 68). Whatever Angkor Wat was modeled after remains conjecture, but there certainly are both Hindu and Buddhist elements represented, together with a liberal dose of king worship.

Those visiting Angkor today should not just set their sights on Angkor Wat. Although dazzling in its own right, Angkor Wat is merely one of many highlights from this prolific age of Khmer temple building. Another capital site, Angkor Thom, has a fantastic temple called the Bayon, which rivals Angkor Wat in size and beauty. Bayon is most famous for the over 200 magnificent, slightly smiling stone faces. Some 70 other temples and monuments adorn the area, only recently opened to foreigners after the removal of unexploded land mines from decades of turmoil. Several temples still retain hundred year-old trees firmly entangled in the structure. The trees cannot be cleared because the roots are so intertwined into the foundation that the structures would collapse if the trees were removed. Giant trees can be seen growing out of the Ta Prohm, Banteay Kdei, and Preah Khan temples, evoking the 19th century ambience of the first French explorers discovering the monuments amid dense jungle foliage.

### Getting to the Temples of Angkor

The many temples of Angkor are located in northwestern Cambodia, situated just north of the town Siem Reap. It isn't the intrepid traveler who ventures to these fascinating temples anymore, but now large tour groups are streaming in and transforming

Siem Reap into a booming tourism town. Only in 1995 Khmer Rouge terrorists still targeted foreign tourists, but today the region is completely safe for travel. From Phnom Penh, there are regular buses, flights and a boat route over Tonlé Sap lake to Siem Reap.

## Phnom Kulen

Before the Temples of Angkor were built, Phnom Kulen was a sacred mountain acknowledged by the first Cambodian king. The mountain was originally named Mahendraparvata, a dedication to the Hindu deity Shiva. Atop this hilltop location, in 802 CE, King Jayavarman II proclaimed independence from Java. The event gave rise to Cambodian independence, and what followed was five centuries of prolific temple construction at Angkor. Although Jayavarman II was a Hindu obsessed with the lingam-cult of Shiva, the summit of Phnom Kulen contains a sculpture of a large reclining Buddha which was carved at a later date into the upper portion of a massive sandstone boulder. Jayavarman II held the first "god-king" ceremony legitimizing his "universal kingship" through the establishment of a royal lingam-worshipping cult. The lingam-cult would remain central to Angkorian kingship, religion, art and architecture for centuries.

> **Phnom Kulen has been the holiest mountain in Cambodia since the ninth century, and remains so today. The summit contains Cambodia's largest image of a reclining Buddha. It was also from this mountain where sandstone was quarried to construct Angkor.**

The lingam-cult in ninth century Cambodia was derived from a sect of the Hindu religion devoted to the god Shiva. In this aspect Shiva is worshiped in the form of a lingam, or a phallic symbol. The lingam is typically depicted inside a square perimeter representing the female vulva. Most of the Hindu temples at Angkor housed stone lingams, inside square boxes, which were attended and worshiped by devotees. In Hindu tradition, water that passed over lingams became sacred, even magical. It was believed that the lingams spiritually "fertilized" the waters that fed the *barays* (reservoirs) and irrigated the rice fields below.

Cutting through the upper plateau of Phnom Kulen is the River of One Thousand Lingams, fed in part by several natural springs. Less than a meter under the river's surface can be found over 1,000 small carvings sculpted into the sandstone riverbed, interspersed by larger sections of bedrock featuring *apsaras* (mythological celestial nymphs), the god Vishnu, and other figures. In the year 1054 King Suryavarman I ordered part of the river diverted temporarily so that hundreds of phallic images could be carved into the sandstone floor. The water became holy by passing over this area before moving downstream to a series of tiered waterfalls. At the top, where

▲ This temple perched on a high rock at Phnom Kulen contains the reclining statue of the Buddha.

Suryavarman I chose to bathe, he again had the river diverted so that the stone bed could be carved with an elaborate rendering of the Hindu god Vishnu. Here Vishnu can be seen reclining on the serpent Ananta, with his consort Lakshmi at his feet and a lotus flower protruding from his navel bearing the god Brahma. This holy place must have been favored during the Angkorian epoch when its waters, after having been washed by gods and lingams, continued downward to the spectacular royal cities of their kingdom. During the reign of King Ang Chan I in the 16th century, the city Mahendraparvata became a worshipping place of Theravada Buddhism. The sculpted Buddha near the summit, set inside a small pagoda, remains a modern-day pilgrimage destination for Cambodians.

### Getting to Phnom Kulen

Phnom Kulen is located 35 miles (50 km) northeast of Siem Reap. The mountain has only recently returned to government hands after the fall of the Khmer Rouge and can be inaccessible or slow going due to poor road conditions, especially in the rainy season. Visitors can walk into the water to take pictures of the lingams but are instructed not to touch the underwater carvings. The reclining Buddha near the summit of Phnom Kulen is the focal point of any Cambodian pilgrimage. It is respectful to remove one's shoes before ascending the stairs to the reclining Buddha sanctuary.

# INDONESIA

Almost all the ancient history of Indonesia lies within the long and narrow island of Java. The first to settle here a half-million years ago was *Pithecanthropus erectus*, a primitive humanoid also known as Java Man. The Indian and Chinese traders arrived around the century of Christ and brought with them their own religions: Hinduism and Buddhism. The great monuments of Java are either Hindu or

Buddhist, or more likely combinations of both. The Buddhist sanctuary of Borobudur and the Hindu complex of Prambanan stand as proud testaments of architectural glory from the eighth and ninth centuries CE. Soon after Islam swept through Java and, still today, remains the official religion of Indonesia.

Early Hindu texts refer to a *Suvarnabhumi*, literally translating into a "Land of Gold." Historians believe the term refers to Java, where the island was central to the cultivation of nutmeg, pepper, and the clove trade for the rest of the world. In the early decades of trade such valued commodities far surpassed their equal weight in gold. Java and some of the surrounding islands took on the name "Spice Islands" during the period of the first European incursions. Undoubtedly, prosperity flourished on Java for many centuries, as the mainland of Southeast Asia could not satiate the world's desire for the spices. Past records confirm that Javanese spices were found as far away as Mesopotamia in 1700 BCE, and featured in Roman literature around the first century BCE.

## Borobudur

On top of a volcanic mound lies a fantastic stupa complex of shrines dedicated to the Buddha. The name is Borobudur, meaning "monastery of accumulated virtue." Philosophically, the association of Buddha and stupa is most neatly stated in an aphorism from a medieval Javanese text: "The body of the Buddha is a stupa." This Mahayana Buddhist stupa-temple is the premier architectural masterpiece of Indonesia. Erected by the Sailendra (Kings of the Mountain) Dynasty in the eighth century CE, the temple structure has nine levels. The building features stone terraces mounted on a pre-existing hill rising 140 feet (43 m) above the surrounding rice fields. On the higher tiers are 72 bell-shaped stupas containing statues of the Buddha. Lower galleries contain more than 1,300 relief panels depicting the symbolic life of the Buddha. The stupa consists of six square terraces that are in turn surmounted by three circular terraces. In all, each facade has 108 Buddha statues, a number that is considered auspicious in Indian numerological systems.

The stupa is a symbolic representation of the Mahayana Buddhist cosmological view of the universe. The lower level depicts humankind's monumental place in the world, bound by rebirth under the karmic Law of Cause and Effect, and owing to humans' unceasing attachment to desire. The higher square terraces have highly artistic relief carvings depicting the life of Gautama (the Buddha) and the Bodhisattvas (high virtue beings destined for Buddhahood). The upper-most square terrace is transitional, passing to three circular terraces bearing 72 latticed dagoba, arranged in a concentric circle around the central structure. The upper

▲ An overview of Borobudur. Its shape resembles a mandala.

▲ The author encounters a mythical beast on one of the lower terraces of Borobudur.

depictions represent the formless states reached by a Buddhist disciple after complete detachment over incredibly long periods of time from the human desires that bind mortals to the wheel of life. To climb Borobudur is to ascend symbolically from hell to the temporal, and finally to celestial worlds.

**Borobudur can be viewed as a physical example of the Buddhist path that humans should follow if they hope to progress to nirvana. It is the largest Buddhist monument on earth.**

From above, the design of Borobudur resembles a *mandala* (a Hindu pattern used in meditation), leading to speculation that the complex was built by Indian Buddhists who were influenced by Hindu beliefs. Viewed from the ground, the mandala comes together to form a mountain of stone. Mountain peaks, according to Buddhist thought, are the place where contact with divine truth may take place. Pilgrims today and yesterday would climb Borobudur level by level, drawing closer and closer to complete infusion by divine wisdom. Essentially, the pilgrim can experience nirvana on earth.

As a testament in stone Borobudur is remarkable, but even without its religious implications the art of the carved reliefs would ensure it a high place among the world's greatest monuments. Unfortunately, Borobudur was shaken severely by an earthquake and much defaced by the Muslims who left it to ruin. It was rediscovered and partially restored by a British expedition in 1815. The structures' foundation was in threat of collapsing until the Indonesian government, with aid from UNESCO and private donations, undertook a major renovation program. The restored Borobudur monument is now nearly restored to its original grandeur, as the work was completed in mid-1983.

### Getting to Borobudur

Borobudur is located 30 miles (48 km) northwest of Jogjakarta, pretty much in the middle of Java. Private taxis are the most convenient mode of transportation, but are expensive. If you go by local bus, first go to the town of Muntilan, and there change to the local bus that passes Borobudur. The round trip by bus takes about four hours from Jogjakarta, about three by taxi.

## Prambanan

The neighborhood of Jogjakarta is well known for its wealth of architectural remains. This region, known as the Prambanan Plain, has the largest concentration of ancient temples in Indonesia—some 50 in all. It was during the middle Javanese or classical period (eighth and ninth centuries CE), when the influences of Indian traditions, especially religions, swept the island. There are numerous sites from this and later periods that spread widely over central Java, the most notable being Borobudur and Prambanan. An inscription dating from 782 was located on the outskirts of Jogjakarta commemorating King Kailasa as a great ruler with a penchant for building temples. Kailasa led the Sailendra (Kings of the Mountain) Dynasty in the eighth century CE, whom the inscription credited the construction of most of the region's temples. His kingdom spread up the Malay Peninsula as far north as Cambodia, and encompassed much of what is modern Indonesia. The first Cambodian king, Jayavarman II, almost certainly visited Borobudur and Prambanan as they were being built, and took many architectural ideas back with him before founding the Khmer empire.

Prambanan is a grouping of temples—mostly Hindu, but featuring some Buddhist images. Most of the buildings were constructed in the second half of the ninth century CE under the Hindu Mataram Dynasty. Nearby are the Buddhist Kalasan Sewu and Plaosan temples completed about the same time as the others. The Candi Sambisari temple was discovered in 1966 when a farmer's plow hit a stone that turned out to be the top of the largest temple to be found intact in Java.

**The three western temples at Prambanan are dedicated to the Hindu Trinity—Brahma, Shiva and Vishnu.**

The temple complex of Prambanan is sometimes called Candi Larajonggrang, named after the statue of the cursed maiden to be found in the north room of the largest building dedicated to Shiva. The statue is easily identified because of her broken-off nose and her shiny black

▲ The entrance doorway of a Prambanan temple.

breasts and belly worn smooth by fond caresses over the centuries. The main complex has a square inner court encircled by a wall. Within this court are eight stone shrines: three in a row along the west side facing east, another row of three along the east side facing west, and two smaller temples between them. The largest temple in Prambanan is the Shiva temple, measuring 174 feet (53 m) in height. The Brahma temple is to the south, and the Vishnu temple is to the north of the Shiva temple. The Shiva temple has four main rooms. In the central room is an image of Shiva, the destroyer and renovator of all things. The southern room contains Bhatara Guru, and the west room the elephant-headed son of Shiva, Ganesha. In the north room is the image of the popular cursed maiden after whom the complex is named.

### Getting to Prambanan

Prambanan is located 10 miles (16 km) northeast of Jogjakarta—the cultural capital of Java—along the Surakarta (Solo) road. Local buses and taxis ply the route hourly from Jogja. Some of the temples are spread far across the Prambanan Plain, so a good location map or tour guide is necessary for taking in the whole site.

### INDONESIA TRAVEL ADVISORY

The U.S. State Department issued a travel warning to all visitors to Indonesia after 202 people were killed in a car-bombing attack on two nightclubs in Kuta Beach, Bali. The two explosions occurred almost simultaneously late at night on October 12th, 2002 and were targeted directly at foreign tourists. The government of Indonesia has since convicted several suspects and greatly improved security measures on Bali and throughout Indonesia. Another terrorist bombing rocked the capital Jakarta on August 5th, 2003. Travelers are advised to be especially alert for potentially risky situations during any trip to Indonesia.

# THAILAND

Some of the earliest traces of human culture can be found in Thailand. It is evident that *Homo erectus* passed through Thailand on his way down the Malay Peninsula, where his remains have been unearthed on the Indonesian island of Java. The earliest traces of inhabitation come from the Ban Chiang culture (4,000 BCE to 500 CE), named after the village of Ban Chiang in northeast Thailand. Here the earliest Southeast Asian high culture emerged by producing impressive jewelry items and weapons out of bronze. The ancient Ban Chiang inhabitants also produced beautiful earthenware pots, some embellished with curving and spiral designs. This early culture must have held a profound belief in the afterlife, because many of these objects were found buried in graves. Like the Egyptians, they buried personal objects with the body so the deceased would have their necessary items in the next world.

The art and architecture of Thailand were largely produced in the service of Theravada Buddhism, which was introduced from India in the fifth century CE.

Thailand is the largest Buddhist nation in Southeast Asia and has nearly 20,000 temples (*wats*) and monasteries scattered throughout the cities and countryside. Although animism is practiced in the ubiquitous Thai spirit houses seen everywhere, its mixture with Buddhism is easily tolerated by the mellow Thai people. The result is the gentlest and most liberal form of Buddhism practiced today. Glittering Buddhist temples and shrines are scattered around Thailand. Most young men continue to embrace monkhood for a short time, usually for one year. Religious festivals and visits to Buddhist temples are an integral part of Thai life, but influence from the West is becoming more and more apparent, such as strip malls and Western fashion.

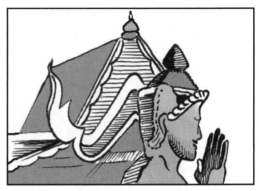

## Sukhothai

The Khmers of Angkor were the first to settle Sukhothai, establishing the site originally as a major frontier post. As Khmer power waned, several rival kingdoms emerged in peninsular Thailand in the 13th century CE, each vying for regional power. The most notable kingdom was Sukhothai, being founded in 1238, when several northern Thailand kings unified to drive the Khmers out of their frontier post. The son of a rebellious king named Ramkhamhaeng rose to power and eventually unified the country. He was Thailand's first great king and chose Sukhothai as his capital. King Ramkhamhaeng ascended the throne in 1278, ruled for 40 years, and became known as a fair and just ruler. His reputation became legendary—much like King Arthur in England—with Sukhothai as his fabled court. King Ramkhamhaeng opened political relations with China, visited Emperor Kublai Khan in 1282, and returned with Chinese artisans and the basis for a new Thai alphabet. Sukhothai came to represent early Thai society in its purest form—a period when citizens were allowed to pursue their chosen livelihood. During his reign there was a high degree of prosperity and happiness. In fact, the name *Sukhothai* translates into "the dawn of happiness."

**Early on Sukhothai emerged as the first independent Thai kingdom. As a result the ancient city became exalted as ushering in the golden era of Thailand history.**

Sukhothai was originally founded by the Khmers, who left behind three buildings and a sophisticated water irrigation system like those they constructed at Angkor, Cambodia. After the Angkorian outpost was evacuated, the Thais moved in and

▲ The stupa-filled Old Sukhothai covers a large area surrounded by earthen walls and moats. The ancient city is highly revered by the people of Thailand.

started constructing their own buildings. First built was a massive wall protecting the inner city, including two moats, three earthen ramparts, and four gates. At one of the gates King Ramkhamhaeng set up a bell, where, if his subjects needed help settling a dispute, they could ring the bell and he would emerge and dispense justice. Within the inner city there were at least 35 monuments, including Buddhist temples and 70 more in the immediate area, most repeating familiar architectural themes. Unfortunately, the Thais eschewed the intricate Khmer irrigation system and when the Yom River changed its course, the city dried up. This is believed to have led to the city's demise after serving as the capital for 120 years.

The Thais of Sukhothai adopted Theravada Buddhism, distinguishing themselves from the Hindu influence of the Cambodian kings. Little remains of the Khmer statues of Hindu gods such as Vishnu and Shiva, while the elegant Theravada Buddha images of Sukhothai — replete with parrot's beak noses and elongated faces — were housed in temples of brick, many of which can still be seen today. A common statue is the characteristic sitting Buddha in a lotus posture with his hands resting in a gesture of meditation, conveying both spiritual strength and solidity. Most statues of the Buddha were carved for placement at a Buddhist stupa or monastery. His elongated earlobes, the lotus marks on his palms, the cranial bump with the flame of wisdom, and the third eye of insight together identify the Thai image of Buddha. Ever since the founding of Sukhothai, Buddhism has been deeply rooted in the Thai way of life.

### Getting to Sukhothai

Sukhothai is located about 267 miles (427 km) north of Bangkok. There is a New Sukhothai of modern buildings and an Old Sukhothai where the ancient capital resides, about seven miles (12 km) apart. Public transportation from other Thai cities access New Sukhothai, where most of the accommodations and restaurants are, while people seeking the ruins of Old Sukhothai usually take a shuttle or tuk-tuk (small taxi) out to the site. There is regular bus service from Bankgkok's Northern Terminal to Old Sukhothai. New Sukhothai is best reached by tour bus, or a private vehicle up Route 1 to Tak, then Highway 105 west.

# VIETNAM

The long coastline of Vietnam was favorable for it to become an important trading center and watershed of religions. Early in its development, China influenced Vietnam stronger than any other Southeast Asian country. Chinese feudalists dominated its southern neighbor for more than 1,000 years, leaving behind its language, writing style, and cultural traditions. Areas in the south drew inspiration from India up until the 16th century. Today, most Vietnamese are Buddhists, but this has not always been the case. Located in southern Vietnam, often on hilltops, are Hindu temples constructed from the seventh to 16th centuries CE. Hindu temple interiors are small, leaving artistic decoration primarily for the exterior. The idea behind these temples was to draw worshippers inside where they could pay homage individually before the Hindu god of their choice, usually bringing incense or flowers to the altar. Buddhist temples of Vietnam, on the other hand, are big on the inside and are usually part of a larger complex. Like Christian monasteries, Buddhist monks have separate living quarters near their buildings of worship. The main hall, dedicated to the Buddha, can be rather large, and many images of the Buddha are placed upon the altar. Similar to Hindu temples, worshippers honor the Buddha individually.

## Cham Towers

The minority Cham people of Vietnam are an interesting and ancient subset of people. Cham people are more deeply pigmented than the Vietnamese and speak their own language (similar to Malay) in addition to Vietnamese. Cham men wear sarongs, short jackets and sometimes very colorful headwear, while the women wear long button-less dresses. There is a strong matrilineal element in their social affairs; for example, some of the Chams are Hindu who eat no beef and cremate their dead, while others are Muslim who eat no pork and bury their dead.

The Hindu-influenced realm of the Chams began in the early fifth century CE and remained a powerful force through much of the later medieval period. The Kingdom of Champa was a Hindu Kingdom contemporary with Angkor, located only a few hundred miles away. At various times of ancient Khmer rule, the Chams were the traditional enemies of the Cambodian kings. Both cultures left behind magnificent religious edifices. Scattered across central Vietnam are a number of characteristic brick towers, remnants of the much grander days of the Chams. The architecture and sculpture of the Cham towers are profoundly influenced by the Indian Gupta technique. Yet some Cham characteristics appear more graceful and refined than the Gupta artistic style.

> **Although Hindu influenced, Vietnamese Cham towers today are representative of all religions. Hindu, Buddhist, Muslim and Christian alike are welcome to make offerings.**

▲ Cham towers near the city of Nha Trang.

Ancient Cham towers can often be found near the many coastal towns of central Vietnam. Cham shrines were the focal points of political, economic and social life, and the ocean or major rivers provided easy access. The Cham temple grounds are usually located in the oldest parts of the cities where they reside. The Po Nagar temple near Nha Trang is one of the oldest towers, built by King Saryavarman in 784 CE. There is an excellent tower just on the outskirts of Thap Cham. Other notable Cham towers can be found at Hung Thanh, further north near Qui Nhon, and especially at My Son, located 19 miles (30 km) south of Danang. Within the My Son Valley is the 10th century CE shrine of Bhadresvara, which was the spiritual center for the Chams. My Son was specifically chosen by King Bhadravarnan in the fourth century to be a religious sanctuary. The valley became a Holy Land and continued to host the building of religious Cham structures for many centuries. Archaeologists found My Son at the end of 19th century, buried deep in the jungle foliage after being forgotten for 400 years. My Son was much grander when it was discovered, but was almost completely lost in the Vietnam War. Before the war, dozens of towers were still in fine condition, but after almost 40 years of continuous war in Vietnam, many were destroyed or damaged.

## Getting to Cham Towers

In 2002, the World Heritage Road project was initiated, aimed at connecting several Cham tower locations, as well as four UNESCO-designated sites in central Vietnam. The World Heritage Road connects the 16th century silk route trading post of Hoi An; the sacred Cham remains in My Son Valley; the Phong Nha caves in Quang Binh province; and the ancient imperial city of Hue. The village of Dran, on the road to Phan Rang, contains relics of the Cham Kingdom in the form of a silk coat, a golden crown and other priceless objects. Other Cham villages are located mostly along the coastal plains in Ninh Thuan province and further north.

## Cao Dai Temple

The fantastic Cao Dai Temple in Tay Ninh is headquarters to one of the most esoteric and bizarre religions on earth. Cao Daism, a sect created in the late 1920's, professes to be a synthesis of the "five faiths" —Animism, Buddhism, Confucianism, Taoism, and Christianity. Members are reported to receive messages direct from the spirit Cao Dai, and an assortment of other historical figures, including French novelist Victor Hugo. In a series of visions following World War I, a Vietnamese nationalist working for French colonialists started receiving revelations from the "Reigning God," or a powerful spirit he identified as Cao Dai. The sect quickly began to dominate southern Vietnam, especially Tay Ninh province. Once numbering over two million adherents, Cao Dai membership lost most of its assets and members during the Vietnam War era. In 1985, the Holy See and several hundred temples in Vietnam were returned to the sect, which is now slowly reviving.

**The Tay Ninh cathedral is the Holy See of Cao Daism. Throughout Vietnam the "Eye of God" symbol figures prominently in all of the sect's temples.**

All around the Great Cao Dai Temple, inside and out, an image of the divine eye appears to be keeping a watch over things. The Cao Dai eye is described by the sect as a "mover of the heart, sovereign master of visual perception." It is most commonly represented inside a triangle emitting beams of light, similar to the back of a

▲ The Holy See Cao Dai Temple of Tay Ninh.

119

U.S. one dollar bill. The symbolized Eye of God is painted on a huge green globe decorated with 3,000 stars, inside the temple on an elaborately carved golden altar. It is also represented on the head garments of all the high priests.

All Cao Daists are strict vegetarians "with pure souls in their bodies." They believe carnivores "fattened by foulness of the flesh" will perish at the coming of the Consoler, a messiah figure who will arrive when a new age of consciousness emerges on earth. Following the Chinese duality concept of yin and yang, there is a male and female god in their heaven, which probably explains why the men and women are split when they proceed into the temple. Cao Dai ceremonies consist primarily of meditation and chanting, followed by intermittent body contortions and wild gesticulation. Services are highly stylized, including the offerings of fruit, wine, incense, and occasionally a sacrifice. Public festivals are colorful and marked by elaborate rituals, yet séances with the spirit world are conducted in private. Cao Dai spirit mediums have reported communication with the founders of all the world's major religions, as well as those who helped shape global civilization. Messages are reported from Jesus Christ, William Shakespeare, Mohammed, Buddha, Vladimir Lenin, and Sun Yat-Sen the founder of modern China. Mediums receive their communication while in a deep trance, written or "caught" by scribes who record the messages for the faithful.

### Getting to Cao Dai Temple

The Cao Dai Great Temple is the main attraction of Tay Ninh, a small city near the eastern border of Cambodia. The temple, built between 1933 and 1955, is located more specifically in Long Hoa, 3 miles (5 km) southeast of Tay Ninh along the main road. Tay Ninh is located 60 miles (96 km) northwest of Ho Chi Minh City (Saigon) in southwest Vietnam. There is regular bus service from Ho Chi Minh City to Tay Ninh every day. Also of fame in the area is Nui Ba Den (Black Lady) Mountain, rising 3,235 feet (986 m) above the surrounding paddy fields.

# AUSTRALIA

# AND THE PACIFIC

*For pilgrimage to make sense —it must represent a complete integration of inner and outer life, of one's relation to oneself and to other men. If we instinctively seek a paradisiacal and special place on the earth, it is because we know in our inmost hearts that the earth was given to us in order that we might find meaning, order, truth and salvation in it. The world is not only a vale of tears. There is joy in it somewhere. Joy is to be sought for the glory of God. —Thomas Merton*

THE FAR-FLUNG ISLANDS IN THE VAST PACIFIC OCEAN have long inspired explorers and pilgrims since people first took to the sea. Egyptian and Phoenician mariners left evidence of their early voyages on islands of the Torres Straits near Australia. Much later and against all odds, Polynesian seafarers colonized thousands of islands in the expansive Pacific basin. From proselytizing Christian missionaries to writers like Herman Melville, James Michener, Robert Louis Stevenson and others, places like Pago Pago, Tahiti and Fiji became synonymous with exotic adventure. The canvases of Paul Gaúguin immortalized the natives of Polynesia, while renowned explorers like James Cook and Abel Tasman mapped the whole region.

To some, Australia and the South Pacific represent the last part of the world relatively untarnished by the modern age. Primitive cultures retain their heritage, wild animals roam freely, and a strong emphasis on conservation is implemented by their mutual governing bodies. Australia, for example, protects nearly all 1,250 miles (2,000 km) of the Great Barrier Reef (GBR) stretching along its northeastern coast. And it's a good thing too, because the GBR is home to 1,500 species of fish, 4,000 species of mollusks and 500 types of seaweed. As observed around the world, Mother Nature provides her share of sacred places—above and below the water.

# AUSTRALIA

E ons ago, the Aboriginal people of Australia—the oldest variety of Homo sapiens and oldest surviving culture —visualized the planetsphere. In their collective consciousness known as "dreamtime," the Aboriginal people could communicate telepathically. Creating a rhythm with two sticks and a hollow branch know as a didgeridoo, the oldest musical instrument in the world, the tribes came together in a unity dance ritual. Using these primal instruments, the Aboriginal people could dance themselves into a deep trance-like state and invoke the energy of Australian sacred sites. Indeed, the Aboriginal people knew of the earth's ley lines, and called them "song lines" in accordance to their invoking musical instincts.

Located in numerous places around the continent of Australia are relics of ancient Egypt. From Egyptian coins and hand tools to buried ships and even pyramids, the evidence suggests that Australia was visited by ancient Egyptian seafarers, who traveled east over the great oceans to the fabled land of Punt. In Queensland a rock statue of a baboon holding a papyrus against his chest was uncovered. The sculpture was discovered near the terraced pyramid at Gympie and likely represents Thoth (the Egyptian god of science), yet no baboons live outside of Africa or Arabia. It is a little-publicized fact that in King Tut's tomb was found a case of gold and inlaid stone boomerangs, which suggests a direct interaction with the Aboriginal people of Australia. Even today, the island inhabitants of the Torres Straits (between Australia and New Guinea) practice many curious customs of ancient Egypt, including mummification and elaborate mask dances.

## Arnhem Land

In the far north of Australia, in the unincorporated Northern Territory, is a highly sacred region to Aboriginal people called Arnhem Land. Here on the "Top End" of the continent resides the last remaining true dreamtime Aboriginals. It is also the first place the Aboriginal people settled, with some artifacts dating 40,000 years or older. Spectacular scenery, wildlife and Aboriginal art make Arnhem Land one of the most extensive wilderness areas on the continent.

Although Aboriginal rock art is found in most parts of Australia, Arnhem Land is the best-known rock art province. In western Arnhem Land are the famous "X-ray" fish painted in rock shelters. They combine a naturalistic profile and visible external features of fish incorporated with a complex infill including bones and intestines. Also found are an older tradition of Mimi figures, which depict detailed scenes of prehistoric life. Hand stencils are common all over Australia and some can be dated to 50,000 years old. Aboriginal rock art continues to be produced in Arnhem Land, making it the world's longest lasting artistic tradition.

**For reasons unexplained, Arnhem Land contains more meteorite craters than any other place in Australia.**

Near the confluence of the Rose and Roper Rivers in the Brimmy Valley just south of Arnhem Land is a lost city associated with the Egyptians. Australian explorers named it the "ruined City of the Moon," or "Moon City." The early explorers recorded similarities between Aboriginal depictions and those of the Masons or the Egyptians. The Aboriginals call the place "Burrangie," the legendary home of giant people who live in the realm of dreamtime. Moon City is considered an ultra-sacred Aboriginal site and is strictly off-limits to outsiders.

▲ Arnhem Land Aboroginals can sometimes be seen traveling around Australia playing the didgeridoo for donations.

The European invasion meant the destruction of Aboriginal society, and most natives have now assimilated into the white man's world. Few Aboriginals completely live their hunter-and-gatherer way of life anymore in Australia. Some of the Aboriginal population living within Arnhem Land are among the last to truly retain their language, culture, and religion of pre-contact times. Their nomadic way of life is reflected in their religious beliefs. In Aboriginal cosmology, the manifested world has its origin in, and continues to be dependent upon, the collective dreaming of the group, known as dreamtime. Aboriginal myth originated with their concept of dreamtime, in which ancestral beings roamed the earth, creating the traditional paths the Aborigines followed and the shapes of the earth itself. While only a few tribes of outback Australian Aboriginals remain in the golden age of dreamtime, most will profess a primordial oneness with the earth. The core of Aboriginal culture and dance rituals is a perceived direct relationship with the rocks, minerals, plants, insects, and animals. Their songs and stories celebrate a strong relationship with their beloved land upon which they exist.

### Getting to Arnhem Land

Arnhem Land is strictly an Aboriginal Reserve and travel to outside persons is restricted. As with other Aboriginal Reserves, visitors must obtain an entry permit. No paved roads exist in Arnhem Land and getting around is very difficult. Swampy marshes, unmarked trails, and estuary crocodiles—some growing to 26 feet (8 m)—make overland travel a hazardous proposition. Most travelers opt to visit only neighboring Kakadu National Park, which is far more accessible, open to tourism, and just outside the city of Darwin.

## Uluru (Ayers Rock)

Centered in the middle of the Australian outback is a massive slab of orange rock known to local Aboriginal tribes as Uluru. Much later, Western explorers named it Ayers Rock after an explorer and the name stuck. Aboriginal people believe Uluru is the origin of life and the center of the universe. The word *uluru* means, "the all-knowing and everlasting" and the giant freestanding rock is indeed the most sacred site in Australia to the Aboriginal people.

## Located in the red center of the continent is Uluru, a huge mass of stone resembling the shape of a human brain on its side.

Ayers Rock is actually the summit of a single buried sandstone rock, measuring five miles (8 km) around the base and rising 1,150 feet (350 m) above the surrounding plain. The elevation from the top of the rock is 2,610 feet (783 m) above sea level. The unique position of Uluru suggests that the rock was once submerged in a shallow sea and ended up in its present position after the sea dried up or drained.

As the center of the universe to the Aboriginal people, Uluru was a pilgrimage and meeting place of the tribes since time immemorial. The tribes would typically gather in the winter when the climate was dry and cool. Aboriginal tribes would follow telluric currents in the earth known as "Song Lines" or "Dreaming Tracks," which are the ley lines of Australia said to converge directly upon Uluru.

Around the base of Uluru are several sacred caves, some forbidden to entry by non-Aboriginal people. Most of the caves are richly decorated with paintings portraying the legends of their collective dreamtime. Depicted are snake-men and lizard-men that fought each other and lived around the rock many eons ago. Aboriginal legend tells of a famous dreamtime battle fought at the rock between mythical creatures, leaving the rock scarred as it is today from that moment in the dim past. In fact, every crack, crevice, hole, lump, indentation and cave has some meaning to local Aboriginals.

Uluru                    Ayer's Rock, AUSTRALIA

### Getting to Uluru (Ayers Rock)

Located almost exactly in the center of the Australian continent, Uluru is a long way from the habitable coastline. Further isolated by desert on all four sides, travelers must be prepared for a sometimes-harsh outback experience. Roads in remote areas are not suitable for conventional cars, and the lack of food, water and gasoline can make travel hazardous even by four-wheel-drive vehicles. Most travelers visiting Ayers Rock opt to take a bus tour from the southern Australian cities. Alice Springs in the Northern Territory is the nearest major settlement to Uluru, some 300 miles (480 km) away. It is about a 45-minute climb to the summit of the rock on the east side.

## Sacred Aboriginal Sites

Twenty miles (32 km) due west of Ayers Rock are the Olgas, a fascinating cluster of rocks also part of Uluru National Park. The Olgas are a huge grouping of cathedral-like domed rocks covering an area of 11 square miles (18 sq. km). The sandstone and granite domes form a circlet of minarets, which the Aboriginals named the Many Headed Mountains (Olgas). The Aborigines believe the physical marks on the Olgas were left by ancestral beings long ago, hardened into rock, and now denote their distinct features and shapes. The Olgas are positioned in perfect parallel with Uluru and another peak called Mount Conner, which resembles the keep of a mediaeval castle.

Mootawingee is a single oasis of permanent water and life with thousands of miles of scorching desert land surrounding it. This oasis was a primary intersection of dreamtime during the dry season. Here, the dreaming would converge all desert people on the same days for water, trade and communal dance. This single energy spot of life in an unforgiving land was a focal point of walkabout for thousands of years. The record of dreamtime is found at Mootawingee and is expressed in chants passed on to the youth in songs at initiation ceremonies.

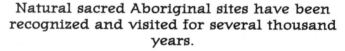

**Natural sacred Aboriginal sites have been recognized and visited for several thousand years.**

Mt.Warning Australia

The Nullarbor Plain, a vast plateau of porous limestone, stretches for hundreds of desolate miles in the south and central portions of Australia. Near the coast where tall limestone cliffs crack off into the ocean, several caves offer shelter in this inhospitable region. The Nullarbor caves, some still unexplored, range in size from narrow mole-holes to chambers so massive that they contain subterranean rivers and lakes. Fresh water meant sustainability for the Aboriginal tribes and protection from the blistering sun. Koonalda Cave contains some of the oldest known Aboriginal rock engravings. Inside the cave are petroglyphs of geometric figures and meandering lines incised into the soft limestone walls. Koonalda Cave is a sacred cavern located along the southern Australian coastline known as the "Big Bight."

The summit of Mount Wollumbin (Mount Warning) is the first place in Australia to reflect the sun's rays each morning. From here, it is believed that whatever is invoked at sunrise will go on to influence the rest of the Australian continent. *Wollumbin* means "Fighting Chief of the Mountains" to Aboriginals, and the mountain is said to possess strong male energies. Tribes would migrate to the triangular land between Wollumbin, Nimbin Rocks and Cape Byron because they could recognize the powerful energies created in this sacred triangle. Aboriginal tribes would use the land within this triangle for ritual purposes rather than as a dwelling place. Captain Cook named it Mount Warning because of offshore dangers.

### Climbing Mount Wollumbin

To reach the top of this 3,795-foot (1,157-m) extinct volcano, it's best to start your trek from Nimbin at least three hours before sunrise. Full moon nights are ideal. The mountain peak is the center of the largest volcanic crater in the world, stretching 39 miles (63 km) across, and extending partly out to sea. The crater's center is Mount Wollumbin, and the core of the crater is replete with mineral deposits and volcanic caves. No mining or souvenir collecting is allowed.

# HAWAIIAN ISLANDS

The Hawaiian archipelago is the most remote population center in the world. The eight main islands are centrally located in the North Pacific Ocean, some 2,500 miles (4,000 km) from the nearest continent. Before the arrival of humans, all original flora and fauna on the Hawaiian Islands came by air, on ocean currents, or attached to migratory birds. The odds were highly against any life form making this long journey successfully, but time is always on the side of evolution. Those species that managed to survive the transition rapidly diversified and flourished due to the temperate climate and limited competition. Species endangerment started when the first Polynesian people arrived with introduced plants and animal species causing many endemic extinctions and near-extinctions, particularly among birds.

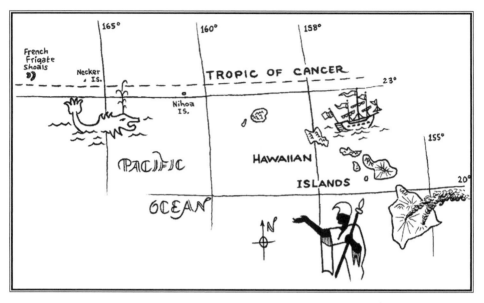

# THE BIG ISLAND HAWAII

All the Hawaiian Islands were created by volcanic activity, but only on the Big Island of Hawaii are those volcanoes still active. Not only is the mass of the Big Island the youngest land in the world, it is the largest single object on earth—that is if the huge bulk of mountain underwater is included. By such calculations, Mauna Kea is also the tallest mountain on earth, standing 13,796 feet (22,211 m) above sea level and 20,000 feet (32,200 m) below water. Without question Mouna Kea is the tallest mountain in the Pacific basin and the only peak in this vast region to have supported glaciers during the last Ice Age. In the shadow of the great mountain the first Polynesians arrived in Hawaii and erected their villages, sacred *heiaus*, and etched petroglyphs (rock carvings) to explain their existence. The first Polynesian voyagers are estimated to have arrived around the second or third century CE, and likely went on to support a population of Polynesians far greater than are found in Hawaii today.

## City of Refuge (*Pu'uhonua o Honaunau*)

The name *Pu'uhonua* is an ancient Hawaiian title for the similar biblical term "City of Refuge," where those guilty of *kapu* (something forbidden) could be absolved of their misdoing, or the innocent could wait out a violent conflict. If a common person looked directly at a chief or got too close, it was considered *kapu*. This strict taboo standard also applied to walking in the chief's footsteps, touching the chief's possessions, landing a boat on the chief's beach, or allowing one's shadow to fall on the palace grounds. Everyday activities, too, were regulated by *kapu*. Women could not eat food reserved for offerings to the gods such as pork or coconut; they could not prepare meals for men or eat with men. Even activities such as gathering wood, fishing or killing animals were all strictly controlled. At the instance of a *kapu* being broken, suddenly everybody in the community was against the *kapu* breaker, lest the gods become angered and take revenge on everyone in the form of volcanic reactions, tidal waves, famine, or earthquakes. The only hope for someone breaking *kapu* was to avoid capture and run to a City of Refuge. Those who survived the chase and got through the heavily fortified compound were awarded clemency for their crime. Upon arrival, a ceremony of absolution was performed by the *kahuna pule* (priest) and the offender could then return home safely, usually within a few hours or the next day. All islanders respected the spirit of the *Pu'uhonua*. Since no blood was to be spilled within its' confines, non-combatants during war, loaded with provisions, would seek the City of Refuge to wait in safety until the conflict was over. Since the object of war in ancient times was to exterminate the enemy, which included anyone who belonged to the opposing side, women, children and the elderly risked execution unless they could escape to a City of Refuge. Similarly, warriors who were undecided on either battling chief could wait for the outcome and then swear their allegiance to the victor. Inside the heavily fortified sacred precincts were high priests and several *heiau* (meaning 'temple' and pronounced 'hey ow') surrounded by a high wall. The Hawaiian word *hei* means to summon, capture or ensnare, and *au* implies a vibration, current, or invisible power or energy. Thus, a *heiau* captures spiritual power (*mana*). Outside the City of Refuge was a fortified compound for the royal chiefs (*ali'i*), which was guarded by armed warriors and a fleet of war canoeists.

**The City of Refuge served as a safe haven for people wishing to stay out of a conflict, or guilty criminals hoping to avoid execution and receive a second chance.**

Each island had at least one, and the Big Island is thought to have had six, yet only three are known: Pu'uhonua o Honaunau, Waipio Valley and Coconut Island in Hilo. Since only the strongest and the smartest could survive this rigid social system, *kapu* was the primary way ancient Hawaiians would "weed out the weaklings." Thus, survival of the fittest was a fundamental principle of ancient Hawaiian law, in which might was usually considered right, unless one could safely make it to the City of Refuge.

The *kapu* system, however, was to be short lived after the arrival of European explorers, and the City of Refuge stood at the crossroads of immense change within the lifetime of a single man. As was typical to most native islanders in the vast Pacific basin, the first Europeans in their tall masted sailing ships came as a big surprise. The islanders had only limited ways of interpreting these arrivals, so they assumed the Europeans were visiting gods and treated them as such. When Captain Cook returned to the Big Island after making initial contact to fix a broken mast, the

▲ Early European explorers were amazed at the spirited and frenzied war dances of the Hawaiians, as can be seen in this 19<sup>th</sup> century depiction.

Hawaiians took this as a bad omen and killed the eminent explorer in a scuffle at Kealakekua Bay, a mere eight miles (13 km) north of the City of Refuge. An impressionable and ambitious man in his mid-twenties named Kamehameha (pronounced 'kah may ha may ha') was present for Cook's first arrival and tragic second landing. It is quite possible that Kamehameha was involved in the brawl that took Cook's life, and present at the ceremony afterward where his body was burned, stripped of flesh, and offered to the gods in exchange for the great navigator's *mana*. Before Cook's death, the young Kamehameha was fascinated by the ship *Resolution*, visiting the vessel several times and even obtaining permission to spend a night on board. What interested him the most were the Western weapons the ship carried, an interest that was to become a determining factor in his successful fight to unify the Hawaiian Islands under one regime. He lived his dream and became known as King Kamehameha the Great, but upon his death in 1819 his wife and son dismantled the *kapu* system forever. Pu'uhonua o Honaunau and all the old pagan temples on the island were either destroyed or fell into disrepair. Fortunately, the temples along the Kona Coast where Kamehameha died were simply abandoned and remain in good condition today. The *pali* (cliffs) above Kealakekua Bay, where Captain Cook met his undignified fate, was a sacred burial location for great chiefs, including perhaps the remains of Kamehameha I and Captain Cook himself. An obelisk on the north side of Kealakekua beach stands to commemorate the spot where the renowned navigator was killed.

### Getting to City of Refuge (Pu'uhonua o Honaunau)

Called the single most evocative historical site in all the Hawaiian Islands, the City of Refuge has adopted the name Pu'uhonua o Honaunau National Historic Park. It is located 25 miles (40 km) south of Kailua-Kona via Hawaii 11 to Hawaii 160 (intersec-

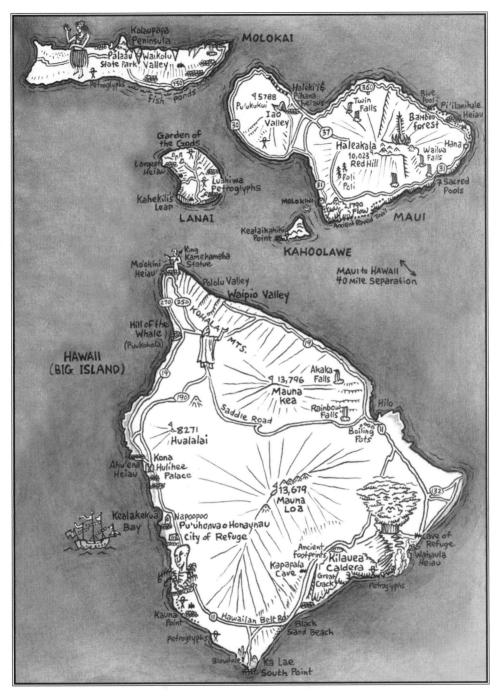

tion is between mileposts 103 and 104). There are alternative routes near the turnoff for the Painted Church, or via the ocean route past Napo'opo'o. There is a small entrance fee to the historic site, administered by the National Park Service. Just south of the City of Refuge is a beautiful public beach renowned as one of the best snorkeling spots on the island. Getting down to Kealakekua Bay requires a strenuous hike both ways, but the views are fantastic and dolphins can often be spotted in the bay. There is no entrance fee to Kealakekua Bay. Numerous snorkeling boats congregate at Kealakekua Bay every day, but swimmers are not allowed to swim ashore.

# MAUI

The first chief to unite Maui in the 16th century from centuries of tribal warfare was a chief named Pi'ilani. He not only united all of Maui, but went on to conquer the neighboring Kahoolawe, Lanai and Molokai islands. Pi'ilani is also credited as the first chief to initiate a road encircling an entire Hawaiian island; wide enough for eight men to walk shoulder to shoulder, and completed by his son Kihapi'ilani. Parts of the modern Pi'ilani Highway follow the ancient route, and near La Pérouse Bay sections of the original road are still intact. The first European to set foot on Maui was the French admiral La Pérouse in 1786, yet he defied orders and refused to claim the island for the French Crown out of respect for the Hawaiian people. The last eruption on Maui occurred four years later, wiping out the village at La Pérouse Bay where the French navigator had just landed.

## Haleakala

Everything in East Maui centers around, or is inside, the massive cone-shaped Haleakala volcano. Rising 10,023 feet (3,007 m) into the tropical sky, from a sea-level base of 33 miles (53 km) in diameter, Haleakala is the world's largest dormant volcano and holds many unusual distinctions. Viewing the huge mountain from top down, Haleakala National Park contains an enormous crater at the summit — an immense bowl measuring 7.5 miles (12 km) long, 2.5 miles (4 km) wide, and .5 mile (.8 km) deep — which could

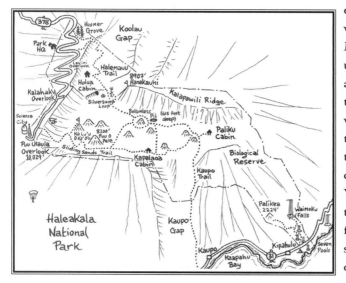

easily accommodate the whole island of Manhattan. Along the upper slopes of Haleakala and inside the crater lives the rarest plant in the world, the silversword. On the southeast slopes lies the greatest climactic change in the world. Within one mile you can travel from a tropical rainforest on the windward side to desert conditions on the leeward side.

Significant archaeological remains have been found inside the crater, yet there is no evidence the ancient Hawaiians ever made their homes in this hostile environment. In pre-contact times they hiked to the summit to mine basalt for adzes, to hunt birds, conduct religious ceremonies, and bury their dead. Lately archaeologists have discovered traces of an ancient paved road that once crossed the crater floor and led down the Kaupo Gap. One of the most spectacular sections of the crater is called Pele's Paint Pot, named after the vivid streak of red sand against a backdrop of brown and yellow mounds.

### Haleakala was a very sacred place to ancient Hawaiians. The literal translation *Hale a ka la* means "House of the Sun."

According to an old Tahitian chant, when the earth was discovered by Polynesians in the primordial ocean, the great god Maui set sail in his fleet of canoes and visited all the Hawaiian Islands, building temples wherever he stopped. Maui Island must have been one of his favorites to derive the name of the legendary demigod. Haleakala Crater is where Maui captured the sun and demanded the sun take longer crossing the horizon every day to allow his mother's *tapa* (bark-cloth) more time to dry. The trickster god Maui caught the sun in a web of ropes and kept it hostage in the "House of the Sun" for many days. The sun agreed to slow its movement, and Maui let it go. Although clouds usually shroud the lower slopes of Haleakala and sometimes fill the

crater, the summit is often bathed in dramatic sunlight. This magnificent display of light is attributed by natives to the demigod Maui. The impression everywhere is of dazzling colors, and viewing the sunrise from the summit of Haleakala is one of the most popular activities for Maui tourists.

The crater of Haleakala is not a crater at all, but the collapsed and eroded portions of a once 13,000-foot (3,900-m) tall mountain. The cinder cones inside the crater are the result of minor eruptions long after the erosion process began. Dowsers and geomancers detect enormous energy coming up through the shield volcano Haleakala. It is believed there is a massive crystal underneath Haleakala; a wedged part of the earth's crystallized core pushed up by the volcano. Maybe this is why there are more New Age healing centers and workshops on the slopes of Haleakala than all other Hawaiian Islands combined.

▲ Haleakala crater is an unusual volcanic landscape. It was a mythical place to the Hawaiian people.

### Getting to Haleakala

Snaking its way up the slopes of Haleakala to the summit is Highway 378, which is an easy drive for any rental car. Haleakala National Park is open every day of the year. The Hawaiian Islands are serviced by many major airlines from all parts of the Pacific Rim. Most flights land in Honolulu on Oahu, but an increasing number are flying direct from the mainland to the Big Island, Maui and Kaua'i. Rental cars and accommodations can be arranged at the airport.

# MICRONESIA

In a cluster of South Pacific islands, located approximately between Japan and Australia, is a fascinating archipelago containing megalithic ruins. The Federated States of Micronesia incorporates the Caroline Islands where most of the ruins are located. Famous sites in Micronesia include: a 5-foot andesite stone head and aligned standing stones on Babeldaob Island in Palau; massive standing latte pillars 18 feet (5.5 m) with capstones on the island of Tinian; the Palau island terraces, some resembling step pyramids replete with exotic "crowns" and "brims" on their summits; and massive walls at Lele on the island of Kosrae. Truk Lagoon on Truk Island is where an entire Japanese fleet sunk in the shallow waters of the central lagoon. The battle of Truk Lagoon has been described as America's surprise attack answer to Pearl Harbor, and today is one of the most famous scuba dive locations in the Pacific. Truk Lagoon is not too far from Feefen, where mysterious underwater archaeological ruins remain.

## Nan Madol

On the remote Micronesian island of Pohnpei is Nan Madol, one of the most bizarre lost cities on earth. Constructed of massive basalt slabs weighing 20 to 50 tons (18,140 to 45,350 kg), Nan Madol is a maze of stacked-rock structures along the tidal flats of a shallow coral reef. The immense megalithic stone city, 17 square miles (28 sq. km) in size, resides above and below the ocean's surface. Next to Nan Madol on the southeast corner of Pohnpei is Madolinihmw Harbor, which is known to contain underwater columns in a straight row and assorted sunken ruins, including a so-called "castle," in 200 feet (60 m) of murky water.

Most of the above water ruins lie upon the 90 to 100 artificial islets in "Nan Madol central," an area of approximately a square mile (2.5 sq. km) bisected by canals and underwater tunnels. The ruins on the artificial islands are mostly square or rectangular in shape, each created out of stacked basalt logs, weighing up to an amazing 50 tons (45,350 kg)! The giant rock slabs are set together like Lincoln Logs, creating walls up to 30 feet (10 m) in height. Strangely, none of the native people on Pohnpei build in stone anymore—today they all live in grass huts, which indicates a regression of culture has taken place.

## Early European explorers called Nan Madol the "Venice of the Pacific" because the ancient city was built upon a coral reef and is intersected by artificial water canals.

The largest building of Nan Madol is called Nan Dowas, a massive open-air complex with an inner sanctum. Underground tunnels connect Nan Dowas to several of the larger buildings. It is believed that some of these tunnels go beneath the reef and exit underwater to caves that can be seen while scuba diving. The walls of Nan Dowas are an impressive 33 feet (11 m) in height, and are constructed of huge

▲ Nan Dowas is the largest of many island complexes at Nan Madol.

stones expertly stacked. Some of the rocks are basalt logs 16 feet (5 m) long in a hexagonal shape, formed naturally through crystallization. Other stones are huge slabs, roughly cut and dressed, and are the largest of the rocks used. Contained within the rock basalt of Nan Madol are large crystals, which are highly magnetized. These heavy basalt crystals are so magnetized that compasses spin out of control when held near the walls.

Among the many mysteries of Nan Madol are the strange mineral findings. During the Japanese occupation preceding World War II, Japanese divers discovered platinum coffins near the underwater stone vaults, pillars and monoliths in *Madolinihmw*, the name meaning "City of the Gods." Among the recorded Japanese exports of Pohnpei were copra, vanilla, sago, mother of pearl and platinum. Strangely, the rock on Pohnpei Island and surrounding islands contains no trace of platinum. Further adding mystery, the Japanese divers reported the source of the platinum were watertight tombs containing very large human bones. Giant people of a highly advanced civilization? Could this be evidence of a very old, sunken continent in the Pacific?

### Getting to Nan Madol

Nan Madol is located on the southeast side of Pohnpei island, which lies about 9,920 miles (16,000 km) northeast of New Guinea. Pohnpei is the capital of the newly independent Federated States of Micronesia, and flights arrive daily from the U.S. territory of Guam and other Pacific Rim countries. Pohnpei is part of the Caroline Island chain, and the nearest island with a sizeable population is Guam.

# NEW ZEALAND

The native people of New Zealand, the Maori, were a seafaring tribe of Polynesian (and slightly Melanesian) descent. The Maori were hunters and gathers. Their prize catches were fish, shellfish, shorebirds and the large flightless moa birds, which eventually became extinct by overhunting. The Maori people, however, were not the first inhabitants of this geologically active country. The first arrivals to New Zealand were the now vanished Moriori tribe, the predecessors to the Maori by several centuries. The earliest traces of the Moriori people can be found near or underneath later Maori settlements. It is likely the Moriori and the Maori people assimilated in race, language, culture and religion. For example, the language of the Maori is Austronesian, a blend of Australian Aboriginal and Polynesian. Captain Cook was astonished when his Tahiti interpreter could communicate with the Maori.

## Mount Cook

The mighty Mount Cook, New Zealand's highest mountain at 12,349 feet (6,175 m), was named *Aorangi*, a Maori term meaning "cloud in the sky." This sacred peak was dominion of the Maori gods, and was never to be climbed by native people. Dominating the range of mountains known as the Southern Alps, Mount Cook and the surrounding region is noted for its glaciers and thrilling scenery. The southern coast is indented by numerous fjords and provides many spectacular hiking trails. And Mount Cook is not alone in its grandeur; a dozen of Mount Cook's sister mountains in the spectacular Southern Alps tower more than 10,000 feet (3,000 m), and the range has more than 200 peaks measuring higher than 7,000 feet (2,100 m). The soaring mountains are testimony to the wonder and sheer natural beauty of New Zealand.

### Adding to the mystique of Mount Cook are the Tasman Glacier and the 4,000-foot (1,200-m) Hochsetter Ice Fall.

Most mountains in New Zealand, especially the volcanoes, are shrouded in ancient legend and are considered sacred by the Maori people. Active, dormant and extinct volcanoes cover the North Island, and many hot springs can be found near their bases. Rising from relatively flat surroundings, North Island volcanoes tower high into the sky and invoke awe into all who gaze upon them. Early European explorers like Tasman and Cook used the peaks as navigational markers.

### Climbing Mount Cook

Mount Cook was first climbed on Christmas Day 1894 by three young and inexperienced men from the neighboring region. Their motive was to reach the summit before anyone from outside of New Zealand could claim it. Tourist buses presently run alongside Tasman Glacier to Ball Hut, the place where most treks depart. From here, access to the glacier itself is comparatively easy. Guided day hikes take parties for a walk on the ice where beautiful glacial caves can be seen. An ice pick, crampons, warm clothes and 12 hours of stamina are required to summit Mount Cook.

## North Island Sacred Volcanoes

Similar to the Aboriginals in Australia, the Maori continue to revere a host of natural sacred sites. Near the New Zealand capital city of Auckland rises a cone formation that can be seen for miles around. At its summit are an obelisk and one lone tree, hence the name "One Tree Hill." The warlike Maori had a large settlement near Auckland and built a fortified settlement, called "Maori Pa" on One Tree Hill. The Maori people of today still consider this land sacred and make annual pilgrimages here to visit their ancestors' spiritual home. Other esoteric spiritual groups, including the Druids, recognize the immense power of One Tree Hill and use the site for solstice celebrations, as well as rituals of music and dance. Sharing title with the obelisk and tree at the summit are three large, breached craters. These indented craters create nice wind shelters and natural amphitheaters. Drum circles sound especially commanding from the inside of any crater on One Tree Hill.

One Tree Hill   Auckland, NEW ZEALAND

Three towering volcanoes, one active and two dormant, reside in the middle of the North Island. These volcanoes are especially sacred. The Maoris consider these three mountains as guardian deities. They are Mount Tongariro, Mount Ngauruhoe and Mount Taranaki (called Mount Egmont by Europeans). Taranaki rises like a perfect cone near the shores of the Tasman Sea, while the active Ngauruhoe smolders near Tongariro in the center of the North Island. Mount Ngauruhoe last erupted in 1975.

**All three volcanic mountains in Tongariro National Park are sacred to the Maori.**

According to Maori legend, the three mountains were once grouped together, but Taranaki departed to his present position because of a domestic quarrel. Maori legend also relates the story of a high priest from Arawa who was climbing Mount Ngauruhoe when he was overtaken by a fierce blizzard. Hearing cries, his priestess sisters turned the mountain into a volcano to bring their brother warmth.

Geological activity and remnants of an old volcano are apparent near Lake Taupo, New Zealand's largest lake. Motutaiko Island in Lake Taupo was a Maori burial place, and some of the interment caves can still be seen there. Surrounding the lake is New Zealand's famous geyser and hot spring region. Here, fire and ice lie close together, and the steam that rises from thermal vents can often be seen from afar. Above the thermal caves at Pohutu Geyser, Maori tribe members built a sacred village where the scalding water was both worshiped and utilized. A nearby graveyard points the way to a maze of geysers and mud pools that the Maori used for cooking and washing. Also near the southern end of Lake Taupo is the enigmatic Kaimanawa Wall. The wall is composed of megalithic blocks with symmetrical corners. The level top suggests it may have been a platform pyramid, similar to those found on several islands in the South Pacific. Until the jungle is cleared and a full excavation takes place, the Kaimanawa Wall remains a mystery.

### Getting to the North Island Volcanoes

New Zealand is widest on the North Island at 250 miles (400 km), and the whole country is about 1,000 miles (1,600 km) in length. Sparsely populated (3.4 million people, half Maori) and not very big, New Zealand is easy to navigate and get around. Public transportation, rental cars and hitchhiking are all easy ways to reach the North Island volcanoes. Auckland is the typical starting point, and One Tree Hill is easy to locate just outside the city. One main road travels south from Auckland and all locations are clearly marked and visible from the road.

# TONGA

The archipelago of Tonga borders the western frontier of Melanesia, yet is distinctly Polynesian in race, culture and language. The actual land area is a scant 269 square miles (433 sq. km) of verdant jungle and sandy atolls. The cluster of 150 coral and volcanic islands (only 36 islands are populated) that make up the Polynesian nation of Tonga were dubbed the "Friendly Islands" by Captain Cook in 1773. Though Cook's visit was soon followed by merchants and missionaries, the island-nation stayed in a time warp of sorts. At the time of European world colonization, Tonga maintained a strong central government and has managed to remain an autonomous, independent nation to this day. Tonga has the unique distinction of being the last Polynesian kingdom in the world.

## Mu'a

On the southernmost island of Tonga, called Tongatapu, are many megalithic ruins from a lost city known as Mu'a. The most visible is a massive stone trilithon called the *Ha'amonga Maui*, meaning the Arch, or Burden, of Maui. This megalithic structure consists of two upright stones supporting a precisely fitted horizontal slab, creating an impressive archway. Elsewhere on the island are several platforms of expertly fitted stones, pyramids, a well-constructed harbor and a road and moat system, all suggesting a highly sophisticated civilization. Pottery shards found on Tongatapu match those found on many islands in Melanesia and are identified with the Lapita People, the progenitors of Tonga and Polynesian culture. Mounting evidence indicates that Tongatapu was the central naval base for a pan-Pacific empire that existed for thousands of years and had only fallen into decline a few hundred years before European contact.

## At one time, Mu'a was the capital of the entire Polynesian realm.

The basis of power at Mu'a was its natural harbor, which housed a huge fleet of seagoing vessels. In times of antiquity the captains of Mu'a navigated and unified the vast Pacific Ocean. The glory of the ancient Sun Empire of the Pacific made its capital at *Tongatapu*, which means "Sacred Tonga" or "Sacred South" in Polynesian. Mu'a was the governmental port city, while nearby Haketa where the Ha'amonga trilithon stands had been a great university of astronomy, navigation, climatology and theological history. This maritime empire traded with powerful countries all around the Pacific Rim, including North and South America.

There has been much speculation about the purpose of the Ha'amonga trilithon. Some thought it a gateway to a royal compound, while others note its resemblance to ancient European monuments such as Stonehenge. However, a notch carved on the top lintel points directly to the summer and winter solstices exactly, confirming that the structure was an astronomical observatory. The area of the trilithon is called Haketa, and the remains of several small platforms can be seen.

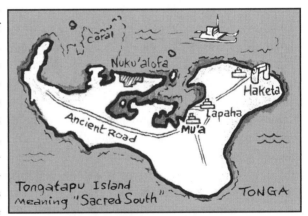

▲ Remnants of an ancient city remains on Tongatapu Island of Tonga.

Haketa was an isolated religious and learning center where students from all over the empire came to study navigation and astronomy for dominion over the great ocean. Indeed, construction of the stone arch alone was a considerable task for a population with limited tools and materials.

The central area of Mu'a was surrounded by a huge canal that offered a sheltered berthing place for smaller canoes and protection from an advancing army. The huge stones at the ancient port on the lagoon side of Mu'a are evidence for the docking of immense transoceanic vessels in ancient times. Mu'a was a planned city that had roads leading from it in all directions. Most of the pyramids at Mu'a are overgrown with trees and bushes growing through the cracks, yet the expert masonry and notched fittings on the famous Tauhala Stone can be seen. The emerging picture of ancient Tonga is one of an extremely advanced culture that built a sophisticated system of roads, canals, monumental pyramids, and other megalithic remains.

### Getting to Mu'a

Tongatapu is the largest island in the Tongatapu Group, the southernmost cluster of islands in Tonga. The capital and international airport are at Nuku'alofa city on Tongatapu. International flights arrive daily and the natural Uta lagoon is a year-round host to yacht travel. The ruined cities of Mu'a and Haketa are located on the eastern side of the island and are easily reached by taxi, bus or bicycle.

# MALDEN ISLAND

On the barren Pacific islet of Malden, completely uninhabited by native islanders since first discovered by European explorers in the early 1800s, lie the remains of a mysterious megalithic culture. From several temple complexes near the center of the island radiates an ancient highway system that spans across the island like a giant spider web. An ancient highway system composed of large basalt slabs fitted tightly together runs across the island, crosses the beach and disappears under the waves of the Pacific. The ancient highways on Malden Island, better described as "paved ways," are very similar to the *Ara Metua,* a paved road on Rarotonga Island, 1,000 miles (1,610 km) to the south of Malden. The *Ara Metua* road on Rarotonga is essentially an island circuit road that goes around the island. Rarotonga, like Malden Island and many others in the Pacific, has a number of pyramid-platforms connected by the megalithic roads.

**Malden Island is a deserted location a thousand miles from anywhere. Why it contains temples, pyramid-platforms and ancient paved paths leading directly into the ocean is still a mystery.**

Several step-pyramids, platforms, megaliths, and strange stacks of stones are scattered across Malden Island. Stepped and truncated pyramids measure in the range of 30 feet (9 m) in height, 20 to 60 feet (6-18 m) in width, and 90 to 200 feet (27-60 m) in length. The pyramids are approached by paved ways from the sea and are capped with dolmens or "compass stones." These 40 stone temples on Malden Island are described as similar in design to the buildings of Nan Madol on Pohnpei, some 3,400 miles (5,475 km) away.

What was the purpose of all these platforms? Were they part of an ancient sun-worshipping cult, altars for Polynesian chiefs, or a "crossroad" meeting place for a seafaring nation? And what of the paved ways leading into the sea? Evidence for the lost Pacific continent of Mu, or Lemuria? Speculation also suggests that Malden Island is positioned on a special power point upon the Earth Grid, acknowledged and venerated by the ancients. This island may have been an important stopover place on trans-Pacific voyages, but the reality is that no one really knows. One thing is for

▲ The desolate Malden Island contains an assortment of megalithic monuments.

certain; some mysterious group put a large amount of effort into building megalithic monuments on an island that could hardly support even a small population.

## Getting to Malden Island

Malden Island is part of the uninhabited Line Islands, which are clustered together with the Phoenix group, and are now part of the Independent Republic of Kiribati. More than 500 miles (800 km) north of Malden is Christmas Island, the only neighboring population center, with only 1,300 people. No tours or charters go to Malden Island, and the only conceivable way to get there would be by a private boat or seaplane. But with no airstrip or amenities, Malden Island would prove difficult to visit for any length of time.

# SOUTH AMERICA

**Feel yourself as pervading all directions, far near.** —*Paul Reps*

OUTH AMERICA HAD A LONG HISTORY OF HIGH CULTURE before the coming of European colonialists. The earliest people, the pre-Inca Viracocha, came and departed mysteriously, only to be usurped by another great civilization, the Inca. Both cultures employed master stone-workers to erect enormous religious and ceremonial centers. When the Spanish and the Portuguese invaded South America in the 16th century, their legions of Christian missionaries were quick to dismantle the heathen religions. However, not all of South America was fully converted to Christianity. Vestiges of pre-Christian religion remain in the nomads of the Andes, the witches of Bolivia, and the tribes living deep in the Amazon jungle.

In the last remaining tribal cultures of South America, the central figurehead of the group is the shaman. He or she is the "doctor of the soul" for both individuals and the community at-large. The primary task of the shaman is to keep the collective spirit healthy, to keep the tribe inspired, and to guide the community in vision. To the shaman, sickness is simply a loss of one's energy, not might or strength. The shamanic teaching is to gain power over oneself and to be in full awareness with everyone and everything. The shaman also sees separation as sickness. An individual can feel separation from community, nature, one's homeland, or from the source. Many South American indigenous people are feeling separated as their land and culture continue to be encroached by the outside world. Now is a crucial period in their very existence.

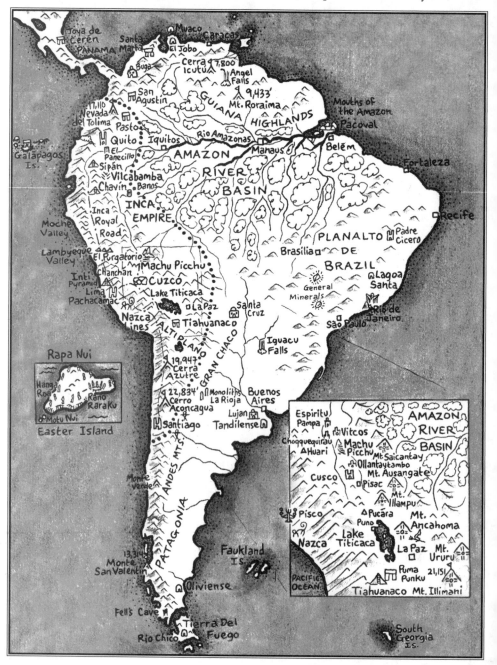

Photo by Karen Tate

▲ Obelisks and megalithic architecture
dazzle visitors throughout Egypt.

Photo by Brad Olsen

▲ A colossal face sculpture at the
Temples of Angkor, Cambodia.

▲ The Temple of Jagannath near Puri, India allows entrance to Hindus only.

▲ The lost city of Hampi is hard to reach, but it is one of the most amazing sacred sites in India.

*Photo by Brad Olsen*

▲ Ultra-sacred Machapuchre, or 'Fish Tail' Mountain soars over the Pokhara Valley in Nepal. The majestic peak rises 22,937 (6,993 m) above sea level.

*Photo by Brad Olsen*

▲ Kathmandu Valley in Nepal features a temple or shrine around every corner.

Photo by Brad Olsen

▲ Inside the Holy See Cao Dai Temple in Tay Ninh, Vietnam.

Photo by Brad Olsen

▲ A characteristic 'elongated' Buddha statue of Sukhothai, Thailand.

▲ Machu Picchu, Peru is a lost city that appears to be floating on clouds.

Photo by David Childress

▲ Tiahuanaco, Bolivia is one of the highest elevation ritual centers in the world.

Photo by David Childress

Photo by Brad Olsen

▲ Bell Rock in Sedona, Arizona is said to contain powerful vortex energy.

Photo by Brad Olsen

▲ Summer solstice sunrise over the astronomically aligned Bighorn Medicine Wheel near Sheridan, Wyoming.

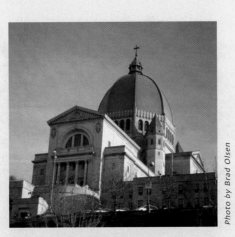

Photo by Brad Olsen

▲ Saint Joseph's Oratory in
Montreal, Canada is a popular
Catholic pilgrimage destination.

Photo by Karen Tate

▲ The Tholos rotunda in the Sacred
Precinct at Delphi was built in the forth
century BCE. What rituals were practiced
here remain a mystery.

▲ The Ggantija Temple on the Mediterranean island of Gozo is one of oldest in the world.

Photo by Karen Tate

▲ The Throne Room in Knossos, Greece is partly restored. The throne, benches, floor and bowl are original.

Photo by Karen Tate

# BOLIVIA

The landlocked country of Bolivia is twice blessed with shoreline along a very sacred lake and some of the last purebred Inca people. The Indians of the *Altiplano* (High Plateau) of Bolivia are some of the most colorful indigenous people in South America. Many Bolivians live according to the age-old traditions established by their ancestors, including the practice of witchcraft. The largest majority of native people live primarily around eastern Lake Titicaca, the world's highest navigable lake at 12,506 feet (3,752 m) in elevation. The Bolivian Indians pasture llamas on the windswept high plains, but gather on the weekends for the colorful "Witch's Market" in La Paz.

## Tiahuanaco

High on the treeless plains just south of Lake Titicaca stand the wind-blasted ruins of Tiahuanaco. Here reside the remnants of a once-great ceremonial center called the "Gateway of the Sun," appropriately elevated on the high Andean plateau. Stone buildings and statues dot the plain 13,000 feet (3,900 m) above sea level. The most notable structure is a doorway carved from several massive slabs of andesite, which once acted as an entrance to the never-completed complex. Carved upon the Gate of the Sun is a central human figure, flanked on either side by three rows of figures that are depicted as half-human and half-bird.

Tiahuanaco was the principal ceremonial center and pilgrimage destination for an advanced Andean people known as the Viracocha. The prehistoric Viracocha are recognized as the original people who brought civilization to South America. It was the Viracocha who were the original builders and sculptors in South America, passing on their masonry skills to the Inca at a much later date. This enigmatic race disappeared as mysteriously as they arrived. Yet, for unexplained reasons, the Viracocha built their greatest ceremonial center at Tiahuanaco, one of the most inhospitable places in South America.

**Tiahuanaco was an important religious pilgrimage site, centered around a big, open plaza designed to accommodate thousands of people.**

What little is known of the Viracocha remains one of the greatest mysteries of prehistory. The megalithic platforms and colossal statues of Tiahuanaco are the best ruins of the Viracocha—a Caucasian race from pre-Inca times. Early Spanish chroniclers recorded stories in all parts of the Inca Empire about the *Viracocha–"runa"* ("people"). From these stories the Viracocha emerge as an ancient race, tall, white and bearded. The Inca ruled over many races of indigenous people and considered themselves descendants of "Manco Capac"—a red-haired, bearded messenger from God. When Francisco Pizarro arrived in 1527 to conquer the Inca Empire for its gold, it was only a small contingent of Spaniards who won the war. The reason the mighty Inca military fell so swiftly was because the Incas erroneously believed the Spanish to be the returning Viracocha people. Even today, Indians around Lake Titicaca still refer to any white skin traveler as *viracocha*.

**▲ The Sun God is carved on the gate leading into the mysterious Tiahuanaco complex.**

The artwork and architectural style of Tiahuanaco undoubtedly influenced the invading Inca people in the 12th century CE, about the same time the Viracocha vanished. The stylized designs symbolizing Tiahuanaco were repeated on ceramics, woodcarving and metalwork throughout most of the Inca Empire. Inca lore relates Tiahuanaco as being the place where the original ancestral god Viracocha was said to have created the first Andean human being.

A recently excavated earth-covered pyramidal mound at Akapana at Tiahuanaco reveals some startling facts about pre-Inca history. The Akapana pyramid is a terraced pyramid predating the Inca Empire by many centuries. It is faced with accurately hewn and artistically joined blocks, which are comparable to those found on Easter Island. This discovery proves that Inca builders learned their impressive craft of masonry from their predecessors in Tiahuanaco. The ground plan of this unfinished pyramid is only slightly smaller than the dimensions of the Great Pyramid in Egypt. Was the Bolivian pyramid an initiation chamber or important link point on the Earth Grid as the Giza pyramids acted?

Another enigma of Tiahuanaco is the stone-lined canal system found near the prehistoric city. Today they neither carry water, nor connect bodies of water. What are these obsolete canals doing two-and-a-half miles above sea level? Speculation exists that the canals once served as a connection between the Pacific Ocean and the geologic Amazonian Sea (which was formerly part of the Atlantic Ocean) before the last polar shift. Could Tiahuanaco be the remains of an Atlantean city?

## Getting to Tiahuanaco

The ruins of Tiahuanaco are located near the southern end of Lake Titicaca, about 45 miles (72 km) from Bolivia's capital La Paz. Most travelers opt for a day trip to Tiahuanaco into and out of La Paz. Buses, taxis and mini-buses ply the route daily from La Paz, but the rough road takes about two hours each way. A ticket to

Tiahuanaco also includes admission to Puma Punku (down the road 1 km), which contains a pair of andesite gates considered to be among the finest examples of stone cutting in South America.

## Lake Titicaca

Many mysteries and legends shroud the shores of this high alpine lake on the border of Peru and Bolivia. Not only is Lake Titicaca the highest navigable lake in South America, it is the world's largest mountain lake at 3,200 square miles (8,288 sq. km), and the second deepest alpine lake with a depth of 1,000 feet (305 m). Lake Titicaca has been a sacred body of water to South America's indigenous people since pre-Inca times. According to Indian lore, the legendary god Viracocha arose from Lake Titicaca and went to Tiahuanaco to create the first Andean human being. It was long rumored that sunken palaces existed at the bottom of the lake, and these rumors were substantiated when modern scientists explored its depths.

**Lake Titicaca was the legendary source of human creation and contains mysterious underwater ruins.**

Scholars have long been intrigued by tales of ancient palaces seen by fishermen during dry spells when the lake level dropped, or of local Indians diving down and touching the roofs of stone buildings. Even early Spanish chroniclers recorded Inca stories of a great flood long ago and ruins on the lake bottom. In 1967, a scientific expedition authorized by the Bolivian government began exploring the depths of Lake Titicaca. The divers found high walls covered in mud and slime and eaten away by the brackish water. Not far from the shore, a number of paved paths led into the lake and connected to a large, crescent-shaped base. The finely cut stone paths, numbering 30 in all, were set with great precision into the ground in a parallel formation. Another expedition in the year 2000 located and documented a 660-foot (200-m) by 160-foot (50-m) temple after following a submerged road, in an area of the lake near Copacabana town. To date, no conclusive answers have been given as to who may have built the monuments before they sank.

Dotting the lake are several islands considered ultra sacred. The Island of the Sun is the largest among the many scattered islands in Lake Titicaca, and contains the above-water Pilko Caima Inca ruins. The Island of the Sun, whose hills are terraced by ancient crop-growing fields, is the legendary home of the supreme Inca god Inti, and contains a sacred stone worshiped as the site of the Inca creation legend. Inca ruins, a nunnery and the Inca goddess Mama Quila reside on the Island of the Moon. Other notable Titicaca islands are Taquile, residence of the last purebred Inca tribe; over-commercialized Suriqui Island; Pariti Island, home to excellent weavers and craftspeople; and Quebraya Island, where pre-Inca *chulpas* "tombs" stretch along its shore.

### Getting to Lake Titicaca

In Bolivia, the road and railway both lead to Guaqui, the main port for Lake Titicaca passenger boats. Public ferryboats interconnect the lake and access the many islands. Private boats can also be rented. Buses travel completely around the lake, and foreigners must remember to bring along their passports when crossing the Peruvian and Bolivian borders. The cities of Puno in Peru and Copacabana in Bolivia are major travel hubs and popular tourist destinations.

# BRAZIL

B razil is the fifth largest country in the world—inferior in size only to Russia, China, Canada and the United States. It contains the most tributaries of the largest river system in the world. The mouth of the Amazon River is wider than all of Belgium. The country itself occupies nearly half of the South American continent, and most of that territory is the Amazon rainforest. Early Portuguese settlers called the country "Vast Land." If Brazil was as heavily populated as Belgium it could house nearly to the entire world population.

## Amazon Rainforest

The Amazon jungle, spanning most of northern and western Brazil, represents the world's largest intact wilderness. Within the Amazon rainforest are 25 percent of the planet's trees, as well as a wide array of indigenous tribes. Nearly two-thirds of all plant and animal species on the planet exist within its confines, several with the potential to cure or limit many human diseases. Not only does the forest contain a large amount of the world's available genetic information, but it acts as the lungs of the planet. Tropical forests absorb large amounts of carbon dioxide and produce life-giving oxygen for the rest of the world. Carbon dioxide, ever on the increase in our atmosphere, is one of the gases that traps solar heat and induces global warming.

The Amazon is the largest of all river systems. The volume of water discharged into the Atlantic Ocean amounts to about 7 million cubic feet per second, enough to fill Lake Ontario in a mere three hours. The outflow is 12 times greater than the Mississippi and 16 times that of the Nile. At least ten of the Amazon's tributaries are larger rivers than the Mississippi. Jacques Coustéau writes in his book *Amazon Journey,* "The awesome alchemy of the jungle produces more than peculiar life forms. New medicines and new raw materials and new foods lie hidden in Amazonia's unstudied sea of diversity ... How tragically shortsighted it would be to eradicate these wonders before they are even discovered."

**Because of its tremendous life-giving properties, the Amazon rainforest is a sacred place to our entire living planet. Here is Gaia at its most abundant.**

The Amazon rainforest is seriously threatened right now by deforestation and mass burning. Over 15 percent of the 2 million square-mile (3,220,000 sq.-km) jungle is already gone. Burning has been so intense in recent years that the normally moist jungle is drying up and people in forest communities are being treated for respiratory ailments. More than half of the Amazon rainforest, even at its pristine core, is a tinderbox ready to go up in flames. "A lot of the Amazon has lost its capacity to protect itself from fire," says Steve Schwartzman, director of the Environmental Defense Fund. "When the forest is this dry, small fires can turn into giant ones and take off. The danger to the rainforest has been taken to another level." Logging, deliberate burning around its edges, and changing global weather patterns have raised the specter of an ecological disaster to possibly affect the entire planet. Its demise would be the loss of our planet's greatest asset and would seriously alter the health and well being of everyone.

Indigenous tribes in the Amazon have long lived in harmony with their surroundings. Shaman of the tribes speak of "communicating better with God" when they blend herbs and roots for spiritual awakenings. In this harmonious state, tribal members can mentally summon insects and animals, rather than have to hunt. This form of telepathic communication occurs when shaman put themselves in a meditative state and tune in with the natural state of the animals. Being so full of life and earth consciousness, the rainforest is a perfect location to learn about telepathy.

### Getting to the Amazon Rainforest

The vast Amazon Valley, with its dense equatorial forest zone known as the "hyleia," can be divided up into three regions for entry: The Guianan Highlands in the north, which rise to a height of 9,094 feet (2,772 m) at Mount Roraima; the Amazon Plain, which boasts the world's most luxuriant vegetation; and the Brazilian Upland Slopes to the south. Of the mighty river's 1,100 tributaries, most are serviced by riverboats, accessible by riverside settlements or airstrips. The larger cities along the Amazon River include Iquitos, Peru; and Manaus, Santarém, and Belém in Brazil.

# CHILE

R eferring to the perpetual snow that crowns sacred Mount Mercedario and other glaciated peaks of the Andes, the name Chile is derived from the Quichuan Indian word *Tchili* or *Tchiri,* meaning cold. Chile was the southernmost part of the extensive Inca Empire that stretched north to Columbia. The empire was kept intact by one of the most impressive road systems in the world. The Inca Royal Road extended more than 3,300 miles (5,300 km) and connected a dominion as expansive as the Roman Empire. Using professional relays running day and night, information could be transmitted from Santiago to the capital Cuzco in six to seven days. A remarkable feat, considering the inhospitable Andean terrain.

# Easter Island

The most isolated piece of permanently inhabited land on earth is a tiny volcanic speck in the South Pacific, which Dutch explorers named Easter Island. The island is home to an assortment of curious statues known as *moai*. Mysterious Easter Island, or *Rapa Nui* as it is called by locals, lies 2,328 miles (3,747 km) due west from Chile. Easter Island has been a dependency of Chile since 1888. This volcanic outcropping is a scant 66 square miles (171 sq. km), with a population of 2,000 people. Most of the inhabitants are of Polynesian stock, yet a few regressive genes still bear Caucasian features among the locals. The island is a treasure-trove of artifacts, especially prehistoric stone houses, wooden tablets bearing an unknown script, burial platforms, and the high abundance of megalithic statues. The *moai* (statues), numbering some 800 on the island, weigh up to 82 tons (83,000 kg) each, and the tallest is equal in height to a three-story building! These mammoth statues of gaunt heads and legless bodies mostly face inland placed upon raised platforms. Their sardonic smiles appear to have an unearthly self-assurance.

All moai statues were variations designed on a single theme: a human figure with prominent angular nose and chin, and elongated perforated ears containing discs. Most were carved from the soft volcanic tuff of the Rano Raraku crater with basalt hammer-stones, then transported to various locations around the island. Some statues were buried, others placed upon platforms. At the most prestigious platforms, statues were given eyes of white coral and a separate *pukao* (top-knot) of red scoria lava rock, which was raised and placed like an oversized hat atop the head. Production of the statues apparently ceased suddenly. The quarry contains nearly 400 statues at every stage of manufacture. One of them, the "El Gigante" moai, is more than 66 feet (20 m) long and, when completed, would have weighed 270 tons (274,000 kg).

## The Easter Island statues are remnants of an unknown civilization, and the builders were a different race of people.

Native Easter Island history relates the story of two distinct races: the original Long-ear people from South America, and the later arriving Short-ear people from the Pacific. Historically, Long-ear people existed only in the east, and none to the west. The megalithic masonry of Easter Island, found nowhere else in Polynesia, is strikingly similar to the great walls constructed in ancient Peru. The elongated statues are comparable to statues found in Tiahuanaco, Bolivia, and to those of the Marquesas Islands, which may have been a further colony west. It is clear, however, that the moai were built exclusively by, and represented only, the Long-ear people.

When Spanish explorers conquered Peru in the 16th century, they soon learned of the "Lost Islands of the Incas." The Inca gave the Spaniards precise directions to Easter Island, which the Spanish never followed. The Spanish conquistadors origi-

▲ A common artistic style of the Easter Island statues are the long ears and legless bodies. There is much debate over where this artistic style originated.

nally called the Inca people *Orejones,* "Big-ears," because of their pierced and artificially lengthened earlobes. Both the Inca and the Easter Islanders enlarged their earlobes by inserting (one piece at a time into an ear disc) similar totora reeds to expand their earlobes.

The discovery of Easter Island was made several centuries after the Spanish conquest of South America, on Easter Sunday 1722, by three Dutch sailing vessels searching for another island. The Dutch made the surprising discovery that the islanders they observed were of mixed racial origin. They found some with a brownish hue, darker than the Spaniards, and others with white skin and red hair. Different ethnic groups were clearly coexisting on Easter Island. Those with fair skin wore large discs in their artificially extended earlobes and displayed solemn reverence for the statues. The Short-ears, or the Polynesians, did not revere the statues the Dutch duly noted.

No outside influence would contact the island for another 48 years after the initial Dutch visit. Finally, after securing the mainland, the Spanish arrived in 1770 to annex Easter Island with their empire. They discovered that the islanders had their own writing, unlike any Polynesian nation at that time, as well as a unique spoken language. The Spanish surmised that this mixed population must have included at least one group with an advanced cultural heritage.

Only four years after the Spanish visit, Captain James Cook dropped anchor off the coast. That short interval brought tremendous change. Cook discovered a new island, one of misery and poverty. The islanders were surprisingly in possession of firearms, and the once-wealthy plantations were now abandoned. To further the impression of disaster, most of the statues had been knocked over and desecrated. Cook called the statues "monuments of antiquity" and wrote, "They must have been a work of immense time, and sufficiently show the ingenuity and perseverance of the islanders in the age which they were built; for the present inhabitants have most certainly had no hand in them, as they do not even repair the foundations of those which are going to decay. We could hardly conceive how these islanders, wholly unacquainted with any mechanical power, could raise such stupendous figures, and afterwards place the large cylindrical stones upon their heads."

Evaluating the historical record it appears that Easter Island is the only meeting place of those people who migrated through the islands of the Pacific, and those who migrated from the Americas. But just who were these earliest people? It was certainly the Long-ears who brought to Easter Island the Caucasian genes, writing, megalithic building techniques and the moai sentinels. Diffusionist theories hypothesize that the first arrivals were the original South American Viracocha people who erected their capital at Tiahuanaco, and were driven out by the Incas. As such, Easter Island and its enigmatic statues quite possibly represent the final repository of pre-Inca Viracocha culture and people. Another theory suggests that Viracocha culture derived from the lost civilization of Lemuria, transplants from a long-ago polar shift, and Easter Island is all that remains of the sunken Pacific continent. While no one knows for certain why the moai statues were built, their silent power continues to pique the curiosity of the world.

### Getting to Easter Island

Easter Island occupies a very remote location in the South Pacific Ocean. Its nearest neighbor is Pitcairn Island some 2,250 miles away (3,620 km). The island is governed by Chile, which lies 2,328 miles (3,747 km) to the east. There are regular flights to Easter Island from Santiago, Chile, or Tahiti, French Polynesia. It would take several weeks or months to travel to Easter Island by boat.

# ECUADOR

From magnificent volcanoes in the Andean highlands to the dense jungles of the verdant *oriente*, natural splendors abound in Ecuador. One of the most famous nature preserves in the world is the Galápagos Archipelago, some 620 miles (1,000 km) west of Ecuador. Most of the Galápagos islands are wildlife sanctuaries and it was here in 1835 that Charles Darwin lived for five weeks, making notes on the varied wildlife that eventually provided evidence for his theory of evolution.

During the colonial era of the Spaniards there was a prolific building phase of churches and monasteries in Ecuador. The Christian buildings were decorated with unique paintings and statuary resulting from the blend of Indian and Spanish art influences. This "Quito" school of art is a greatly admired Ecuadorian style of art and architecture in South America.

## Vilcabamba

Nestled in a verdant valley tucked away in the Southern Andean highland is a location long revered by indigenous people. Vilcabamba has been termed the "sacred valley of longevity," whose average inhabitants are said to live 100 years or more. The oldest have reported ages from 120 to 134 years old, yet these claims have not been substantiated scientifically. The native people live a simple, hard-working life and subsist on a diet of non-fatty foods. Vilcabamba is one of five places on earth where people live to 100 on a routine basis. The people's longevity is also attributed to drinking the clustered mineral glacier water that hydrates the human cells. There are two rivers in the valley that flow all year. This mountain water contains valuable minerals and nutrients, and also creates deep and rich topsoil. These reasons, coupled with an excellent local climate, may be why the local people of Vilcabamba live so long.

**The sacred valley of Vilcabamba is best known for the good health and longevity of its inhabitants, as well as a rumored lost treasure.**

After the Inca Empire was crushed by the Spaniards, one last refugee group settled in an unknown location called Vilcabamba to wage guerrilla warfare against the European invaders. Spanish forces eventually found the refuge city of Vilcabamba and captured its ruler. In 1572, the "Inca problem" was finally put to rest when the Inca

▲ Vilcabamba was rumored to be a wealthy city, similar to the Inca capital Cuzco, pictured above. Hiram Bingham hired local Indians to help him find this elusive refuge of the last Incas.

rebel Tupac Amaru was taken to Cuzco and executed. The last known flicker of Inca resistance was finally snuffed out. The Spaniards had hoped to discover even more vast treasures of the Inca Empire upon capturing Vilcabamba, but this was not to be. Few of the precious relics, en route to free the captured Inca ruler Atahuallpa, have ever been recovered. Much of the treasures of the Inca Empire are still rumored to be buried somewhere in the Andes. It was to find the lost city of Vilcabamba that Hiram Bingham set out on his famous expedition in 1911. He discovered Machu Picchu instead.

### Getting to Vilcabamba

Bus transportation is excellent in Ecuador, and several buses per day run from the neighboring cities of Loja and Zumba to Vilcabamba. The town of Vilcabamba is located in the province of Loja, only 30 miles (42 km) south of Loja city. The drive from Vilcabamba to the disputed border of Peru is beautiful all 78 miles (125 km) of the way, but the border is impossible to cross. Visitors must return the way they came.

# PERU

The Inca Empire was at its height in the 16th century when the Spanish first arrived in South America. Under Francisco Pizarro, the Spaniards landed in the northernmost Inca city and used the remarkably well-built Inca Royal Road to move south. The Inca ruler at the time, Atahuallpa, met the Spaniards with a force of 40,000 men. Atahuallpa was so overconfident in his force that he unwittingly allowed himself to be captured by the Spanish contingent of less than 200 men. Atahuallpa promised a roomful of gold for his release, whereby the whole Empire sent their wares down the Inca Royal Road to free their ruler. In one of the most famous ransoms in history, the Spanish took all the gold and still executed Atahuallpa.

The Inca people were largely Aymara and Quechua Indians from the highland regions of the Andes Mountains. Inca lore relates their royal line had intermarried with an important group of white-skinned and bearded Long-eared people. These Long-ear people had come down the coast from the North and taught the Inca megalithic building techniques. This mysterious white clan known as the Viracocha also taught the Inca how to pierce and lengthen their earlobes, which only the distinguished royalty were allowed to practice (in the 16th century when the Spanish arrived). As mysterious as these advanced teachers were, they departed in a similar fashion. The Incas specifically told the Spanish historians that the Long-ears had left from South America to go westward into the Pacific (Easter Island).

## Machu Picchu and Cuzco

Although the Spanish did their best to stamp out Inca culture, they could not erase all the magnificent buildings left behind. Cuzco became the acting capital during Spanish occupation, yet Machu Picchu was mysteriously abandoned, not to be discovered by archaeologists until the early 20th century. Even though the "Inca Trail" had linked Cuzco with Machu Picchu, the Spaniards inexplicably never discovered this mountain-top community. When the inhabitants left, the jungle swallowed up the trail and all clues of its very existence. It became so forgotten that when Hiram Bingham from the United States first discovered Machu Picchu in 1911, he was convinced it was the lost Inca city of Vilcabamba.

Before the Spanish conquest, Machu Picchu was just another small Inca town. It was home to about 1,000 people, held a royal estate, and was away from the main routes that connected their mighty empire. The town is dramatically laid out on a flat mountaintop, next to sheer cliffs on three sides, in an emerald green valley. Surrounding the town on many levels are terraced plantations for cultivation and subsistence of the community. There was enough space in Machu Picchu for the houses to be arranged around a large cen-

▲ The impressive Machu Picchu is one of the best preserved ancient cites in the world.

tral plaza. In the center of the plaza resides the stone known as the Intihuatana, dedicated to the sun-god Inti. The stone was used as a sundial and may have served as a device to create alignments with the sun's rays during the solstice.

**The trail along the Urubamba River below Machu Picchu was considered sacred to the Inca. The distance was a four- or five-day walk from the capital Cuzco.**

The ruins of Machu Picchu—staircases, terraces, temples, palaces, towers and the famous sundial—are some of the best-preserved artifacts of ancient Inca culture. Similar to the lost city of Pompeii in Italy, Machu Picchu is an ancient center almost wholly intact. Also like Pompeii, Machu Picchu is centered around a main plaza and has a massive mountain looming nearby. The mountain overlooking the site, Huayna Picchu (on which there are some ruins), has steps to the top for an amazing overview of the whole complex. The climb to the top takes an hour and should not be attempted on rainy days, or by those afraid of heights.

Cuzco was the center of the world to the ancient Inca. Like Rome in Europe, all roads in western South America led to the capital. Although the Spaniards destroyed most of ancient Cuzco, many fine examples of Inca masonry still remain. The master stone workers of ancient Peru constructed walls, roads and buildings with huge trapezoidal blocks. This characteristic style of architecture is prevalent in both Cuzco and

▲ The stonework surrounding Cuzco is unrivaled in South America. It features some of the largest hewn stones in the world. Evidence suggests the largest cut stones are also the oldest.

Machu Picchu. In Cuzco, most of the best Inca walls and ruins are right in the middle of the old part of the city. Don't miss the walls of the House of the Women, directly across from the Palace of the Serpents. The temples of the Stars and of the Moon are both relatively intact. Some of the most famous cut stones, including the "stone of twelve angles," are refashioned in Cuzco's many cathedrals. Unfortunately, Cuzco's most sacred Inca building, called the Temple of the Sun (Coricancha), was almost entirely dismantled by the conquistadors. It contained fantastic treasures, all looted by the Spaniards, and is rumored to contain subterranean vaults and a tunnel complex extending hundreds of miles north and south underground, possibly as far as Chile and Ecuador.

Said Bingham of Cuzco: "One of the most interesting places in the world is Cuzco, the ancient capital of the Empire of the Incas. In the days of the Spanish conquest of Peru, it was the largest city in (South) America. On a hill back of it is an old fortress, a place of refuge for centuries. The northern wall of that fortress is perhaps the most extraordinary structure built by ancient man in the Western Hemisphere." Like Hiram Bingham, most visitors agree that the most fascinating relic of Cuzco is the great wall of Sacsayhuman. This massive wall of "cyclopean" masonry contains perfectly fitted stones of epic proportions. Hundreds of stones weigh from 100 to 300 tons, and the largest weighs an amazing 440 tons (400,000 kg)! No mortar is used, and no two blocks are alike. Interestingly, the oldest stones remaining are generally the largest and most perfectly cut. The masons of ancient Peru, either Inca or pre-Inca, were some of the finest stoneworkers of all time.

### Getting to Machu Picchu and Cuzco

Cuzco, located in a fertile valley high in the Andes, rises 11,444 feet (3,490 m) above sea level and is an hour flight from Lima, the southern capital of the Inca empire. Modern Cuzco is a bustling city with an airport, a train station and many roads leading to the ancient capital, now a modern tourist hub. Machu Picchu, at an elevation of 8,000 feet (2,450 m), has the most spectacular setting of any ruin in the world. Machu Picchu located is in the southwest Andes, about 60 miles (100 km) north of Cuzco. Access to the lost city is by train and then bus from Cuzco. Another way to get to Machu Picchu is the famed Inca Trail. The hike from Quoriwayrachi takes three to five days.

## Nazca Lines

On a high plateau between the Pacific Ocean and the Andes, covering an area of 200 square miles (520 sq. km), lie hundreds of enormous geometric patterns. The enigmatic patterns range from straight lines to huge animal shapes spanning across many miles of landscape. Most of the designs can be found on the surface of the Pampa Colorada desert near Nazca in one of the driest places on earth. Very little rain has fallen here in the past 10,000 years and the ground blemishes quite easily. All the Nazca lines and figures were shaped by scraping away the topsoil and rocks to reveal the yellow soil beneath. The land's ease of mark-ability has earned Nazca the title, "the greatest scratch pad in the world." For this reason, nobody is allowed to walk or drive anywhere near the designs.

The Nazca Lines are the largest works of graphic art in the world. The lines vary in width and length, fan out in all directions, and often cross over one another in a seemingly random fashion. More than 100 giant designs of animals, humans, plants, intricate mazes and abstract patterns are represented. Some of the lines are more than five miles (8 km) in length and the longest is 40 miles (66 km)! Massive geometric shapes of rectangles, triangles, spirals and trapezoids scatter the landscape, and a series of two long parallel lines in several locations suggest an airstrip of some sort.

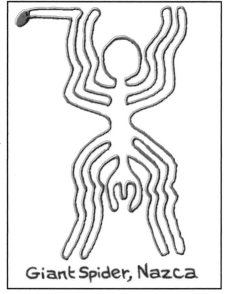

Giant Spider, Nazca

**From ground level it is very difficult to discern the larger design of the Nazca Lines. From the air, the patterns are easily recognizable.**

Most interesting is the wide variety of figures depicted on the desert floor. They include a monkey, a whale, a tree, a snake, a flower, a llama, a lizard and several species of birds. Most of these figures are larger than two football fields in size. Some of the designs represent sacred pictures of humans, such as hands in prayer or a man with a halo. One of the most astonishing figures is the representation of a giant spider of the genus *Ricinulei,* one of the rarest spiders in the world, found only thousands of miles away in the Amazon rainforest. What makes the giant spider design especially interesting is the accuracy of its representation. The depiction shows the creature with one leg extended and its distinctive reproductive organ attached to the tip of one leg —a copulatory mechanism visible only under a microscope.

One common feature of the Nazca Lines is that a single uninterrupted line outlines them all. Sometimes the figures will connect to a geometric pattern, such as two long parallel lines, which determine conclusively that the two patterns were constructed simultaneously. Another aspect of the lines is how precisely straight and perfectly proportioned they are. It is a mystery how the ancient Nazcans were able to retain their precise accuracy over large distances—some lines deviate only a few feet over several miles.

## Getting to Nazca

The small colonial town of Nazca is located 280 miles (452 km) southeast of the Peruvian capital Lima. Public and private buses travel along the Pan-American Highway from Lima to Nazca several times per day. Just north of Nazca town the huge markings begin, but ground access is not permitted. Some of the lines can be viewed from the side of the Pan-American Highway, but the best way to view the lines is by air. Several airplane tours from Nazca town take passengers out to see the famous lines every day.

# CENTRAL AMERICA

*La verdad padece pero no perece.*
*"Truth suffers but never perishes." —Mexican proverb*

THE UNIQUE PREHISTORIC CULTURE OF CENTRAL AMERICA developed over many thousand years in relative isolation. Beginning some 3,500 years ago, the Olmec were the first to build large cities and megalithic carvings in stone, leaving behind the beginnings of a culture soon to influence later civilizations. An interesting aspect of the Olmec is their distinct negroid features, which suggests an African connection. The Zapotecs borrowed from the Olmec culture, as did the Maya, the Toltecs, then followed by the Aztecs. One common thread of all prehistoric cultures following the Olmec was the ceremonial ball game. Players were required to skillfully manipulate a heavy rubber ball with hips, thighs and shoulders, but not arms or hands. The ball game was a sport as well as a sacred ritual, and human sacrifice was often the final outcome. The ball game was played throughout Mesoamerica (Middle America) by many overlapping civilizations. Stone-carved ball courts can be found at most sacred cities in Central America.

In one of the greatest historical mysteries of all time, an enlightened people emerged, then all but vanished in the span of a thousand years. The ancient Maya were among the most advanced cultures—a people who understood the physical cosmos, had a complex written language and developed an extraordinarily accurate way of understanding time. Around the third century CE, the Mayas were building tall, gleaming pyramid-temples of stone and mortar amid their corn patches in the steamy Guatemalan jungles. The Classic period of the Mayas suddenly faltered and began fading out around the 10th century CE. Eventually, the beautiful ceremonial cities in the southern lowlands stood silent and deserted. Yet, less than a century later, the Maya were back, this time with the Toltec in the northern part of the Mexican Yucatán Peninsula. Here, the Post-Classic renaissance reigned until 1450, when the Maya faded away once again for all time. By the time the Spanish arrived in 1527, the finest buildings of the Maya renaissance were already abandoned and overgrown ruins.

# GUATEMALA

What is today Guatemala was once the heart of the Classic Maya world. Excellent sites of Maya ruins and culture can be found amid the dense jungle atmosphere. In the towns and villages are colonial churches, yet the local religion is a unique compound of image-worshipping paganism combined with outward forms of Catholicism. Guatemala is the most populous of the Central American republics next to Mexico, and the only one that is largely Native American in culture and language. The scenery of the Indian regions around the capital, Guatemala City, is full of color and life.

## Tikal

The grand city of Tikal was the primary capital for the Classic period Mayas. At least 10,000 people once lived within the mapped portions of the city, which encompassed six square miles (10 sq. km). The maps reveal 3,000 separate constructions, including temples, palaces, shrines, ceremonial platforms, ballcourts, terraces, plazas, causeways and residences. In the main ceremonial precincts stand 200 elaborately carved *stelae* monuments. *Stelae* were carved stone statues featuring a form of writing, glyphs, and other images.

The Great Plaza of Tikal, overlooking the dense Guatemalan jungle, has to be one of the most awe-inspiring city squares ever built. This Classic period Maya city had an imposing Great Plaza dominated by the huge Temple of the Masks and the Temple of the Giant Jaguar. The plaza was paved and flanked by lesser shrines and features sculpted stone time markers. The impressive pyramids of Tikal, some measuring 150 feet (44 m) in height, were made of lime concrete faced with cut limestone blocks, quarried in the nearby hills, and covered with dazzling white coats of plaster.

**The most striking feature of Tikal are the massive steep-sided pyramid-temples soaring high above the dense Guatemalan rainforest.**

Like the other big Maya centers in the Classic age, Tikal was a location for ceremony and worship. Tikal was selected as a sacred site by Maya priests long before the time of Christ, but reached its zenith in the fourth century CE as a fully functioning ceremonial center. Tikal was constructed upon a slight hill above a swampy lowland, which may be why the original Maya settled on this spot around 700 BCE. Five massive

▲ The Great Plaza at Tikal was one of the largest in the Central American ancient world.

pyramids dominate the near square-mile of Tikal's holy city, with dozens of other temples and shrines complementing the overall sanctuary. New ground-penetrating radar has revealed a labyrinthine of underground tunnels under the Maya pyramid complex at Tikal. The complex system has been mapped and extends a full 500 miles (800 km) to the opposite side of the country.

From the lowliest grower of corn to the highly exalted priest, all believed they were under the direct control of many gods. These gods could only be understood by the stars. The priest-astronomers of Tikal spent most of their time studying the stars, then consulting their calendrical tables in beaten-bark manuscripts to discover ways to overcome the wrath of the gods. Sacrifices were made to appease the gods, usually in the form of jungle animals, but sometimes they were human. The idea of human sacrifice appears to come from the barbaric Toltecs, a wandering band from central Mexico, who relished the sight of spilled blood. Tikal has provided a wealth of artifacts—in addition to the buildings and monuments, more than 10,000 tools, ceremonial objects, personal ornaments and other items have been uncovered.

### Getting to Tikal

The Tikal ruins are located in the middle of Tikal National Park, a wildlife preserve covering 222 square miles (378 sq. km) and the first such park established in Central America. Most travelers visiting Tikal opt to stay in the lakeside villages of Flores or Santa Elena. From these two neighboring villages, buses and minibuses travel the 44 miles (71 km) to Tikal several times daily. There is also a landing strip nearby for small aircraft. Virtually all international flights land in the capital Guatemala City, then passengers usually take the 14-hour overnight bus to Flores.

## Piedras Negras

On the banks of the Usumacinta River, across from Mexico but within Guatemalan territory, lies the enigmatic Piedras Negras, one of the most important cities of ancient Maya civilization. At this site scholars discovered the historical nature of Maya hieroglyphic writing and compiled the first authoritative list of Maya kings. During archaeological work in the 1930's, researchers from the University of Pennsylvania developed one of the first ceramic sequences of the Maya region. The site also produced some of the finest examples of Maya sculpture. The level of realism is unsurpassed, prompting one researcher to describe them as "reminiscent of Greek art." Trenches and pits helped archaeologists establish a more sophisticated understanding of how monumental buildings were constructed, modified and implemented. Indeed, Maya archaeology as practiced today heavily depends on discoveries and methods developed during the Piedras Negras excavations.

The Piedras Negras complex seems to have been an independent Maya city-state for most of the Classic period, however at times it was in alliance with other city-states in the region and perhaps payed tribute to others. It had a known alliance with Yaxchilan, some 25 miles (40 km) up river. Ceramics show the site was occupied from around 650 BCE to 850 CE. Its most remarkable period of sculpture and architecture dated from about 608 through 810, although there is some evidence that Piedras Negras was already a city of some importance earlier. The artistry of the late Classic period sculptures of Piedras Negras is considered particularly exquisite.

**Piedras Negras means "Black Rocks" in Spanish, but the original name of the city is lost. Underneath the city may be the Yucatán Hall of Records prophesied by Edgar Cayce.**

The "Sleeping Prophet" Edgar Cayce made several readings about the ancestors of Atlantis landing in the Yucatán and importing their high culture. Among their gifts to humanity, according to Cayce, were several artifacts detailing the long history of world civilization in the form of a "Hall of Records." Cayce named three locations worldwide where identical records were stored: Giza in Egypt below the Sphinx; inside a collapsed temple under the Atlantic Ocean near Bimini; and below a temple in the Yucatán. Although Cayce never named Piedras Negras by name, or any other site in the Yucatán as the specific location of a Hall of Records, it is quite possible that Piedras Negras is built atop a much older temple. Cayce specifically named the Yucatán as the location of Iltar's covered temple. Iltar was a high priest who

▲ The sophisticated hieroglyphic writing style of the Maya was deciphered largely because so much of Piedras Negras remained hidden and preserved in the jungle.

attempted to preserve the records of Atlantis by transcribing their ancient history in stone. In his famous reading of December, 1933 Cayce said, "these stones are now — during the last few months — being uncovered." The stones Cayce referred to were associated with crystal "firestones" that apparently gave the Atlanteans their power. Further along in the reading Cayce says that an emblem representing the stones would be carried to the Pennsylvania State Museum. If Cayce's time frame is correct, the only excavation in the Yucatán region for all of 1933 was the University of Pennsylvania team who were conducting excavations at Piedras Negras. Several artifacts were taken back to Pennsylvania in the year Cayce mentioned, including a calcite vessel and fragments of a paramagnetic stone known as hematite. To date, the Hall of Records has not been discovered at Piedras Negras, nor anywhere else in Central America.

### Getting to Piedras Negras

Piedras Negras is one of the most remote of all ancient Maya cities in Guatemala and consequently one of the least visited and best preserved. Piedras Negras can only be reached by canoe, including portages through the treacherous tropical jungle. All food and drinking water must be brought in, and all travelers must be in top physical condition to endure the journey. Several outfitters make the arduous trip. For overland travelers the Restaurante Vallescondido leads river trips to Piedras Negras and is located in Mexico on kilometer 61 of the highway between Palenque and Frontera Corozal.

# HONDURAS

Present-day Honduras was the southeastern most extension of Maya territory. It is a rugged and mountainous country, shrouded in dense tropical jungles. Offshore on the Atlantic side are the magnificent Bay Islands, ideal for scuba diving and fishing. Most of the towns and villages in Honduras bear evident reminders of the Spanish colonists who first settled the region in the 16th century.

## Copán

The ancient city of Copán is considered the artistic capital of the Maya empire. Rich in temples and carved-stone *stelae*, this Classic period Maya city was at its peak around 725 CE. The famous stelae of Copán grace the complex, and some of these decorated pillars stand 13 feet (4 m) tall. Images of Maya gods also dot the Copán complex, along with recognizable pyramidal structures. Above and beyond beautiful architecture and artwork, the people of Copán were keepers of a highly advanced culture, employing a complex and sophisticated religion enhanced by astute observation in the cycles of the earth and the cosmos.

The Maya elite and the commoners were able to read and write, and were especially advanced in their knowledge of astronomy. Perhaps the greatest achievement of Classic period Maya civilization was the intricate calendar they developed. It is the most precise calendar ever conceptualized by humans, even more exact than the Gregorian calendar, which is widely used throughout the world today. A good analogy of how the Maya calendar works is the gear mechanism of a motorized watch, where a small wheel meshes with a larger wheel, which in turn meshes with a mega-wheel to record the long passage of time. The elaborate calendar system the Maya employed was premised in part on the idea that history repeated itself. Thus, Maya priests believed they were able to simultaneously record the past and predict the future. Maya astronomers were able to calculate the length of the solar year, the Venus year, and the lunar month with exceeding accuracy. Further calculations enabled them to pinpoint solar and lunar eclipses to the exact second. It is no wonder the Maya knowledge of the heavenly bodies was inexorably linked to their religion. As such, both the sun and moon were worshiped, and the city of Copán was constructed in strict accordance to celestial movements.

## The primary function of Copán was a ceremonial center. There is also evidence that it was used as a university — perhaps the first established in the Americas.

Maya calendar glyphs are found extensively at Copán, as well as a profusion of inscriptions and well-preserved sculptures. Many clues indicate that Copán was a center of learning, astronomy and ceremony. The large, open spaces in the two main plazas could accommodate a great number of citizens, while only a few select people would attend the ceremonies that took place on top of the pyramids. Common people could read their collective history alongside the aristocracy on the carved-stone stelae in the plazas. High atop the imposing pyramids, priests and officials communed with the heavenly bodies. These lords of Maya city-states portrayed themselves and their cosmology on the stelae monuments. Placed in the plazas before the palaces and pyramids of the Copán ritual center, these sculptures recorded royal inaugurations, military triumphs, marriages, deaths and religious events of the agricultural cycle. Stelae provide critical information about Classic Maya civilization between 200 CE

▲ The Teobert Mahler glyph shows a Maya priest escaping the destruction of his city. Some believe this is a depiction of Atlantis in its final hours.

and 900 CE. It is a complete mystery as to why this astronomically and mathematically advanced race suddenly disappeared.

### Getting to Copán

Copán is in eastern Honduras, just over the border from Guatemala. Buses can be caught from San Pedro Sula to La Entrada, and from La Entrada to a small town near the site called Sta. Rosa de Copán near the *Copán Ruinas*. Alternatively, it is accessible by chartered plane from Guatemala City, San Salvador, or the Honduran capital Tegucigalpa.

# MEXICO

As the largest country in Mesoamerica, Mexico has been host to ancient cultures for thousands of years. Several distinct cultures emerged at different time periods. The first, the Olmec, carved colossal stone heads and thrived along the Gulf of Mexico. The next civilization was the Zapotecs, who were influenced by the Olmecs and lent much to the next culture, the Maya. Of all the Mesoamerican cultures the Maya were the most prolific builders, creating several sacred cities before they faded away around 900 CE. The Maya re-emerged, coupled with the war-like Toltecs to create a Post-Classic period (900-1450) on the Yucatán Peninsula. Finally, the Aztecs took the stage in central Mexico, only to be defeated by the invading Spaniards.

## Guadalupe

Immediately following the Aztec defeat to Spanish forces, the colonial New World was established under the auspices of the Catholic Church. Less than 20 years later, some nine million Mesoamerica inhabitants, who for centuries professed a polytheistic and human sacrificing religion, become new converts to Christianity. The transition from paganism to Christianity was difficult for the natives, and perhaps the new converts needed a sign. According to legend, the Holy Virgin appeared to an Indian farmer named Juan Diego who saw her at the foot of the hill, *Cerro Del Tepeyac*, on December 9th, 1531. Ever since that day his whole Indian community accepted the Virgin as their patroness. Even today the Virgin of Guadalupe, as she became known, plays an important role in the religious and social life of most Mexicans. To Catholic Mexicans, the Virgin is even more important than Jesus Christ.

The story of Juan Diego, the seer of Guadalupe, has long captivated the faithful of Latin America. Juan was a recently baptized adult convert, aged 57, when Mary appeared to him at Tepeyac hill, formerly the site of a pagan temple devoted to the Aztec mother goddess Tonantzin. The year was 1531, a mere decade after the demise of the Aztec nation. As he was walking near the hill Juan began to hear celestial music and saw in front of him an intense glowing light surrounded by rainbows. Suddenly, a beautiful dark-skinned woman emerged from the light and spoke to him in Nahuatl,

Juan's native tongue but also a language forbidden by the Spanish. She declared herself to be the Virgin Mary, the mother of Jesus Christ, and addressed him as "my littlest son." After reassuring Juan Diego that he had nothing to fear, she urged him to return to the city to request the bishop construct a new church on the hill. The bishop did not believe him at first and it took two more appearances by the Virgin Mary in front of Juan Diego before he had some proof of a miracle. On the third appearance, the Virgin emblazoned her image on Juan Diego's cactus fabric cloak. This evidence was enough to satisfy the bishop that a miracle had occurred and a basilica was constructed in her honor.

> **Guadalupe is the site of the oldest recorded miracles in the New World. Our Lady of Guadalupe has become know as the Patroness of the Americas. Her shrine is the most visited religious site in Mexico.**

Mexico's most celebrated festival is held annually every December in honor of Our Lady of Guadalupe (also known as the Virgin of Guadalupe), Mexico's patron saint. Although celebrations commence on December 1, December 12 is the official day of honor for the Virgin of Guadalupe, and is also a Mexican national holiday. The festival paying homage to Our Lady of Guadalupe has been celebrated in Mexico for hundreds of years, and today millions of pilgrims proceed to the site of the ancient temple of Tonantzin, (now known as the Basilica of Guadalupe) in Mexico City to pay their respects. The Miracle of Guadalupe was officially recognized by the Vatican in 1745, although in 1555 the apparitions were officially approved. Juan Diego died in 1548, aged 74, and was beatified in 1990.

### Getting to Guadalupe

Guadalupe is located 5 miles (8 km) north of the Mexico City center. From downtown Mexico City, or from most of the metropolitan area, Guadalupe is easily reached by bus or Metro. The bus stop and the nearest Metro station are both called La Villa station. It is a short walk from there—just follow the crowds. Juan Diego's cloak with the image of the Virgin Mary has been preserved and set in gold. Visitors may view the cloak in the modern *Basilica de Guadalupe,* next to the old colonial basilica, now a museum.

# Palenque

The temple-filled city of Palenque was once a major seat of religious and political power in Maya society. While not as expansive or elaborate as other Maya ruins, its decoration and architecture are of equal par. Palenque flourished from 600 to 800 CE under the initial rule of a king named Pacal who laid the larger foundations for this magnificent city. Under his rule, many plazas, pyramids and governmental buildings

▲ The Temple of Inscriptions conceals the passageway down to the tomb of Lord Pacal.

were constructed within the 12 square miles (20 sq. km) of the city. The word *Palenque* means "Palisade" in Spanish and has no relation to the ancient city's real name, which remains unknown.

Hieroglyphic inscriptions at Palenque predicted Pacal's reign thousands of years prior to his ascension. They also predict that he would be celebrated far into the future and that the city would once again be used as a ceremonial center.

The ceremonial center of Palenque is one of the most impressive of all Maya sites. Arranged around a central plaza are three temple-pyramids: the Temple of the Sun, the Temple of the Cross, and the Temple of Inscriptions. Each temple is built upon a stepped pyramid and contains beautifully carved hieroglyphs of the various gods they were used to worship. The most remarkable building at Palenque is the Temple of Inscriptions, faced with a steep, 65-foot (23-m) stairway ascending the front of the pyramid. Inside the temple are four supporting pillars bearing relief sculptures of life-size figures, each holding either a baby or small child.

The Temple of Inscriptions is considered a funerary monument because it was constructed as a tomb for Lord Pacal. Mexican archaeologist Alberto Ruz Lhuillier discovered a hidden stairwell in 1952 that led from the top of the pyramid down to Pacal's crypt, which sits exactly at ground level. Lord Pacal's funerary crypt lies behind the pyramid's front stairway and is inscribed by relief carvings of guardian gods of the Underworld. Most interesting is Pacal's sarcophagus itself, whose elaborately carved lid depicts a central figure in an unusual position surrounded by rich symbolism. Some claim the famous portrait is the Lord's spirit voyaging into the realm of the dead, others see Pacal as an astronaut riding in a space capsule.

Diagonally opposite the Temple of Inscriptions is the labyrinth of buildings and corridors known as the Palace. Dominating the Palace is a four-level tower used by Maya royalty and the priestly class to observe the sun falling directly into the Temple of Inscriptions on the winter solstice. It is also believed that the tower was used for astronomical observations and as a vista point for farmers on the fertile plain of the

River Usumacinta. The tower and the Palace are well endowed with fine stucco relief sculptures on the walls. Exquisite jungle trails surround the ruins and make for fantastic hiking trips.

### Getting to Palenque

The town of Palenque is four miles (6.5 km) away from the archaeological site. Minibuses and taxis travel from town to the ruins every 15 minutes. Palenque town is serviced by regular bus service from dozens of Mexican cities, including the 16-hour bus ride to Mexico City. A small airstrip and a train station a few miles north of town also access Palenque.

## Chichén Itzá

In the flat, sun-baked region of Mexico's Yucatán Peninsula, an interesting hybrid of two cultures emerged. First was the Maya, with advanced knowledge of the cosmos, then around 1000 CE the Toltec, who brought the cult of a feathered serpent god. Chichén Itzá is filled with images of the serpent Quetzalcoatl, which is a morphed version of a peaceful Maya god. This yin-yang age is called Post-Classic Maya, but has a very strong Toltec influence. While the Maya philosophy that deified the stars and worshiped time remained, the Toltec placed increasing emphasis on human sacrifice. They co-existed from the 10th century CE until the 15th century before their mixed culture virtually vanished. By the time the Spanish conquistadors arrived in 1527, all that was left were abandoned buildings and a few minor city-states continually at war with one another.

Chichén Itzá in its heyday was not only a ceremonial center, but a residential city with a bustling market. Trade with other Yucatan cities prospered under a strict rule. Everything was controlled by the astrologer-priests, who maintained forced labor of the local peasantry. Religion and politics were one and the same, and Chichén Itzá was the theocratic capital.

*Chichén Itzá* **means "Home of the Holy Ones." It was a sacred city to both the Maya and Toltec peoples.**

The city complex of Chichén Itzá houses many unique monuments, including one of the most fascinating pyramids on earth. The El Castillo step

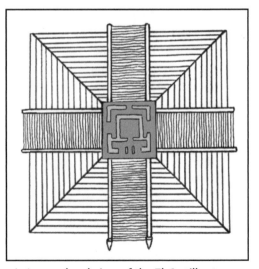

▲ An overhead view of the El Castillo step pyramid.

▲ Spring and Fall Equinox dates reveal the serpent in the El Castillo pyramid.

pyramid is the centerpiece of Chichén Itzá, a very sacred place used in many Maya and Toltec ceremonies. Other major ruins include the Temple of the Warriors, and the Caracol Tower, a round building with a small observation chamber at the top. The Caracol Tower has its main axis aligned to the rising and setting of Venus. Other astronomical observations include the vernal equinox, and the moon setting at its most southern and northern declinations. Another dominant area in Chichén Itzá is the plaza housing the ball court. A sacred ritual called *pok-ta-pok* in Maya was played to the death here. The object of this sacred ritual was to bounce a hard rubber ball through stone rings on either side of the court without the use of hands or arms. Relief sculptures in the ball court show the unfortunate fate of a beheaded squad.

The El Castillo pyramid is fundamentally the Maya calendar formed in stone. In order to calculate the appropriate time for rituals and planting, the astrologer-priests relied on the highly advanced knowledge of Maya timekeeping—the most accurate calendar system developed by humans to date. The pyramid was specifically designed to represent the solar calendar and its attributes. The brilliance of the El Castillo design is seen in how it was constructed to show the shadow of a serpent only on the spring and fall equinox days. The serpent was originally a Maya symbol of divine wisdom and is featured in practically every stone structure in the Yucatán. The four flights of the pyramids' four stairways have 91 steps each, 364 in all, to which there is one final step up to the temple's sanctum, for a total number equal to that of the solar year. Despite some damage along the sides, El Castillo stands relatively intact. The pyramid we see today was rebuilt upon an older, previous pyramid. The larger pyramid was superimposed over a smaller structure by the Toltecs. Other notable Toltec additions are the warriors represented in temple carvings at the top. The El Castillo temple incorporates an inner sanctum containing a jaguar throne and a supreme Toltec figure.

After the Yucatán Peninsula was invaded by the Toltec, information recorded in stone reveals the new rainmaking ceremonies and other major sacrificial rites became a theater of blood. The primary deities were aspects of nature and creation, and from atop the pyramid the priests would often request rain, fertility and a plentiful harvest of corn. During the ceremonies, worshippers would assemble at the base of the pyramid, while the nobles would pierce their own tongues and ears and deliver their blood on pieces of bark for presentation to the gods. Splendidly attired priests divided into different orders to officiate the ceremonies. One order held the arms and legs of the victims —usually prisoners of war—while another split open the chests to remove their still-beating hearts. The lifeless bodies were then hurled down the pyramid steps where they would be deposited in a nearby well, along with offerings of gold, jade and copper. At times of famine or prolonged drought, live sacrifices, preferably children, were thrown into the 130-foot (40-m) deep "Well of Sacrifice." The artifacts located at the bottom of the well revealed a blood-thirsty culture, among the offerings of priceless jewels and medallions.

### Getting to Chichén Itzá

Chichén Itzá lies in the northern region of Mexico's Yucatán Peninsula. The ruins are just west of Valladolid and 75 miles (110 km) east of the major city Merida. Buses run on a regular basis from Valladolid and Merida, and all the major resorts near Cancún access the famous archaeological site. There is also an airstrip nearby.

# La Venta

The first advanced civilization to prosper in Mesoamerica were the Olmec, a people who established their capital at La Venta. Unfortunately, little remains of their cities, but what is known is that the Olmec inhabited the lowland regions along the Gulf of Mexico and flourished from 800 to 500 BCE. The Olmec capital La Venta, originally constructed as early as 1500 BCE, was built on an island where the Rio Tonala River runs into the Gulf. The Olmec were the first civilization in Central America to develop numbers and a written hieroglyphic language. They also devel-

oped a 365-day calendar known as the Vague Year calendar. The legacy of the Olmec was further characterized by their rendering of enormous heads sculpted from basalt. The heads weigh up to 60 tons (54,420 kg) and are all sculpted with characteristic "jaguar mouths" and enigmatic negroid features. These basalt statues are at least 3,000 years old and are similar in appearance to both African art and Southeast Asian art, such as that found at the temples of Angkor in Cambodia. Like the ancient Khmer of Cambodia, the Olmec sculpted the heads as a memorial and tribute to their leaders. They transported the heads from a quarry some 70 miles (100 km) away to La Venta without the

▲ The Olmec appear to have African facial features.

use of the wheel. Furthermore, the colossal stone heads of the Olmec were carved entirely without the use of metal tools.

## La Venta was capital to the first people who brought high civilization to Central America.

The tropical forest had engulfed the architecture of La Venta, and the memory of the Olmec had long drifted out of memory by the time the Spanish arrived in the 16th century. Archaeologists discovered the site of La Venta in 1925 and the Olmec, meaning "people from the land of rubber" in native Nahuatl, were finally revealed to the world. Additional discoveries conclusively proved that the Olmec were progenitors of Mesoamerica's other high cultures, a position held until then by the Maya. Although it is presumed that the Olmec were trampled by successive waves of invaders, many aspects of their culture survived. The Olmec bequeathed upon their Maya predecessors important religious symbolism —not only the idea of a pyramid-temple, but sculpted images of their gods. The best example is the jaguar, a symbol central in Maya culture, which was originally an Olmec symbol.

### Getting to La Venta

Unfortunately, most of the original site of La Venta has been closed due to petroleum excavation. While a few less-important pieces remain at La Venta, the overall impression of this site has been greatly reduced by the sight and sounds of active oil rigs and refineries. The most significant artifacts have been moved to the nearby city Villahermosa in a hard-to-find outdoor museum called *Parque-Museo La Venta*. The park is rightly considered one of Mexico's great archaeological exhibits, but since it is removed from its original location, the setting is not quite the same. Villahermosa is the capital of Tabasco and is accessed by many roads and an airport. La Venta is 90 miles (130 km) from Villahermosa as a bird flies, but is more difficult to find because no main roads go near there, and the oil companies discourage tourism.

# Monte Albán

In the sacred Valley of Oaxaca, a pre-Maya culture called the Zapotecs started building a civilization with a highly advanced writing system of hieroglyphics. Here, around 700 BCE, the Oaxaca Valley witnessed a building boom concurrently when the city of Monte Albán developed on a mountain plateau, partly stimulated by contact with the Olmec. Here, in the ancient Indian capital city, local inhabitants built a huge complex of ceremonial buildings consisting of pyramids, walls, terraces, tombs, staircases and intricate sculptures.

Zapotec culture shows many affinities with the Olmec and Maya, yet their history relates no mass migration or invasion. The three cultures were similar, yet quite distinct. For example, the Zapotecs uniquely believed themselves to be descended from trees, rocks and jaguars. By the time the Spanish arrived in 1519 and quashed the ancient civilization in the Oaxaca Valley, the Zapotecs had already long abandoned their city. Their lasting legacy was a high level of urban and agricultural development, as well as a refined artistic style, advanced mathematics, cal-

▲ The serpent is a central motif in most Central American prehistoric cultures, including the Zapotec.

endrical science and their language. More than 300,000 native Oaxacans continue to speak Zapotec as their first or second language.

## Megalithic architecture, undeciphered hieroglyphs, and a honeycomb of miniature tunnels and staircases under the main pyramid are some of the central mysteries of Monte Albán.

Monte Albán is an enigmatic ruin that had been occupied, reorganized and built onto for thousands of years. The city is constructed on an artificially flattened mountaintop 2,000 feet (600 m) above the valley of Oaxaca. Underneath the city is a complex network of stone-lined tunnels, far too small to be used by adults or even children of average stature. These tiny passageways, most no more than a foot high, lead to miniature flights of steps and chambers containing human skeletons and funerary objects. How and why these items were placed there remains a mystery.

Like most sacred cities of Mesoamerica, Monte Albán had a central plaza flanked with ceremonial buildings. The remarkable rectangular plaza, 650 by 980 feet (200 by 300 m), is rimmed by large ceremonial platforms. Surrounding the plaza is a ball court, a palace, a wide staircase leading to a high platform, and the Temple of the Dancers, which is richly endowed with basalt reliefs, glyphs and calendar signs dating from the fifth century BCE. The sacred city lasted until the 10th century CE before it was mysteriously abandoned and became a burial place. Interesting tombs can be explored in and around the ancient city. Tombs on the far northern end of the city were built of megalithic slabs, and inscribed in them were ceramic sun symbols and corn gods. Also in the ceremonial city of Monte Albán is one of the most unusual structures in Central America. There is an oddly shaped structure that has no two sides or angles that are equal. It is completely random in design and may have been used for astronomical purposes. Slabs on the outside of the building are inscribed with hieroglyphs that have not been fully deciphered.

### Getting to Monte Albán

Monte Albán is about six miles (10 km) uphill from Oaxaca city. Mini-buses ascend the route four times a day from the big hotels in Oaxaca, but hiking up the footpaths to the ancient city is highly recommended. The city of Oaxaca is well serviced by buses coming to and from many Mexican cities. The valley of Oaxaca exemplifies native Indian culture and is home to many other interesting ruins.

## Tenochtitlán

After the mysterious decline of the Maya and abandonment of their great cities, it was only a matter of time before another culture would rise up and take their role as masters of Mesoamerica. That other culture was the Aztec, whose first traces began in the 13th century CE. The Aztec had a barbaric ancestry linked to the Toltec, and thus had a wandering life. The Aztec people would not, nor could not, ascend to power before they built their prophesied capital.

Aztec legend relates the story of their travels and founding of a magnificent city. The Aztec god Huitzilopochtli told the Aztec people to wander until they came to a place where they would see an eagle sitting upon a cactus eating a serpent; it would also be a place where fish would swim. The Aztec wandered for a hundred years before witnessing this auspicious confluence on the swampy banks of Lake Texcoco. Here, the Aztec began to build *Tenochtitlán*, which means "the Place of the Cactus."

Like Venice in Europe, Tenochtitlán was a water-based city with an elaborate network of canals. The city consisted of narrow and wide canals dividing a multitude of islands surrounding the sacred precincts in its heart. Built on reclaimed land on the shores of Lake Texcoco, Tenochtitlán rose to great power largely due to its strategic location. The surrounding lake acted as a protective moat from ground assault, while the skillful mariners could thwart any attack by water.

▲ The exact location of Aztlan is unknown. The homeland of the Aztec was somewhere far to the north. This image is supposedly Aztlan.

All three causeways entering Tenochtitlán converged upon the sacred precincts, an area protected and surrounded by a high wall. In the heart of the sacred precincts was the Great Temple, a Maya-style pyramid tall enough to dominate the entire city. Two temples adorned the top of the Great Temple, one dedicated to Huitzilopochtli, the Aztec patron saint and god of war and conquest, the other to Tlaloc, god of rain and agriculture. Complimenting the Great Temple were a dozen other various temples, as well as a ball court where the ritual ball game played by the Maya and Toltec continued to be enacted. Human offerings were apparent with the finding of a skull rack containing hundreds of piled-up skulls from sacrificed victims. Just before the Spaniards arrived, it is recorded that Aztec priests slaughtered no fewer than 20,000 captives in one festival at the central pyramid in the ancient city.

## The foundation of modern Mexico City was laid on the ruins of the magnificent Aztec capital Tenochtitlán.

Early Spanish explorers in 1519 CE were amazed by the size and advanced state of building the Aztec had achieved. For a short while, the Spaniards were allied with the Aztec and were allowed to walk freely in the magnificent Tenochtitlán. But when inevitable hostilities broke out between the two forces, the city was eventually sacked and completely destroyed by the Spaniards. Easily outnumbered a thousand to one, the Spaniards were able to conquer the mighty Aztec primarily because of the prophecy of a returning god. The Aztec, under Montezuma, presumed the bearded leader Cortés was the returning god Quetzalcoatl, and welcomed his small army into the "Kingdom of Gold." Cortés struck with blinding violence and treachery, and deposed both Aztec throne and theology as he systematically destroyed the city and took Montezuma captive in order to extort the empire's gold. Cortés succeeded, and Aztec civilization died a quick death, soon to be replaced by the enforced Spanish language, religion and government. Within two years of Cortés' 1519 arrival in the pre-conquest capital of Tenochtitlán, its population had dropped from 60,000 to about 18,000.

### Getting to Tenochtitlán

Located directly in the center of Mexico City are the Aztec ruins of Tenochtitlán. So thorough were the Spaniards in their destruction of Tenochtitlán that the exact site of the Great Temple remained unknown until 1978, when a subway excavation crew accidentally came upon the site. Since this recent discovery a massive excavation and reconstruction effort has taken place, and this once sacred site has re-emerged. A large section of Mexico City had to be demolished to make way for the Great Temple Project, which is easy to find in the sprawling city. The most important finds are located in the *Museo de la Ciudad de Mexico* in Mexico City.

# Teotihuacán

Some of the most remarkable ruins of Mesoamerica, if not the whole world, are the relics of an ancient civilization located just north of Mexico City. The holy city of Teotihuacán is traceable over an area of two by four miles (3.5 by 6.5 km) and is dominated by two massive pyramids. The twin pyramids are the largest artificial mounds on both American continents. The Pyramid of the Moon, a half-mile away (1 km), is half the size. The Pyramid of the Sun at Teotihuacán, which is aligned with the solstice, is as old as any Maya structure and 20 times as big. The Pyramid of the Sun is 208 feet tall (64 m) and is about one-half the size, in total volume, of the Great Pyramid in Egypt. The sacred peak of Cerro Gordo, (Fat Hill) looms in the distance overlooking the ancient metropolis.

Located on the largest pyramid are the so-called "glimmer chambers," which are rumored to be hidden behind padlocked doors. These little-known inner rooms may have been initiation chambers, but admission is not permitted and there is now evidence that this section has been recently sealed up with concrete. The Pyramid of the Sun was built directly over a four-chambered lava tube in the second century CE. The sides of the Pyramid of the Sun are terraced, and wide stairs lead to the summit. Unfortunately, the surface was restored using the wrong materials to wrong specifications in 1910, and has become a distorted version of the original appearance.

> **The name *Teotihuacán* means "City of the Gods." A thousand years later, the Aztec wandered into the Valley of Mexico and declared it "the place of those who have the road of the gods."**

Of all the peoples who created the Mexican upland cultures in Maya times, only those in the Valley of Mexico and the Zapotecs built lavish burial chambers, while the people of Teotihuacán raised mighty pyramids. By 300 CE, Teotihuacán was the religious and civic center for 100,000 Mesoamericans, boasting plazas lined with palaces and avenues, paved with polished stucco and drained by an elaborate system of underground conduits. The Plumed Serpent Quetzalcoatl is a sign and ornament found all over Mexico. The cult of Quetzalcoatl may have originated at Teotihuacán, but certainly the later conquering Toltecs spread the symbol throughout the whole of Mexico, especially to the cities of the Maya renaissance on the Yucatán peninsula.

Pyramids of the Sun + Moon  Teotihuacán, MEXICO

▲ The Pyramids of the Sun and Moon are the largest freestanding structures in Central America.

All that stands today of this magnificent sacred city is a mere fraction of its former glory. Nine-tenths of Teotihuacán is still buried under layer upon layer of periodically rebuilt buildings and landfill. The city was constructed according to a remarkably precise urban plan set around quadrangles and ceremonial areas. Bisecting the city is the wide Avenue of the Dead, with the Pyramid of the Moon at one end, the Pyramid of the Sun off the center and more than 100 smaller religious buildings positioned along the avenue. On either side of the Avenue of the Dead are grid-shaped rows of residences

176

where the noble elite and priestly caste lived, all positioned on the axis followed by the sun as it sets. The Avenue of the Dead is aligned with the rising of Pleiades, which is directly overhead at this latitude. This well-planned center of commerce and religion was deliberately plundered and burned in the seventh century CE, with its influence elsewhere suddenly ceasing. In its heyday, this first of all American cities was even larger than Caesar's Rome, and had a population to match its size.

### Getting to Teotihuacán

Teotihuacán is located in the central section of the Valley of Teotihuacán, 25 miles (45 km) northeast of Mexico City, and makes a perfect day trip. Tour buses ply the route nearly every hour from Mexico City until the site closes around sunset. Note that many of the locals refer to the site as *Pirámides* meaning pyramids, rather than its name, Teotihuacán.

# NORTH AMERICA

If one advances confidently, in the direction of his own dreams
and endeavors, to lead the life which he has imagined, he will
meet with a success unexpected in common hours.
—*Henry David Thoreau*

UNLIKE ASIA, EUROPE OR AFRICA, THE NEW WORLD of the Americas contains no deposits of human fossils other than Homo sapiens. This fact suggests that humans arrived independently to North America via the Bering Strait land bridge during the last Ice Age, or possibly from the east or west by boat. These first American settlers hunted woolly mammoth and other large mammals with weapons comparable to those used in Siberia. Agriculture and domestication of animals provided the subsistence base on which civilization could develop. In North America, high civilization developed in select farming cultures, most notably the Anasazi in the Southwest and the earlier Mississippian culture in the Midwest and South. Throughout the rest of North America isolated tribes survived on fishing, hunting, gathering and growing corn until the arrival of the Europeans.

# CANADA

Scattered across the plains of Canada, especially Alberta, are thousands of circular stone structures. Most of these are simple circles of cobblestones that once held down the edges of the famous teepees of the Plains Indians. Most of these circles are known as "teepee rings," but other stone structures are of a more esoteric nature. Extremely large stone circles—many greater than 40 feet (12 m) across—may be the remains of sacred ceremonial centers. Sometimes the cobble arrangements form the outline of human figures or give shape to abstract forms. Perhaps the most intriguing rock constructions are the ones known as medicine wheels. The word "medicine" implies a magical or supernatural function, yet is applied for want of a better word. Medicine wheels are so old that their original use is unknown. (See: Big Horn Medicine Wheel, page 205.) When European settlers arrived in Canada they also imported their religion, as well as a perception of sacred sites. Native American sites were originally disregarded by the new arrivals, but in time the ways and practices of the "First Nation" people became acceptable to modern Canadians of European descent.

# QUÉBEC

After a French commissioner traveling with Italian navigator Giovanni da Verrazano sailed into New York harbor and Eastern Canada in 1524, the king of France was notified that there was abundant territory free for the taking. The king sent Jacques Cartier to explore the new lands in 1534 and again in 1542, attributing French names to the places he discovered and lay claim to all the northern territories in the name of France. He was on his way home when he passed the shipload of French colonists under Sieur de Roberval coming to attempt the first, ill-fated settlement. Later Samuel de Champlain, Louis Joliet, Father Marquette, Robert La Salle, and others were to move westward and establish New France in what is today Canada and the Mississippi Valley in the United States. From 1604 until his death in 1635 Champlain was the foremost French colonizer. In 1608 he founded the fortified village of Québec, the first permanent settlement in French America. Although Québec City earned the nickname "Gibraltar of America" because of its strategic hilltop position, the British managed to capture the city and all French holdings east of the Mississippi in the 1756 to 1763 French and Indian War. In a stroke of colonial wisdom, the British passed the Québec Act in 1774 allowing the French subjects to retain their old laws and the freedom to worship as Roman Catholics. This explains why the province of Québec remains largely New France, with a Catholic majority of French speakers who have yet to lose hope of someday achieving their political autonomy from Canada. In the northeast, the Gaspé Peninsula of Québec is an attractive rural region of scattered small towns and villages that retain strong French influences and traditions. This is where the northern section of America's Appalachian Mountains meets the ocean. In the language of the original inhabitants, the Micmac "Indians of the Sea," *Gespeg* means "land's end," and the Gaspé Peninsula offers the kind of rugged beauty in a place where mountains collide with the sea.

## Saint Joseph's Oratory

The world-renowned basilica dominating the southwestern Montreal skyline started out as a small wooden chapel on Mount Royal. The founder was a simple brother who lived a childhood of poverty, and was orphaned at age 12 along with 11 brothers and sisters. His name was Alfred Bessette (1845-1937), a physically frail man with little education, yet with a big heart and healing touch that would one day inspire millions. Growing up a poor French Canadian orphan, he was forced in his teens to be a migrant worker in the textile mills of New England. He returned to his native Québec province in 1867. Three years later he joined the priesthood, but because of his weak condition was relegated to the responsibility of a doorman. Once accepted as a novitiate of the Holy Cross Order at age 25 he was given the name Brother André, a name which took on spiritual consequences when his healing prayers to Saint Joseph for others began to manifest physically. His blessings were most appreciated by the poor and sick who would come to Brother André in a saddened and oftentimes desperate condition. He invited them to pray with him to Saint Joseph to obtain favors, and in a short time many people reported that their prayers were being answered, yet always when Brother André was not present. He was a modest man who took little credit for his efforts, solely attributing all the healing power to Saint Joseph. In 1904, Brother André helped pay for a small wooden chapel by cutting hair at the Holy Cross. The small chapel was crowded from the beginning and too small for the amount of people who flocked to the site. Brother André moved into an apartment over the chapel a few years later to accommodate the steady flow of pilgrims. By 1914, a major basilica was being built near the small chapel, but construction was halted several times due to financial constraints. Brother André died in 1937 at the ripe old age of 91 and was buried in the crypt of the unfinished church. A million people came to his funeral during a bitter winter storm. The magnificent Saint Joseph's Oratory was finally completed in 1955. Brother André was beatified in 1982 by Pope John Paul II, the final honor before being declared a saint. Although the basilica is a powerful tribute to Saint Joseph, devotees from all over North America come as much to honor Blessed André's shrine and pray for sickness cures.

**The massive dome of Saint Joseph's Oratory is the largest in North America, second only in the world to Saint Peter's in Rome. Its prominent location in Montreal and the healing tradition founded by Brother André attract more than two million pilgrims per year.**

▲ Pilgrims begin their solemn ascent to the Oratory from the Saint Joseph statue.

The Catholic Church regards the Oratory as the world's most important sanctuary devoted to Saint Joseph. As father of Jesus Christ, Saint Joseph is represented as the model of workers, guardian of virgins, support of families, terror of demons, consolation of the afflicted, hope of the sick, patron of the dying, and protector of the Church. Brother André had a strong devotion to Saint Joseph based on their mutual experiences as impoverished exiles and unskilled laborers. Despite the passing of Brother André, the sanctuary still retains its reputation as a healing center. Hundreds of thousands of pilgrims arrive each year to prostrate themselves at the long flight of stairs leading up to the Oratory. The middle staircase is constructed of wood so pilgrims may ascend the staircase on their knees. Canes, crutches and other objects hang between pillars in the Votive Chapel, as well as on the walls of the little wooden chapel founded by Brother André. His loving and ever-optimistic spirit endears the legacy he left as a humble servant to Saint Joseph whose ability to inspire others became legendary.

### Getting to Saint Joseph's Oratory

Saint Joseph's Oratory is located on the slopes of Mount Royal, in the southwest region of Montreal. The address is 3800 Queen-Mary Road, a few blocks from the *Côte-des-Neiges* metro station. Saint Joseph's Oratory overlooks the twin sprawling cemeteries called *Cimetière Notre-Dame-des-Neiges* and the *Cimetière Mont-Royal* on the backside of Mount Royal. The little wooden chapel is on the grounds next to the massive oratory.

## Sainte-Anne De Beaupré

From the earliest times of Christianity, believers had an interest in knowing more about the historical family of Jesus Christ, especially his mother, father and grandmother. Despite no mention in the Bible, the Virgin Mary's mother has long been regarded as a Jewish woman named Anne. She is first mentioned in a Greek manuscript called "the Revelation of James," probably written around the year 160 CE by a non-Jewish Christian. The James account speaks of Mary and her parents Joachim and Anne. Although the story was most likely fictional, the cult of Saint Anne has nevertheless influenced millions of Christians worldwide.

In Canada, devotion to Saint Anne goes back to the beginning of New France, and was brought to Québec by the first settlers and early missionaries. The original parish on the present site dates from the year 1650 and achieved legendary status when several shipwrecked sailors on the Saint Lawrence River attributed their deliverance to Saint Anne. A few years later, on March 13, 1658, a foundation was dug for a larger stone-built chapel, which by general consent, would be dedicated to the beloved Saint Anne. On the first day of construction the spirit of Saint Anne demonstrated how favorably she viewed the undertaking by healing Louis Guimont, an inhabitant of Beaupré who suffered terribly from rheumatism of the loins. With little strength but for his confidence in Saint Anne, he came forward and placed three more stones in the foundation, at which time he found himself suddenly and completely cured of his ailment. Shortly thereafter the French-Canadian tradition of pilgrimage to Sainte-Anne De Beaupré began for the sick and despondent, making it the oldest pilgrimage destination in North America. By 1707 the site had gained importance with Saint Lawrence Indian tribes, also called "First Nations" in Canada, who came to venerate the one they called "Grandmother in the Faith." Popular for centuries due to the high status they afforded to grandmothers, the Micmac and other tribes make an annual pilgrimage to Beaupré every June. The largest pilgrimages come for the feast of Saint Anne (July 26th) and the Sunday closest to the feast of the Nativity of Mary

(September 8th). From July 17th pilgrims make a *novena*—nine consecutive days of private prayer and public worship—ending in a candlelit procession on the eve of the festival. On the feast day the sick are anointed outside the Basilica, then come inside to pray at the Miraculous Statue, an impressive oak carving of Saint Anne and a young Virgin Mary. Over the centuries the miraculous cures have rendered the site comparable with the great pilgrimages to Lourdes, France or Fátima, Portugal. Sainte-Anne De Beaupré has been described as "the Lourdes of the New World." Until 1875 the yearly number of pilgrims did not exceed 12,000, but to judge by the heap of crutches left at the saint's feet, there must have been many marvelous cures wrought at Beaupré.

**Although the present Basilica at Sainte-Anne De Beaupré dates from 1926, it replaced the older, more endearing church of 1676. On either side of the main doorway are crutches, walking-sticks, bandages, and other offerings left behind by the faithful who have gone home healed.**

Pilgrims come to the cathedral not only for miracle cures, but to view the sacred relics of Saint Anne. The oldest is a finger bone of Saint Anne, which was first exposed for veneration on March 12th, 1670, and has ever since been an object of great devotion. Other

relics of the saint have been added in later times to the treasures of this shrine. Perhaps the most visible object in the Basilica is the Miraculous Statue of Saint Anne holding a young Virgin Mary. Pilgrims direct their prayers to God through the intercession of the saint. This important statue stands on a pillar in the north transept, where it can be seen from almost every point in the Basilica. In 1892, Cardinal Taschedreau presented a "Great Relic" to the Basilica, the four-inch (10-cm) long wrist bone of Saint Anne. When the wrist bone was brought over from Rome it stopped in New York City, where an epileptic was cured on its first appearance, causing a tremendous excitement in the city. Ever since, American pilgrimages have increased exponentially to Sainte-Anne De Beaupré. The road from Québec City, the tradi-

▲ One of the oldest established Catholic traditions in North America originated at the site of the present cathedral.

tional pilgrimage route still walked by many (particularly on the feast days), is marked by wayside shrines and bread ovens.

### Getting to Sainte-Anne De Beaupré

The huge Catholic Basilica and associated religious buildings form their own village just south of the town Beaupré along the shores of the Saint Lawrence River. Sainte-Anne De Beaupré is located 22 miles (35 km) north of Québec City on Canadian Highway 138. The picturesque surrounding area includes Ile d'Orleans between two branches of the Saint Lawrence, the Chute Montmorency (a waterfall twice as tall as Niagara Falls), the Mont Sainte-Anne ski resort and the Sainte Anne River emptying at the town of Beaupré. The official pilgrimage season runs from early June to early September, with around a million and a half visitors each year.

# THE UNITED STATES

I n the past few hundred years, the land comprising the United States has gone through tremendous change. Before European contact, Native American tribes lived peacefully off the plentiful abundance of the land, growing maize, hunting and offering thanks to the Great Spirit. The open land of the Indians gave way to European colonists who divided the land into property deeds and created productive agricultural communities. In turn, agriculture gave way to the Industrial Revolution as the growth measure of America. Today the United States is a lone global super-power in the dawn of the Information Age.

# ARIZONA

A rizona has the largest Native American population of any state. Its name comes from the Indian word *arizonac,* meaning "small spring." One of the fastest growing states in the country, Arizona is home to such famous natural wonders as the Painted Desert, the Petrified Forest and the Grand Canyon. The Navajo and Hopi reservations corner the northeastern part of the state in a vast land marked by towering red rock formations, spectacular canyons and green, forested mountains. Navajo territory, the larger of the two, completely surrounds the Hopi land, and overlaps into western New Mexico and southern Utah. In this part of Arizona primitive Navajo *hogans*, Hopi mesa homes, traditional attire and lively ceremonies color the atmosphere. The Navajo and Hopi reservations are a place of limitless horizons, stark mesas, and reflective inspiration.

## Sedona Vortices

The Sedona landscape is commonly described as magical, with its red-rock canyon walls standing majestically against the clear, blue sky of central Arizona. The mesas in the region are stark and tall, and dominate the panorama. Sedona is a popular New Age center, attracting millions of tourists from around the world every year. Nearby, the canyon opens up into a gorgeous, rock-rimmed amphitheater, and south of the city stands the famous Chapel of the Holy Cross. Yet most people come to Sedona to experience the unique energies residing here, called vortices.

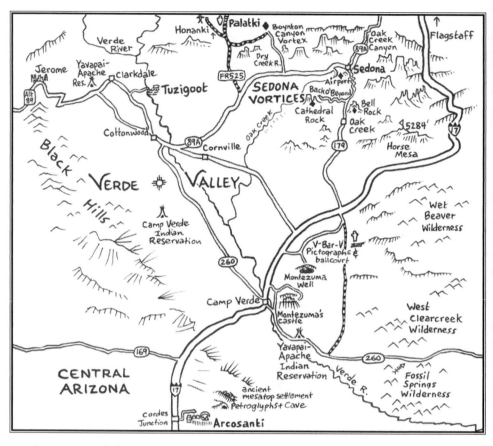

A recent study by Northern Arizona University concluded that 64 percent of the near four million annual visitors to Sedona came seeking some sort of spiritual experience. The surrounding red rock country is believed by many to be a vortex meditation site. Such sites are defined as specific places of power in the rocks that enhance prayer, contemplation, and reflection for people of all faiths. A vortex is a place where the earth is at its healthiest and most alive. The energy of a vortex acts as an amplifier, working to enhance or magnify any physical, mental, emotional, or spiritual levels brought near it. This amplifier effect of the vortices supposedly helps augment thoughts and intuitions, heighten emotions, or may allow unexpected insights at an interpersonal or spiritual level. One scientific explanation of vortices has suggested that the mineral composition of the red rocks creates a magnetism that can have an discernable effect on people. As a result of their popularity, vortex sites are among the most visited and impacted places in the Coconino National Forest.

**Sedona, Arizona has been deemed the New Age capital of the United States, mainly because of at least four major energy vortices that have been**

identified in and around the town. The vortices of Sedona are some of the strongest and most readily apparent in the world.

Most of the natural features in the Sedona area were held sacred by prehistoric people who recognized the energies of the land. Native Americans say that the Grandmother Spirit of the world still lives in Sedona, welcoming her family home. The veneration of a sacred place by people of more than one cultural tradition is very apparent at Sedona. Native American legends abound in the region. Now that Sedona is a New Age

▲ On the trail to the Boynton Canyon vortex.

mecca, it attracts artists, writers and spiritual seekers from all walks of life. The strong energy vibrations from the surrounding area enhance the feelings of people on a vision quest, and seem to be quite conducive to attracting others of a like mind. Several medicine wheels of stacked rocks have been constructed in the area, both by visitors and native peoples.

## Getting to Sedona Vortices

There are four main energy vortices in the Sedona area. Boynton Canyon Vortex is located 3.2 miles (5.2 km) west of Sedona on Highway 89A past the Highway 179 junction. Follow the signs for Boynton Canyon. Well-marked trails will lead you to a 30-foot-high (10-m) knoll where the energy is strongest, a place called "Kachina Woman." The Bell Rock Vortex emanates up from the base into a near perfectly symmetrical butte. Bell Rock has a distinct shape, and is easy to spot just north of the village of Oak Creek on Highway 179. Airport Vortex is the closest vortex to the town itself. Going 1.1 miles (1.8 km) west on 89A, turn south on Airport Road and park a half-mile up at the distinct curve before the road continues to the top of the mesa. The vortex is a small hill with twisted junipers and a clear view of Sedona on both sides. Finally, there is the Cathedral Rock Vortex. This vortex is located 4.3 miles (7 km) west on 89A past the junction of 89A and Highway 179. Turn west on Back O' Beyond Road to the car turnoff and the trailhead to Cathedral Rock. It is now required of all motorists to obtain a "Red Rock Pass" before parking at any of the vortex turn-off areas. The cost is $5 per day or $15 per week and is available in numerous park service and Chamber of Commerce offices in the Sedona vicinity.

# CALIFORNIA INDIANS

The original native people of California were ancestors of the Great Plains Indians, who likely crossed the Alaskan land bridge during the last Ice Age. The largest tribes from north to south were: the Modoc; Shasta; Nongatl; Washoe; Maiduu; Yuki; Miwok; Ohlone; Yokuts; Salinan; Chumash; and the Serrano. The

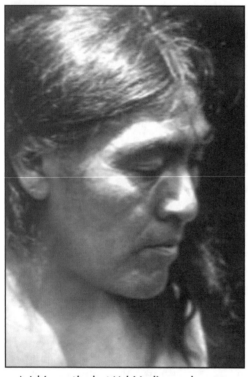

▲ Ishi was the last Yahi Indian, only emerging from the Sierra foothills in the early 19th century.

California tribes seem to have traveled over the inland barriers centuries later, then established themselves in relatively isolated groups. On the coast there was no long distance pattern of contact or communication among them, unlike their Central and South American brethren. For many centuries, the California tribes lived in isolated harmony with the land and made pilgrimages to localized sacred sites. Hot springs and wells were particular favorites of the native tribes.

The single most destructive element to California Indians was the discovery of gold. Hundreds of thousands of immigrants from around the world descended upon the gold fields of California to seek their fortune. Nothing would block their way, especially native people who were viewed as more of a nuisance than anything else. Few California tribes were fortunate enough to retain even a small fraction of their land, let alone their way of life. The missionaries also played a large role in subjugating the Indians and encouraging them to forget their cultural ties. Most California tribes died of disease, genocide, starvation, warfare, or were relocated far away from their native homelands.

## Mission Trail

The first sea explorers to reach California were mostly touch-and-go, primarily seeking supplies and safe harbor before setting off again. The Spanish were the first to make land claims on California, soon to be followed by the English explorer Sir Francis Drake in Northern California, and later the Russians at Fort Ross. In order to shore-up their possessions, the Spanish needed to establish a land trade route and permanent settlements. Under Spanish rule, the California Mission Trail was established

188

in 1769 to link the coastline from north of the Bay Area to the southern tip of Baja. The Baja region was known as Baja California and the region north of Baja was known as Alta California, much of which today is the state of California.

Before the Mission Trail, several Catholic colonies were established on the west coast of California, some as early as the

▲ The San Gabriel Archángel mission helped establish commerce in Los Angeles.

15th century. The Mission Trail in Alta California, known as El Camino Real, connected each mission within a day or two's travel on horseback. Visitors to California are often amazed by the abundance of Spanish saints among city names throughout the state. The names of the saints of the day were often applied to newly discovered localities, whether rivers, bays, mountains or valleys. Spanish saints' names were also chosen for presidios or forts, pueblos or towns, and of course, the Franciscan missions. Today, most all of these early missionary settlements are thriving urban centers. From north to south, visit the old missions in the modern city centers of: Sonoma, San Rafael, San Francisco, San Jose, Santa Cruz, Carmel, San Juan Bautista, San Luis Obispo, Santa Barbara, Los Angeles, San Juan Capistrano and San Diego.

## The Mission Trail unified California in the name of proselytizing Christianity.

Most missions were instrumental in California's early development. Perhaps the most significant was the Los Angeles mission called San Gabriel Archángel, located just south of Pasadena. San Gabriel was the first land link with the capital Mexico City in 1774, and became the chief point of contact with Mexico for many decades. Its strategic location made San Gabriel the wealthiest and most prosperous of all the missions, which resulted in the building of a beautiful church, peaceful gardens and an expansive art collection. The founder of the Mission Trail, Father Junipero Serra lived most of his life and died in the Carmel mission, one of the most scenic and best-preserved missions in this historic chain. Father Serra is currently being considered for canonization. If he becomes a saint, Catholic pilgrims could soon be flooding the Mission Trail in record numbers.

### Getting to the California Missions

The old missions are a proud and historic part of every California community where they reside. Most are located in the middle of the oldest sections of town, and roads

▲ The Carmel mission was home to Father Junipero Serra for most of his life.

with names like El Camino Real and Mission Street usually lead right to their doorsteps. The country missions are equally fascinating. From north to south, roughly paralleling Highway 101 between Carmel and San Diego, look for: Mission Nuestra Senora de la Soledad Ruins near Soledad; Mission San Antonio de Padua on the Hunter Liggett military base; Mission San Miguel Archángel near San Miguel; La Purisima Mission State Historical Park near Lompoc; Mission San Buenaventura near Ventura; and Mission San Luis Rey de Francia near Oceanside. Sunday masses are held in some of the old basilicas, or a nearby Catholic church on the grounds. All have become museums of sort, and a small donation is always appreciated.

## Mount Shasta

The landmark Mount Shasta is the 14,162-foot (4,249-m) centerpiece of northern California, rising like a giant diamond in a field of evergreens. Long regarded as a place of intense energy, Mount Shasta has a visible and majestic presence. New Age mystics believe it represents our three-ring chakra, located above our head, connecting the mountain to our collective survival. In fact, Mount Shasta is situated at the intersection of three mountain ranges: the Sierra Nevada to the southeast, the Cascades to the north, and the Klamath to the west. Shasta is the second highest of the Cascade Range volcanoes and is home to California's largest glaciers. It rises more than 10,000 feet (3,000 m) from its base and is visible for hundreds of miles in all directions on a clear day. This cone-shaped volcano is relatively young, as is evident by the lack of extensive glacial erosion. Tiny hot springs just below the summit of Mount Shasta suggest this dormant volcano is merely taking a short nap.

To the Modoc Native American tribe, Shasta was the center of the universe. "Before there were people on the earth," begins a Modoc legend, "the Chief of the Sky Spirits grew tired of his home in the Above World because the air was always brittle with an icy cold. So he carved a hole in the sky with a stone and pushed all the snow and ice down below until he made a great mound that reached from the earth almost to the sky. Today it is known as Mount Shasta." This lengthy creation story goes on to explain how he formed the trees, rivers, animals and rocky hills, bestowing all the features of the mountain with spiritual significance. The towering volcano was located in the southwest corner of Modoc territory before the tribe was displaced in the

1850s, when gold was discovered in the region. The Modoc have prophesied that when Shasta loses all its glaciers and snow, it will again erupt. When Shasta erupts, according to tribal elders, the world will go through major reformations and climac-

▲ Hikers near the summit of Mount Shasta.

tic changes. During recent California drought years, Mount Shasta becomes nearly devoid of glaciers. Could the Modoc have foreseen today's global warming and changing weather patterns?

Any Indian tribe who came into view of Mount Shasta held the mountain in very high esteem. Tribes such as the Karok, Modoc, Yurok, Shasta, Wiyot, Yuki, and the Wintun revered the mountain as a spiritual center. Others would travel great distances to catch a view of *Wyeka*, or "Great White." The dormant volcano is believed to contain powerful Earth Spirit energy where the Great Spirit himself sometimes resides. Large mountains like Shasta were not to be climbed by native peoples because the power of the Great Spirit was too strong there. Since the lodge of the Great Spirit is on peaks such as Shasta, he demands respect and only those of a pure heart can climb to the summit and not be harmed. That is why most native people today do not climb to the peak, although on the lower slopes, such as Panther Meadows, purification rituals and sweat lodge ceremonies are still held on the mountain.

**Mount Shasta is a very powerful beacon to the indigenous peoples of Northern California and Oregon. It is also the rumored home of Bigfoot, citizens of Lemuria, The Great White Brotherhood, and a variety of UFO sightings.**

Shasta is said to be the abode of many different spirits and beings, both present and past. The energy of Mount Shasta is so powerful that it has been described by New Agers as the "Epcot Center" of sacred sites. Almost all stories tell of the mountain's interior, which is home to several mysterious and legendary beings. Keep a lookout for the Lemurians, the Yaktayvians, Gray Aliens, and one white-robed character named Phylos who can materialize himself at will. This is Mount Shasta, a.k.a. the "gentle giant" whose interior is rumored to be a massive cavern with gold-lined offshoot caves. The Lemurians were a pre-Atlantic race believed to have lived on the

Pacific continent of Lemuria around 14,000 years ago. The Lemurians were survivors of a great flood and thus became early ancestors of Native American tribes. The Yaktayvians are another mysterious race said to be living inside the mountain, who use their magic bells to keep humans away. Extraterrestrials are said to use the peak for landing, refueling and entering the mountain inter-dimensionally. Sightings of ape-men and hooded phantoms are reported every year. Such stories only enhance the mystery and legend of this powerful mountain.

## Climbing Mount Shasta

Mount Shasta is not a technical ice climbing mountain, and several routes to the summit make the ascent relatively accessible for those lacking mountaineering experience. This is not to say the ascent is easy, because it certainly is not. Weather and season often determine difficulty and, on average, half of those attempting the summit turn back. Altitude sickness is a primary reason for not reaching the summit, second only to foul weather. Since the mountain is so huge, weather patterns develop here, and it is not uncommon to be caught in high winds and/or heavy snowfall. If there are large, rounded lenticular clouds forming over the summit, a storm is likely brewing and it may be time to start descending. The ideal months for climbing Mount Shasta are July and August, although the potential to climb exists from late spring to middle autumn. Consult the ranger's station in the town of Mount Shasta for permits and updated weather forecasts. Also in Mount Shasta or Weed along the I-5 are several places to rent crampons, boots and ice picks—essential for any summit climb no matter what season. To acclimate in higher elevations, spend at least one day and one night on the mountain, either at Sierra Club's Horse Camp, or at the 10,000-foot (3,000 m) Helen Lake campsite.

# FLORIDA

According to legend, Florida was discovered by the Spanish explorer Ponce de León on his quest to find the mythical Fountain of Youth. Whether Ponce de León actually found the fountain history will never know, but what is known is that the eminent explorer organized an expedition from Puerto Rico in 1513 CE to a land he named *Pascua Florida*. While the Ponce de León expedition was exploring the Florida coast it discovered the Gulf Stream and several islands in the Bahamas, and was the first to chart the Yucatán Peninsula. The northeastern Florida city St. Augustine was one of the landing sites for Ponce de León in 1513, and in 1565 it became occupied continuously, making it North America's oldest permanent city.

## Coral Castle

The mysterious Coral Castle in south Florida was built single-handedly by an eccentric loner named Ed Leedskalnin—a 5-foot-tall (1.5 m), 100-pound (45 kg) Latvian native. Ed was born in 1887, and at the age of 26 was engaged to marry a 16-year old Latvian girl named Agnes Scuffs. The day before the wedding young Agnes decided to cancel because she thought Ed was too old, or maybe she was in love with someone else. Heartbroken and alone, Ed left his beloved Latvia for the United States always thinking of Agnes as his "Sweet Sixteen." With only a 4th grade education, he drifted from job to job until he came down with tuberculosis and moved to Florida for its favorable climate. During his travels he became interested in science, astronomy, and Egyptian history, spending most of his time reading books on magnetic currents and cosmic forces. Ed was a frugal man, collecting old mechanical pieces and saving money any way he could. Eventually he bought a 10-acre (4-ha) plot of land in Homestead and set about excavating, carving, and moving many tons of coral rock by himself. His monument would be devoted to his lost love, his Sweet Sixteen.

**Using only simple tools, a slight immigrant from Latvia single-handedly moved over 1,100 tons (997,700 kg) of coral blocks and constructed an engineering marvel called the Coral Castle.**

Ed's coral carvings are symbolic of everything that mattered to him: love, astronomy, nationalism, family and magnetism. He created huge block walls surrounding a courtyard of theme tables and other whimsical stone attractions. Many people witnessed Ed hauling his original sculptures from Florida City to Homestead, but no one ever saw how he loaded or unloaded the trailer. He refused to allow visitors while he worked and had a kind of sixth sense which alerted him when someone was coming to spy. Ed was a very private man who did much of his work entirely alone in the quiet of the night. For 28 years, with only crude winches, block tackles, and iron wedges, Ed labored tirelessly on his monument. He cut coral from a quarry in front of the castle and moved enormous stones by lantern light. The Obelisk stone weighs 28.5 tons (25,400 kg / 57,000 pounds) and is taller than the Great Upright at Stonehenge, positioned single-handedly into place by Ed. The Tower consists of 243 tons (220,400 kg) of coral rock with each block weighing four to nine tons (3,630-8,170 kg). The average weight of the individual stones at Coral Castle is greater than those used on the Great Pyramids in Egypt. Perhaps the most astonishing characteristic is the perfectly balanced Nine-Ton Gate that can be turned by the touch of a child. Although the gate is uneven in its dimensions, Ed was able to locate the precise center of balance and easily swing the heavy stone on top of a recycled automotive gear.

Ed had a keen interest in astronomy and his sculptures were inspired in part by celestial objects and their movements. Always pointing to the North Star in Ursa Minor, the Polaris Telescope stands 25 feet (7.5 m) high and weighs 25 tons (25,400 kg). Polaris is a fixed star that is always visible at night through the opening in the telescope. It helped Ed plot the earth's path around the sun and enabled him to design and construct a sundial that also indicates the solstice and equinox days. The sundial is so accurate that it is possible to determine Standard time within one or two minutes all year round. His celestial sculptures range from an 18-ton (16,330 kg) carving of Mars and another of Saturn, to enormous crescent moons, a Sun Couch, a Throne Room, and a Moon Fountain. Since Ed had a personal belief that there was life on Mars, he placed a Palmetto plant in the Mars sculpture as a symbol life.

▲ Ed Leedskalnin poses in front of one of his massive coral sculptures.

The extraction and lifting of such incredible amounts of coral rock — without the use of electricity or modern cranes and using only handmade tools — by a single man seems impossible. Baffled engineers have compared Ed's secret method of construction to Stonehenge and the Great Pyramids. Many people asked the diminutive Latvian how he was able to carve and move such heavy stones. He would only say that he understood the secrets of how the Great Pyramids were built. Was it possible that Ed was a reincarnated Egyptian architect who retained past life knowledge of secret levitation techniques? Some might argue there is no other explanation.

### Getting to the Coral Castle

Nestled between the Florida Keys and Miami, the privately owned Coral Castle is open for self-guided tours from 9 am to 9 pm every day. Conveniently located at 28655 South Dixie Highway on the main drag in Homestead, the Coral Castle is centrally located only "a stones throw away from Exit 5 South," according to the tourist brochure. Just outside of Homestead are the fantastic natural preserves of Everglades National Park and John Pennekamp Coral Reef State Park.

# ILLINOIS

The name Illinois is a French corruption of Illini, meaning the land of great men or warriors. All traces of the mound building Mississippian culture had disappeared by the time the French explorers Father Marquette and Louis Joliet traveled down the Mississippi River in 1673. Returning north up the Illinois River, the French explorers were led by their Indian guides to a strategic portage into Lake Michigan near the present-day Chicago suburb Lyons. A small tributary called Portage Creek flowed into the Des Plaines River just east of Harlem Avenue from Mud Lake, an ancient swamp that accessed the shortest overland portage into the South Branch of the Chicago River. Soon after charting this route, the French established several missions and trading posts at La Salle, Marseilles and Champaign, assimilating various Indian tribes and converting them to Christianity.

## Cahokia Mounds

Located on an expansive flood plain near the confluence of the Illinois, Mississippi and Missouri rivers is the preserved central section of the largest prehistoric Indian city north of Mexico. Cahokia Mounds contains 65 hand-packed earthen mounds, a wooden sun calendar, several burial tombs, and was once home to 20,000 residents at its height in 1250 CE. At that time, the city of Cahokia had a larger population than the city of London. The Cahokia Mounds are also renowned as being the birthplace of archaeoastronomy, the science of identifying astronomical alignments within the architecture of prehistoric structures. Archaeoastronomy became a part of North American archaeology following Warren Wittry's discovery of Cahokia's several woodhenges in the 1960s. Wittry demonstrated that these wooden features were solar observatories and determined that its builders had an integral understanding of celestial movements.

The Mississippi River system once supported an advanced early American civilization that mysteriously disappeared. The Mississippian culture thrived for 500 years, emerging around 900 CE beside the Mississippi River and its many tributaries. The cultures' lasting legacy is the variety of mound cities to be found from Wisconsin down to the Gulf of Mexico. Many of these early settlements were developed later as modern cities; for example, St. Louis was originally termed "Mound City." The people are known as the "Mississippian Culture Mound Builders" because no recorded name exists. Similarly, the name "Cahokia" is taken from a sub-tribe of the Illini Indians because no knowledge of the original name exists. Like the Maya in Central America, this advanced culture went into decline, then all but vanished by the time modern Europeans explored the area. Suggestions as to why Cahokia was abandoned include natural resource depletion, climactic change, war, disease and social unrest. What actually became of the people remains unknown. Later tribes lacked the oral traditions or knowledge of the site to link them to the actual builders, yet Cahokia was perhaps the largest city of the Mississippian people. Ceremonial activities such as human sacrifice and sun worship took place at Cahokia. Atop the pyramids were astronomical observatories, sometimes burial crypts, and sometimes ritual buildings where a priest-king would officiate various ceremonies.

## Monk's Mound at Cahokia is the largest prehistoric structure in North America. Originally more than four city blocks long, the sacred pyramid had a base larger than Egypt's Great Pyramid.

At first glance, the layout of prehistoric Cahokia is remarkably comparable to the layout and design of Central American sacred cities, arranged in rows surrounding open plazas. The central precinct facing Monk's Mound was enclosed by a high stockade wall. A wooden sun calendar was erected to determine the seasons and to schedule ceremonial activities where games were played. Cahokia is sometimes referred to as "the City of the Sun," with a birdman priest, similar in appearance to Quetzalcoatl, as the high priest of the city. But perhaps the greatest similarity to Central American cultures lies within the enormous earthen mounds shaped like pyramids. The largest

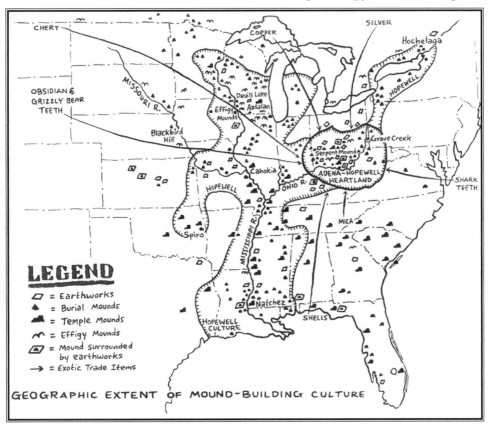

LEGEND

▱ = Earthworks
▲ = Burial Mounds
⬣ = Temple Mounds
ⵥ = Effigy Mounds
▨ = Mound surrounded by earthworks
→ = Exotic Trade Items

GEOGRAPHIC EXTENT OF MOUND-BUILDING CULTURE

▲ The expansive walled city of Cahokia was one of the largest prehistoric settlements in North America.

pyramid at Cahokia is called Monk's Mound, erroneously named after French Trappist Monks living in the region much later than the Mound Builders. Monk's Mound is the largest prehistoric earthwork in the Americas. This ancient pyramid once had a base of 16 acres (6.4 ha), making it larger than the Great Pyramid in Egypt. The earthen mound once stood 10 stories tall, yet due to soil settlement and erosion it is now only 35 feet (11 m) in height. Important ceremonies were held on two levels of the great mound. At the top, a priest-king lived in a wooden shrine, dedicated to the sun god.

Recent drilling into Monk's Mound has revealed an unsuspected find. In January 1998, workers broke a drill bit when they struck a hard surface while probing into the mound. According to archaeologists, the find could be remnants of a ceremonial structure, a burial tomb, a cache of tools, or some sort of drainage system. What makes this interesting is that the Mississippian people were not known to have used stone for their construction, at least not at this site. The find could be an older structure pre-dating Monk's Mound. It is common throughout the world for ancient sites to be located on top of older structures or their original foundations.

### Getting to Cahokia Mounds

The 2,200-acre (880-ha) Cahokia Mounds State Historic Park can be found a mere 12 miles (20 km) from St. Louis, Missouri. In ancient times the mound city would have been just a short canoe trip down a tributary creek to the Mississippi River. The proximity to the Illinois, Mississippi and Missouri rivers made Cahokia a crossroads for early boat traffic. Yet most motorists today will find the World Heritage Site Cahokia Mounds located just outside of St. Louis, across the Mississippi River, in Collinsville, Ill. Interstate 55 / 70 runs very close to the site, and well-marked signs direct motorists from Exit 6 to the ancient city.

# NEW HAMPSHIRE

The White Mountains of New Hampshire, which extend from the Canadian border south to well below the center of the state, are the highest, most celebrated, and most impressive peaks in all of New England. Among the several ranges are eight mountains over a mile (1.6 km) high, with Mount Washington, at 6,288 feet (1,886 m), the highest point in New England. The mountains give the state its nickname the "Granite State," suitable for rock slabs and building material for the early megalithic cultures who sailed over from Europe in prehistoric times.

## America's Stonehenge

On a hilltop near the Massachusetts border are a series of low stonewalls and cobbled rock chambers called America's Stonehenge. The entire complex covers about 30 acres (12 ha) of hills and woodland, around which extends an apparently haphazard collection of walls interspersed with tall, triangular standing stones. The site's central feature is Mystery Hill, situated on a single acre, which contains 22 stone chambers (dolmens) and other megalithic features. Immediately surrounding the central site are upright stone monoliths aligned to predict prominent astronomical sightings.

In the central part of Mystery Hill are several engaging points of interest. The centerpiece is a T-shaped chamber with internal structures similar to a chimney and hearth, as well as a "couch" sculpted right out of the living rock. From the couch, a pipe-like hole called a "speaking tube" ascends to the surface and runs directly below an enormous rock table weighing 4.5 tons (4,080 kg). The tube may have been used for some kind of spooky oracle because it distorts voices from below, and the table may have served as a sacrificial altar because of the carved gutters on top surmised to catch blood. Surrounding the "Oracle Chamber" are more than 20 stone chambers of various sizes, which may have been used as shelter for the Bronze Age inhabitants or

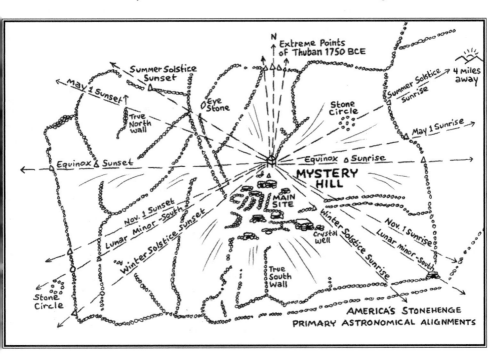

AMERICA'S STONEHENGE
PRIMARY ASTRONOMICAL ALIGNMENTS

some kind of religious ceremonial center. There is evidence that the entire complex is built over a natural cave system, but no entrances have yet been located. Instead, deep well shafts have been discovered, and the most intriguing pit leads not to a cave, but to a natural fault where a cluster of quartz crystals were recovered. The crystals may have been mined nearby, or were placed ritualistically into the well to indicate this site as a power point. It is known that crystals were worshiped or used for tools by ancient cultures.

### America's Stonehenge has been determined by several independent surveys to be a very accurate astronomically aligned calendar.

The hilltop position of the megalithic "beehive" chambers and walls suggests a defensive settlement. The arrangement of its walls and structures also functioned as an observatory. The Summer Solstice Sunrise Monolith is situated where the sun rises over an upright slab of granite on June 21 of each year. The top of the stone is uniquely shaped to match the landscape on the horizon where the sun rises. The place to view this is in the middle of a stone circle, where other astronomical computations can be made. Nearby the stone circle there is a tall rock called the True North Stone, which was determined in 1975 to have lined up with the pole star Thuban around 1750 BCE, and is on the main central axis from which other alignments can be calculated. These alignments include the annual summer and winter solstices (June 21 and Dec. 21) and seasonal equinoxes (March 22 and Sept. 22), as well as specific solar and lunar events of the year. Several of the low stonewalls also indicate true north-south and east-west alignments. It is interesting to note that all astronomical sightings at America's Stonehenge are in a position to accurately predict their events around 1500 BCE—the difference is due to the earth's changing tilt over several thousand years—which is further evidence in determining the age of the site.

Formerly known as the Mystery Hill Caves, America's Stonehenge is more of an academic problem child than a mystery. Professional archaeologists who refute any European contact before Columbus or the Vikings routinely dismiss this sprawling complex as a fraud, ignoring even the most basic evidence. For instance, a white pine tree found growing through one of the walls conclusively determined its tree-ring age to be at least 30 years older than the birth date of farmer Pattee, the first homesteader on the hill. Jonathan Pattee purportedly created this megalithic complex as a hoax in his spare time, then after all his work, turned around and started dismantling and selling the larger slabs for spare change. Yet how Pattee could have erected megaliths weighing 15-20 tons (13,600-18140 kg), dug drainage canals through the bedrock without using modern tools, and aligned markers to indicate solstices and equinoxes was never explained by the stodgy academia. It is known that at least 20% to 50% of the site was devastated by quarrymen in the 1920s who hauled away "cartload after cartload" of the megalithic stones to build sewers and curbstones in Lawrence,

Massachusetts. All that's left today are the skeletal remains of a much larger site. Perhaps the most startling evidence indicating the real age of America's Stonehenge is the carbon dating of charcoal debris excavated for analysis. Two separate tests in 1969 and 1971 determined the age of America's Stonehenge to be at least 3,000 and more likely 4,000 years old. In addition, pottery shards found at the

▲ One of several megalithic chambers at America's Stonehenge.

site seem unrelated to anything Viking, Irish or Native American, suggesting even older voyagers visiting New England in the Bronze Age. The seafaring Mediterranean Phoenician and their Celtic allies from the Iberian peninsula seem the most likely candidates. Along with the characteristic megalithic stone-slab chambers and associated henge stones marking celestial events, rune-like inscriptions have been deciphered as Iberian Punic and read as a dedication to the Phoenician sun god Ba'al. Other inscriptions identified at the site bearing the Celtic Ogam script refer to Bel, The Celtic sun god, long suspected to be the same god as the Phoenician Ba'al. Just the terrifying thought of such pagan gods being worshiped on the Puritan shores of New England has kept the Semitic and Celtic people excluded from their deserved role in American prehistory. Beyond a hoax, the picture of America's Stonehenge emerges as a thriving first century BCE Celtic community, Punic trading post, pagan religious center and Iberian astronomical observatory.

### Getting to America's Stonehenge

Located in North Salem, America's Stonehenge is only about an hour's drive from downtown Boston, and 18 miles (30 km) from the Atlantic Ocean. Boat captains of antiquity would have reached the hilltop location by navigating up the Merrimack River to a tributary that runs just below the site. Most visitors today drive to America's Stonehenge and take Exit 3 off the I-93 to Route 111. Motorists should follow the signs from North Salem. The land around North Salem, New Hampshire is becoming increasingly urbanized by the encroaching urban sprawl of Boston.

# NEW MEXICO

Among the contrasting energy spots of New Mexico are Native American pueblos, breathtaking canyons, atomic energy centers, sacred mountains, top-secret missile bases, and rumors of a crashed UFO near Roswell. New Mexico has a rich Native American history going back at least 10,000 years. Remains of the advanced civilizations that flourished in the region can be seen in the form of well-constructed cliff dwellings. These houses, apartments and whole villages still stand and give a fine view of the advanced states achieved by these early Indian nations. Yesterday as today, the Tiwa Pueblo Indians hold Taos Peak near the village of Taos as ultra sacred. Blue Lake near the summit is off-limits to non-Native American people, as it is regarded as an entrance to the Tiwa spiritual underworld.

## Chaco Canyon

Called the "American Cradle of Civilization," Chaco Canyon represents the most important concentration of archaeological remains in the United States. The 12-mile (19-km) long and one-mile (1.6-km) wide canyon was a thriving urban center 900 years ago, and home to approximately 4,000-6,000 people. The stone-built towns in Chaco Canyon were individual complexes known as "Great Houses." The largest Great House is called Pueblo Bonito, a complex that contained both dwellings and ceremonial centers. The ancient people inhabiting Chaco Canyon are commonly known as the Anasazi—or Ancestral Puebloan —a tribe who designed intricate irrigation systems, outstanding earthenware pots and a city laid out in the manner of a modern apartment block.

The canyon was first inhabited around 100 CE when the nomadic tribe began planting crops and settling down. A thousand years saw this ingenious people go from hunters and gathers to sophisticated urban dwellers. Chaco's most active building period began around 1020 CE and continued at a rapid pace for several decades. By 1111, this power was consolidated at several of the outlying communities where a Chacoan Great House would preside over smaller farming domains. For hundreds of years Chaco influence dominated northeastern New Mexico, and beyond. The Anasazi had trade and spiritual contacts with their Toltec/Maya cousins to the south. The Chaco inhabitants were known to keep macaw parrots from Central America.

Radiating out from the Chaco complex is a mysterious arrangement of straight lines and wide roads that extend 10 to 20 miles (16-32 km) into the desert. Most of the

roads link up to some 75 other Ancestral Puebloan Great Houses, while others seem to go astray. The longest northbound roadway extends for 42 miles (68 km), leading up to the prehistoric communities of Salmon and Aztec. Most of the roads are arrow straight regardless of terrain and were wide enough for eight men to walk abreast. They go directly over mesas (table-top mountains), up

▲ Casa Rinconada kiva in Chaco Canyon features astronomical alignments.

and down vertical cliff faces, and along courses that oftentimes make them impractical for travel. Aerial photographs reveal more than 400 miles (644 km) of roads, visible almost exclusively from the air in the early morning or late afternoon when the sun casts deep shadows. Inspecting the roads at ground level it is evident that they were expertly engineered, planned, and involved a significant amount of labor in their construction and maintenance. The extensive link of roads, some as wide as 30 feet (10 m),

▲ Pueblo Bonito was the largest "Great House" of the Anasazi.

demonstrates that the Anasazi people had a well-developed network for trade and distribution of goods. Some researchers suggest another purpose, such as a charting of the region's ley lines. It is known that north is a point of origin to most Puebloan people, and the Great North Road is almost perfectly straight and astronomically aligned. Others argue that the markings represent an out-of-the-body experience familiar to ancient native shamans. Archaeological research does confirm that most of the lines lead to small shrine-like structures where evidence of religious and shamanistic activity took place. It seems reasonable to suppose that these roads, prior to recent erosion, could have been followed across great expanses of land, thereby delineating an enormous grid or map of shamanistic geography. These mysterious lines, often apparently between no particular places, are found in many parts of the Anasazi realm. The roads certainly provided open communication between communities and demonstrate an advanced social structure.

### Chaco Canyon was home to the first centralized civilization in North America, and for the Anasazi inhabitants, Pueblo Bonito was the center of the universe.

Chaco Canyon was the spiritual center of the Anasazi people and nation. Scattered across Chaco Canyon and especially in the Great Houses were several round *kivas*, or ceremonial rooms. The scale of the kiva ceremonies was immense; 400 people could attend each of the 15 great kivas, while 100 smaller kivas could accommodate 50-100 others. The largest kiva in the Southwest, the Casa Rinconada, has a special window for viewing the summer solstice on June 21st. Also marking the longest day of the year is a spiral petroglyph near the top of Fajada Butte carved behind three upright slabs of rock, which cast a different interplay of light to give calendar markings for the equinoxes and solstices. Large seasonal ceremonies may have attracted "pilgrims" to Chaco along a ritually used road system that connected Chaco to distant communities and to the sacred landscape. The tradition of holding ceremonies in a large round room passed on to the Pueblo Indians, most notably the Hopi, Ute and Zuni tribes.

Many clans still trace a direct relationship with Chaco, including the Navajo who are not even Pueblo Indians. Oral traditions relate stories of clans migrating from Chaco to the surrounding Four Corners area. Ten Hopi clans trace their ancestry to Chaco. As a result, modern Pueblo people share a strong physical and spiritual connection to Chaco and revere the canyon and all its ruins as extremely sacred. Modern Southwest Indians believe that the spirits of their ancestors still inhabit Chaco Canyon, and thus it is a spiritual place to be deeply honored and respected.

The largest Chaco Canyon Great House is a "D-shaped" complex called Pueblo Bonito. The name *Pueblo Bonito* means "pretty village" in Spanish, but like all the ruins in the valley, the original Anasazi names are unknown. From Pueblo Bonito, trails and stairways crisscross Chaco Canyon to the other 12 major ruins in the canyon. Designed for communal domestic life, its other functions probably included religion and ceremony, storage, hospitality, trading, signaling, star observations, and burying of the dead. The complex had more than 600 rooms, numerous two- and three-story buildings, several kiva complexes, and supported a year-round population between 100 and 400 persons. Some of the alignments that can be made from the structure of Pueblo Bonito itself are rather impressive. For example, there are two walls dividing the pueblo, exactly aligned to north, south, east, and west. The east-west wall divides the seasons at the fall and spring equinoxes. Elaborate lunar and solar alignments are featured in the construction of other Chaco Canyon pueblos, including many that integrate noon sun alignments. As advanced as they were no one is sure what happened to this advanced culture: From tree-ring dating, it is known that a period of severe drought came upon the Four Corners area in 1250 CE, causing the abandonment of Chaco Canyon. Rediscovered in 1849 by U.S. Army soldiers on military reconnaissance, the site was severely vandalized for 70 years until it was made a national monument in 1907.

### Getting to Chaco Canyon

Chaco Canyon is located in northwestern New Mexico, about 100 miles (160 km) northwest of Albuquerque and approximately the same distance from Santa Fe. Pueblo Bonito and the other 12 main archaeological sites are collectively known as Chaco Culture National Historic Park. From Albuquerque, take Highway 44/550 north and west to the turn off at County Road 7900. This exit is at mile marker 112.5 and 3 miles (5 km) south of the town Nageezi. County Road 7900 will lead to another turn off on a maintained dirt road. The route has many signs and is not difficult to navigate. Rain and snow can make the roads impassible, so it is best to check the local weather forecast before departure.

# WYOMING

Claimed at different times by Spain, France, and England, Wyoming fell into the possession of the United States, like most of the Rocky Mountain states, after the Louisiana Purchase. Fur trappers were the first outsiders to explore the vast region, living with and learning from the Apsalooka (Crow), Lakota (Sioux), Shoshone, and other tribes. The tides would turn on the Indians when emigrants followed along on the Oregon Trail, then in 1867 when the nation's first transcontinental railroad began to lay track and establish towns across southern Wyoming. During the 1860s and 1870s, Sioux, Arapaho, and Cheyenne fought for control of the Black Hills and the Powder River grasslands. After the inevitable defeat of the Indian tribes, settlement and ranching helped lay the groundwork for Wyoming's modern economy.

## Bighorn Medicine Wheel

On a shoulder of Medicine Mountain is the most famous medicine wheel in North America. Described as a sort of American Stonehenge, Bighorn Medicine Wheel was famous with local native tribes as a location for sunrise and sunset rituals, as well as other celestial observations. The medicine wheel consists of a collection of half-sunken stones in the shape of a wagon wheel. The middle cairn (stone pile) is a meter tall with 28 uneven spokes

▲ The Bighorn Medicine Wheel commands an impressive mountain top position.

radiating to an outer rim. The 28 spokes may represent the 28 days of the lunar cycle. Each spoke is about 36 feet (11 m) long, the outer ring is about 80 feet (24 m) in diameter and 245 feet (74 m) in circumference. Around the rim are 6 smaller cairns about a half meter tall and open on one side. The center cairn and another outside the rim establish an alignment with the rising sun on summer solstice, and one more measures the setting sun on the same day. The other cairns line up with the stars Sirius, Fomalhaut in the constellation Pisces, Rigel in the constellation Orion, and Aldebaran in the constellation Taurus. All these star readings fall within one month of the summer solstice. The hollowed out center cairn may have contained an offering bowl, a buffalo skull platform or some kind of lost instrument used for celestial navigating. No one knows how old the wheel is; some estimates date it back thousands of years, but the best guess puts it around 800 years old.

**The Bighorn Medicine Wheel near the summit of Medicine Mountain marks the sunrise and sunset of the summer solstice and the rising of prominent summer stars. Its astrological alignments represent a profound understanding of seasonal and celestial navigation.**

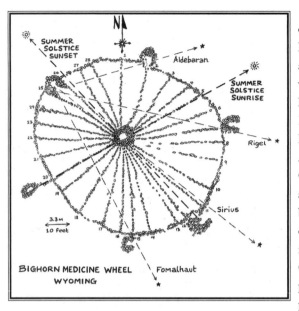

SUMMER
SOLSTICE
SUNSET

Aldebaran

SUMMER
SOLSTICE
SUNRISE

Rigel *

Sirius

3.3 M
10 feet

BIGHORN MEDICINE WHEEL
WYOMING

Fomalhaut

From the impressive elevation of 9,640 feet (2,892 m), the Bighorn Wheel alignments appear to link the distant plains with the heavens. The site has a long history with the Plains Indians and other tribes in the Rocky Mountains. The Crow, Arapaho, Shoshone and Cheyenne all have oral histories about important ceremonies being held here. Crow youth came to the wheel as a place to fast and seek their vision quest. Other tribes came to pray for personal atonement, healing, or pay respect to the Great Spirit. Chief Joseph of the Nez Percé came to Bighorn for guidance and wisdom as his people were transitioning from freedom to reservation life. Today a fence surrounds the Bighorn Medicine Wheel, with prayer offerings attached to the fence. For North American native people the circle represents the cycle of life. The circle is seen as a symbol of eternity—with no beginning and no end—denoting the interconnectedness of everything. The medicine wheel could also represent a microcosm of life, a sort of starting point for all otherworldly aspects. Along with astrological alignments, the circular pathway includes the four cardinal compass points. The four compass points can also be seen as the four seasons, where spring would represent the east, summer the south, autumn the west, and winter the north. The number four also corresponds to the four sacred elements of earth, wind, water, and fire.

## Getting to Bighorn Medicine Wheel

The archaeological mystery and sacred native site is located high atop Medicine Mountain within Bighorn National Forest, 25 miles (40 km) east of Lovell, Wyoming. The nearest city is Sheridan. Medicine Wheel National Historic Site is located just west from Burgess Junction, on US 14A, open from June until October. The site is inaccessible most of the year due to snow pack and winter weather.

# SUB-SAHARA AFRICA

Hatred is like rain in a desert —it is of no use to anybody.
—*African proverb*

ISTORY BEGINS IN AFRICA. Just the name conjures up images
exotic. From the empty expanses of the Sahara Desert to the
dense rainforests of the Congo—Africa represents all things wild.
The continent has been termed the "Cradle of Humanity," where our first
humanoid ancestors ventured from the jungle into the savanna. Here, in
the Great Rift Valley of eastern Africa, massive volcanoes soar overhead
and wild animals roam as they have since the dawn of humanity. Between
safaris and mountain climbs, the traveler is also seduced by many fascinating native tribes, spectacular scenery, and ruins from ancient civilizations.

As the second largest continent, Africa is a place of great diversity over wide expanses
of land. The continent was a meeting point of the Arabic and Christian world with primitive cultures, followed by European colonists who set modern boundaries, oftentimes
with little regard to tribal territories. Despite the trauma of colonization, which indeli-
bly changed the lifestyles of native Africans, many of their religious habits continue in
some fashion today. The landscape of Africa varies as much as the tribal people who
inhabit the land. Yet, many obstacles must be overcome before setting out. All travelers
to Africa must be acquainted with possible setbacks, including exotic diseases, extreme
poverty, political upheavals, rough overland travel, high expenses in some countries and

a lack of amenities. For a complete rundown of travel in Africa, see *World Stompers: A Global Travel Manifesto* by Brad Olsen. In a nutshell, Africa offers a world of contrasts with more than its fair share of problems. Welcome to the Dark Continent.

# SAHARA DESERT

The immense Sahara Desert, the largest desert landmass in the world, stretches over 3,000 miles (4,900 km) from the Atlantic Ocean to the Red Sea. In parts it extends more than 1,200 miles (2,000 km) from north to south. The entire desert covers some 3 million square miles (4,830,000 sq. km), and continues to expand into new parts of Africa every year. The desert name means "wilderness" from the Arabic word *sahrá*. Weather conditions can be extremely harsh, especially during the periodic deadly sandstorms.

Some of the most impoverished nations in the world today are the African countries within and just below the Sahara Desert. In order for people living in extreme poverty on the fringe of the desert to survive, an overtaxing of the fragile land on which they depend has been the result. The desert moves in, the people move to a new forest zone, and the process continues its reckless course. The

▲ A rare desert oasis in the Sahara.

problem is these people, and we as a planet, are running out of farmable land. Could this be a microcosm of modern earth's present dilemma?

## Ancient Rock Drawings

Spanning the middle of the Sahara Desert is a string of mountains with high plateaus and towering cliffs forming a triangle between Tassili (Southern Algeria), Acacus (Libya), and Ennedi (Chad). In 1933, French Foreign Legionnaires were mapping and scouting the central Sahara region when they stumbled upon some of the oldest representations of human artwork. The painted and carved images they found in several different locations are among the greatest archaeological treasures of African history. Stone Age tribes created magnificent artwork on the walls of mountain caves and cliff overhangs. These ancient rock drawings are a pictorial legacy of mythical beings, wild game and impressive images of everyday life. The images clearly depict the Sahara as a blooming garden, replete with nomadic people hunting wild game.

About 10,000 years ago, the central region of the Sahara Desert was a much different place than it is today. Life-size rock carvings in the Sahara highlands depict elephants, giraffes, ostriches, hippopotamus, rhinoceros, evergreen trees and pasture animals that could not possibly survive there in today's hostile conditions. The pre-

▲ This "Mushroom Dance" rock drawing at Tassili, Algeria is about 10,000 years old.

historic human inhabitants of this area were originally hunters. The pictoglyphs, some dating as far back as 8000 BCE, seem to be placed along very early travel routes that passed now extinct lakes, forests and swamps, all teeming with wildlife. On one windswept plateau in the Tassili n'Ajjer Mountains in Algeria is a spectacular site called Sefar. Even today the narrow streets and squares of what was probably the Stone Age equivalent of a city can be seen. Paintings on rock walls show horned giants, exotic animals, and warriors with headdresses resembling those of ancient Egypt. Another site in the Tassili region called Jabbearen boasts murals containing over 5,000 figures. Archaeologists who have examined the pictography at Jabbearen believe the various styles mark the passage of as many as 12 different civilizations over several thousand years. At a period of later development the murals show the hunting tribes becoming sophisticated farmers who herded cattle, rode in chariots, tilled gardens, and made pottery. Other paintings show intimate family scenes, and what appears to be the domestication of dogs.

**Most stunning of the ancient rock drawings in the Sahara are pictures of anthropomorphic beings engaged in ecstatic dance, and having a strong association with a mushroom cult.**

On top of the Sahara Plateau, at an altitude of 6,500 feet (1,950 m), there exist pictures depicting mythical beings alongside growing mushrooms. These deities appear with masks and horns and are seen holding mushrooms in their hands, or the mushrooms are attached directly to their body parts. Further adding mystery to the Stone Age mushroom cult are the images of anthropomorphic beings with mushroom-like heads. One striking rendition is at Tin-Tazarift in the Tassili region of Algeria, which features a picture of a masked being engaged in ecstatic dancing. This figure is most interesting because of the dashed lines that connect a mushroom with the center of the dancer's head. Perhaps these lines represent the mushroom's influence on the human soul, or a flow of energy. Most experts agree that these pictures clearly indicate psychotropic mushroom use. Despite their age, the colors in the rock drawings have retained much of their brilliant hues. Pictures of the mushrooms were drawn in white, as well as several shades of ochre and blue. In nature, these colors are associated with the bluing *Psilocybe* and *Panaeolus*, each a psychedelic, dung-inhabiting species of mushroom that grows primarily on top of raw compost.

The ancient rock drawings indicate that the desert regions of northern Africa were once fertile lands covered with grass and trees. Over-hunting and deforestation likely prompted the transformation of the temperate landscape teeming with wildlife into an inhospitable desert. The massive climactic change took place between 3000 and 1500 BCE, and resulted in the extinction of many animal and plant-life species. All of this only increased the size and severity of the Sahara, which continues to overtake once-fertile territory by leaps and bounds.

### Getting to the Ancient Rock Drawings

The ancient rock drawings of the Sahara are extremely difficult to visit. First off, Libya and Algeria are openly hostile to foreigners, even to the point of kidnapping travelers and killing them. Second, there are only poor roads or no roads whatsoever to access the sites. Third, they are located in rather inhospitable mountain regions with no travel amenities. For the truly intrepid, Libya has prehistoric caves in the Acacus Mountains, Algerian sites are located in the southeast region of Tassili n'Ajjer, and Chad in the northern Tibesti Mountains. Chad is the only country issuing foreign travel visas, but the Tibesti Mountains are dangerous to visit because of uncharted landmines and a long-standing border dispute with Libya.

## Timbuktu

Before Portuguese mariners charted the sea route around Africa's southernmost Cape of Good Hope in 1498 CE, trading with Africa could only be conducted along the harsh Sahara trade routes. One city in particular became fabulously wealthy because of its position on the main caravan routes. The city of Timbuktu, whose name still rings a bell, became the stuff of legend in the collective mind of curious European merchants. Beyond being a major caravan center, Timbuktu was also a major cultural center where a great many doctors, priests and scholars resided with the king in his stately confines. To the king, manuscripts and written books from the Mediterranean nations held greater value than any other merchandise, including gold. At its peak, Timbuktu was home to one million people. Of those million, 25,000 were students at its university, coming from all parts of the Arabic world.

> **Timbuktu, in spite of its barren and remote setting, managed to amass building materials and a diligent work force from afar because of its spectacular wealth.**

The most prominent buildings in Timbuktu were a grand temple and the king's princely palace. Both were made of the finest stone with lime mortar, and constructed by the foremost workmen from Granada, Spain. In 1559, a Spanish Moor known as Leo Africanus, gave this account of the royal court's magnificence: "The rich king ... hath many plates and scepters of gold, some were of weight 1,300 pounds; and he keeps a magnificent and well-furnished court."

▲ The unique architecture of Timbuktu features temples of wood and dried mud.

Gold and slaves from the interior of Africa were the staples of the trans-Sahara trade. Being on the border of the Niger River and the wide-open desert, Timbuktu was the main crossroads for the Sahara trade. Even after it was sacked in 1468 by the Songhai army, the new rulers adapted the Mali mantle and the city remained a cultural center. It wasn't until world sailing routes were firmly established and slavery became abolished in Europe that Timbuktu fell into sharp decline. Alas, today little is left of its former glory, but the legend of Timbuktu remains in its dusty streets and the nomadic tribes who still roam on the fringes of the world's largest desert.

## Getting to Timbuktu

Timbuktu is located on the southern fringe of the Sahara Desert in the country of Mali. It is possible to fly into Mali's capital Bamako and then take a connecting flight on an old Russian turboprop to Timbuktu. The extreme adventure is to take a chartered riverboat down the famous Niger River to Timbuktu. Otherwise, Timbuktu is accessible by bus or camel caravan from the capital or surrounding countries. Mali has economic agreements with France so the cost of travel is relatively high compared to the rest of Africa.

# ETHIOPIA

Most impressions of Ethiopia are of an impoverished, backwater nation. This is far from reality, as Ethiopia is one of Africa's oldest nations, with a long and proud history. The famine reports in the 1980s were mostly localized events. The interior landscape is mountainous and green. Called Abyssinia until a military dictatorship took over, Ethiopia was also known in antiquity as the "Hidden Empire," and a probable home to the fabled Prester John, a model of medieval Christian values. Biblical tradition describes the Queen of Sheba meeting King Solomon around 1000 BCE and bearing a son named Menelik I, who became the king of Ethiopia. The Solomon bloodline of rulership remained unbroken for 3,000 years until the death of Emperor Haile Selassie (born Ras Tafari, 225th Solomonic ruler) in August 1975. He had been under house arrest by the Military Council, which upon his death usurped power and rules Ethiopia to this day. Interestingly, it is Haile Selassie (the Lion of Judah) who is the central figure in the Jamaican Rastafarian cult.

# Axum

The holiest city of the Ethiopian Orthodox faith, Axum was founded over 2,000 years ago and is capital to one of the most glorious empires in history. The numerous churches and monasteries of Axum feature richly endowed icons and crowns of ancient emperors. The 16th century Cathedral of Saint Mary of Zion was likely built on the location of an earlier fourth century church, and is recognized as the holiest church in Ethiopia. In the sanctuary below the cathedral is said to rest a duplicate, or possibly the original Ark of the Covenant. The city of Axum is filled with sacred relics from its glorious past. Near Saint Mary's is the Obelisk Park featuring magnificent carved stelae and massive obelisks, the tallest standing 75 feet (23 m), weighing more than 200 tons (203,200 kg) and hewn from solid granite. Another obelisk of equal proportions is supposed to be returned from Italy soon. Equally impressive in Axum are the graves of King Kaleb and King Gabre Meskal, and the legendary Queen of Sheba bath building.

The Axumite Empire flourished as a sanctuary for Coptic Christians shortly after the time of Christ. Even though Ethiopia was surrounded by the enemies of its religion, the people clung to the Coptic Christian faith, a religion that teaches karma, reincarnation and a perspective that Jesus was actually an Archangelic being from the sixth plane of existence. Like the Gnostic and Nestorian Christians of Europe, the Coptics did not sign the Nicene Creed in the fourth century CE, and were essentially banished from participation in the new Christian order put forth by Emperor Constantine. The Coptics neither recognize the Pope, nor the subsequent editing and censorship of the original New Testament.

**Axum is famous for being the first Christian kingdom outside of the Mediterranean. Its enormous obelisks and the ruins of the Queen of Sheba's palace only add to the mystique.**

Passing through Axum is the famous Historic Route, considered the greatest treasure of Ethiopia. The route accesses Axum to Lalibela, the medieval castles at Gondar, and Bahir Dar & Bale National Park. Lalibela is a unique location, featuring 13 rock-hewn churches carved out of solid rock dating from the 12th century. King Lalibela is credited with the building of these remarkable edifices scattered across a rugged landscape. 34 miles (55 km) from Axum, the Historic Route passes by the 2,500-year old Yeha Temple and the massive walls housing Judaic relics and historic

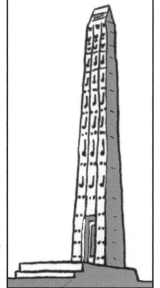

▲ One of the unique obelisks of Axum.

artifacts. The rise of Islam in the seventh century caused Ethiopia to withdraw itself from the capital Axum and move to the inner highlands.

### Getting to Axum

Axum is located near the northern border of Eritrea, which has an ongoing border dispute with Ethiopia. Travel is restricted and unadvised until real peace is achieved. Once in Ethiopia getting around, and local transport from the capital Addis Ababa to Axum, is relatively easy. Lalibela may be inaccessible during the rainy season (June-August). The rock-hewn churches of Lalibela are best discovered on horseback or four-wheel drive.

# TANZANIA

Home to some of the best wildlife reserves on the planet, Tanzania offers up nature as few other destinations can. Here is where Mount Kilimanjaro soars into the sky and wild animals roam in Serengeti National Park. Especially noteworthy is Ngorongoro Crater, which is one of the largest craters in the world and full of wildlife. Complementing the inland animals are the tropical fish and coral reefs on the coast. Mellow towns and nice beaches make Tanzania one of the top tourist attractions in Africa. A warning to travelers: It is uncertain what the August 1998 bombing of the U.S. Embassies in Tanzania and Kenya will mean for internal travel and safety. However, it appears this terrorist act was an isolated political statement and individual travelers are not being targeted.

## Mount Kilimanjaro

Towering 19,340 feet (5,895 m) above sea level, Kilimanjaro dominates the Serengeti Plains. Visible for hundreds of miles in all directions, the view from the top is considered by mountaineers to be the greatest panoramic view available anywhere on earth. The Masai named the mountain "House of God," early colonizers called it the "Crown of Africa," but just about everybody else knows it as Kilimanjaro.

▲ The Coptic religion of northern Africa influenced the tribal cultures of eastern Africa.

Mount Kilimanjaro is one of the largest freestanding volcanoes in the world — so massive that its weight measurably depresses the crust of the earth. The base of Kilimanjaro stretches 50 miles (80 km) along the Tanzania-Kenya border, a product of lava erupting from faults and fractures in the Great Rift Valley. The mountain is a geological infant at 750,000 years old, and consists of one collapsed and two dormant volcanoes.

*Uhuru*, a Swahili word for "freedom," is the name of the tallest peak on Kilimanjaro. Uhuru is the highest point on the African continent. The summit of Kilimanjaro is eerily isolated, a forbidding dome of glaciers and rust-red rock looming over the windswept moors.

The great Alexandrian astronomer and geographer Ptolemy first located Kilimanjaro in the second century BCE while charting the known world. Ptolemy described it as "a great snow mountain" back in an age when the sun was believed to circle the earth. Renowned for the marvel of its equatorial ice and unforbidding angle of its slopes, Kilimanjaro has always been legendary to native tribes who have lived in its shadow. In Chagga tribal mythology, the peak was crowned with silver that would melt in hand, guarded by spirits who would inflict pain and chills on anyone who ventured too high.

**The Masai tribe calls Kilimanjaro *Ngàje Ngài*, meaning "House of God." It is the tallest free-standing mountain in the world.**

Indeed, Kilimanjaro is the roof of the African continent, both in fact and in legend. Native people describe it as a place where spirits seek everlasting rest on its lofty summit. It is the setting of Ernest Hemingway's short story "The Snows of Kilimanjaro," where a dying writer contemplates the portents of death as buzzards and hyenas move in on him. Long regarded as a holy place, Kilimanjaro is an exalted promised land, a recognizable entity, a place where a leopard might lay down to die. This sacred mountain casts a long shadow on the location where humankind's evolutionary adventure first began.

## Climbing Mount Kilimanjaro

Summiting Mount Kilimanjaro can usually be done in two or three days. Some 30,000 tourists attempt it every year, with about half of those turning back largely due to altitude sickness. Ninety percent of climbers follow what is called the tourist or Coca-Cola route, which starts at the Marangu Gate on the southeastern flank of the mountain. This route roughly parallels Hans Meyers' first ascent in 1889. The Coca-Cola route is linked with three bunk-and-kitchen huts for typical tour groups in a five-day, four-night round-trip. With its non-technical slopes, abundance of porters and mild temperatures, the climb is considered moderate by serious mountaineers. A Tanzania National Park service guide is required by law, so the cheapest way is to pick one up at the village of Moshi near the foot of the mountain before ascending.

International flights arrive in Nairobi, Kenya, and Dar es Salaam, Tanzania, every day. From these respective capitals take a local bus or tourist shuttle to the base of the mountain. There are also local and international flights to Kilimanjaro International Airport, located near the mountain and the town Arusha.

# Laetoli Plain

On a dry savanna in northern Tanzania 3.6 million years ago, three early human ancestors went for a walk. Anthropologist Mary Leakey pieced this together by discovering a trail of human-like footprints in the region called the Laetoli Plain. These three barefoot hominids (*Australopithecus afarensis*), supposedly a short man, a woman and a child, walked closely together. They set their tracks on moist volcanic ash and tuff, soon to be covered by another layer of ash. On that epic day, long before our earliest ancestors chipped their first stone tools, it rained. Also preserved are pockmarks of the raindrops that fell beside the three walking hominids.

Leakey uncovered almost 90 feet (26 m) of the three hominids' steady footprints intact. No one can tell where they were going or why. Along the course of their walking, the woman paused and turned left, briefly, before continuing. "A remote ancestor," said Leakey, "experienced a moment of doubt." Possibly, she turned to watch the Sadiman volcano erupt, or perhaps she took one last look at a place she knew would be lost before they left.

The Laetoli footprints prove conclusively that walking on two legs was well established before 3.6 million years ago, and that this, rather than larger brains or the manufacture of stone tools, constituted the earliest ascent on the road to humanity. This sacred place is a record of the first proto-humans taking their first steps on the evolutionary ladder. The prints show a pattern of weight distribution, as well as the position and relative size of the toes, indicating a two-legged stride much like our own, rather than the rolling gait of the Great Apes who rarely walk upright.

▲ Tribal culture lives on in the artwork of Eastern Africa.

**An interesting snapshot of humankind's evolution is marked on the Laetoli Plain. Here, between Lake Victoria and Mount Kilimanjaro, the first proto-humans emerged from the jungle.**

At the Olduvai Gorge near the Laetoli Plain is the richest store of human and prehuman remains ever discovered. Olduvai has been labeled one of the most important archaeological sites in the world. Successive layers suggest this site had a continuous period of habitation extending over hundreds of thousands of years. Australopithecus, meaning "southern ape," is the earliest proto-human ape ever to be discovered. Well-preserved remains of Australopithecus have been uncovered at Olduvai. The most intact Australopithecus has been named "Lucy," a 4-foot (1.2-m) tall female with an ape-like head who walked erect. Its brain size, smaller than the later evolving *Homo erectus*, was larger in proportion than any ape's brain living today. It is also known that *Australopithecus* used splintered antelope bones as weapons and tools. Evolutionists hail Lucy as an intermediate species that proves the descent of man from apes.

### Getting to the Laetoli Plain

After archaeologists studied the stretch of ancient footprints for several years, they buried the location again for preservation. While exposed, the elements threatened to re-claim this long strip of record. Now the footprints are buried as they were and are hard to locate. Like the important digs at Olduvai, there is nothing really to see, or else these sites are restricted dig sites. The real thrill of this sacred place is just taking in the ambiance of where our earliest ancestors emerged onto the planetscape. Some Tanzanian safari companies make a stop at Laetoli or Olduvai, but the best option is to hire a private taxi from Arusha to the site.

# Zanzibar

A popular Tanzanian side trip is out to the island of Zanzibar, where the traveler will observe many people of different racial backgrounds co-existing peacefully. Most apparent is the strong Arabic influence. The Arabs followed the Portuguese who came as traders and slavers. The old Stone Town on Zanzibar is a fascinating labyrinth of ruined palaces, forts and Persian baths from the 15th century Omani period. Many of the buildings in Stone Town are rumored to be haunted. The indigenous people of Zanzibar are the handsome Swahili people, whom early slave traders deemed a fine catch. Slavery was the top economic export of Zanzibar for centuries, until it was finally outlawed worldwide in 1907. The name *Zanzibar* is Portuguese, but is derived from an Arabian word meaning "the region of the black peoples."

Zanzibar is a quiet island with a population more polyglot than that of any other place of comparable size in the world. To walk the streets of old Stone Town is to be part of a place where the Middle East, Africa, Asia and Europe all became fused. Intermingling with turbaned Arabs and proud Africans in native dress, Hindus in colorful saris, are Moslem ladies in heavy black *burka* dresses and Europeans in tropical khaki safari clothes. Zanzibar is quite an anthropological experience.

▲ The old slave forts and jails have now become museums of reconciliation and peace.

### Zanzibar island offers a glimpse of world unity — very different races and cultures living in balanced harmony.

The Peace Museum in Zanzibar Town tells the story of the island's tumultuous history and development. While the story of the island is not always harmonious and had been openly racist, Zanzibar changed its ways, and now offers equality for all. Black people today reside in old slave trader homes, Hindus live in one of the town's biggest hotels that was once an Arab merchant's home, and all are welcome to worship at the Anglican Cathedral, despite it being the last open slave market in the world. Lest history repeat, Zanzibar was the last vestige of slavery worldwide, and now represents an equal rights monument for all.

### Getting to Zanzibar

Zanzibar Town is a 30-minute flight from Dar es Salaam, the Tanzanian capital and main city on the eastern coast. Ferryboats ply the route from the mainland to Zanzibar Island, and some people find passage on private crafts. Most travelers agree that Zanzibar is one of the most idyllic and relaxing places in all of Africa.

# ZIMBABWE

Once called Southern Rhodesia, Zimbabwe declared independence from its British colonial masters in 1965. After a long civil war cooled down, Zimbabwe came close to harmony between black and white, and achieved one of the highest standards of living in Africa before the current political situation sent the country spiraling downward into anarchy. The country is rich in minerals, manufacturing and agricultural industries, and the abundant wildlife provides for numerous game parks. English is widely understood from the centuries of colonial rule. Also in Zimbabwe is the spectacular Victoria Falls, named in the African language *Mosi-Oa-Tunya*, meaning "Smoke that Thunders."

## Great Zimbabwe

Throughout much of sub-Sahara Africa are the remnants of ancient villages, fortresses and castle-like structures made of intricately fitted stones. Few are addressed in mainstream travel literature. The ruins of Great Zimbabwe are undoubtedly the best preserved and most famous of all the ancient ruins. Great Zimbabwe resides in the same country that took its name, and is perhaps the greatest compliment ever paid to an archaeological site.

Travelers visiting the ruins of Great Zimbabwe are awe-struck by the enormous conical tower, called the Elliptical Temple, in the center of town. It was the focal point of the community, and steps up to a platform in front of the tower suggest it had been

▲ The ancient Great Zimbabwe complex as it would have appeared when occupied.

used for ceremonial purposes. The Elliptical Temple's shape is reminiscent of a grain bin, yet the tower is built of solid masonry. Its function appears to be that of a symbolic grain bin, where subjects would bequeath crops to the priest-king in favor of another plentiful growing season. Enclosing the Elliptical Temple compound is a double wall. The outer wall is superbly built and decorated along the top with a zigzag "chevron" pattern, while the inner wall is more crudely cut and has been partially dismantled. There is also an acropolis in the city.

When the community of Great Zimbabwe was last occupied in the 14th century CE, Europeans were still far from reaching this remote region in southern Africa. In its prime, Great Zimbabwe was a successful agriculture and trading center. The city produced highly skilled craft workers who designed exceptional tools in iron, and jewelry in copper and gold. Yet, sometime before the 16th century, the city was all but abandoned. The decline of the city seems to correspond with the coming of Europeans who hoped to find gold mines in Africa, and thus cut off key trading routes. Agricultural failure is another suggestion. Whatever cause, the abandonment of Great Zimbabwe remains a mystery and the fate of its highly skilled citizens an enigma.

**No one really knows when or by whom the tall stone structures of Great Zimbabwe were built, but it is possible that they are 3,000 years old or more.**

Unfortunately, much of the site was looted by private treasure-seekers in the early 20th century, so by the time archaeologists reached the site it was pretty much stripped bare. Only speculation remains as to what high culture may have constructed the city. Some archaeologists link the granite structures of Great Zimbabwe to megalithic structures such as Tiahuanaco, Bolivia, or Stonehenge, England. Others find a similar pattern to the Queen of Sheba's palace in Yemen, a massive stone fort on the Aran Islands off Ireland, or King Solomon's temple at Mount Moriah in Jerusalem. Whoever the builders, Great Zimbabwe appears to be very old, yet not one single item has been found to back up the claim of Bantu tribal origin and a medieval construction date.

### Getting to Great Zimbabwe

The ruins of Great Zimbabwe are a few miles south of the city Masvingo. A well-traveled road connects Masvingo to the Zimbabwe capital Harare (formerly named Salisbury) 160 miles (250 km) to the south. Buses make regular connections from Masvingo. Several South African safari companies operate tours of Great Zimbabwe combined with wild-country safaris and a trip to the spectacular Victoria Falls.

### ZIMBABWE TRAVEL ADVISORY

The deteriorating political situation in Zimbabwe has devastated the economy, causing high rates of unemployment and inflation. A sharp rise in crime has also occurred, including the targeting of travelers. Nationwide fuel shortages have disrupted transportation and getting around can be difficult and dangerous. Nearly half the population faces food shortages and possible famine. The U.S. State Department advises only essential travel should be undertaken in Zimbabwe.

# EUROPE

When you go in peace, when you move in peace, exist in peace, the mind is still, the soul serene, and the heart is tranquil; and you move in harmony with the rhythm of the spheres, partake of the sense of oneness of all that is, and realize the connection between yourself and the divine. *—Pythagorus*

THE EUROPEAN CONTINENT HAS LONG BEEN THE CROSSROADS for countless generations of wanderers and mystics. From Paleolithic Cro-Magnon hunters painting animals in European caves to the rise of indigenous pagan rituals and eventually monotheistic faiths — European paths became the interchange for cultures and religions. During the Roman era it is believed Jesus Christ himself traveled overland from the Holy Land to Glastonbury, England, along with his merchant uncle, Saint Joseph of Arimathea. After Christianity swept the continent many centuries later, pilgrim routes converged on sacred cathedrals all across Europe.

Because of its wide appeal to so many people, Europe has something for everyone. This is usually the circuit for pilgrims seeking a high concentration of significant and ancient sacred sites. Start a first-time European adventure in Ireland or Great Britain where the people speak English, albeit with a rather thick accent in some places. The

# SACRED PLACES AROUND THE WORLD

British Isles are loaded with history and history in the making —more crop circle
appear every summer in southern England than any other place in the world. Try to tim
a visit during July and August when the crop circle season is in full bloom.

**LEGEND**

- ooo = Stone Circles
- = Roman Ruins
- = Castle or Cathedral
- = Viking Ruins
- --- = Celtic Footpaths
- = Alignments
- = Megalithic Ruins

# EUROPE

Mainland Europe can sometimes seem like a world apart. Hundreds of individual cultures and languages remain huddled together in the form of countries and dialects, each taking on unique characteristics that have evolved, yet remained, throughout the march of time. Travelers from large homogenous countries like Canada, Australia and the United States are routinely amazed at how quickly everything can change in such a very short distance. By itself, Europe is a treasure-trove of diverse Western culture with a dazzling array of sacred places.

# BRITISH ISLES

The first people to cross the English Channel and settle in Briton were small bands of hunters from Europe. This initial migration took place around 4000 BCE and little remains of these earliest arrivals. Another wave of immigrants came around 3000 BCE, and these new people brought with them basic stone tools and a mysterious new religion. The religion focused on the sacred henge—a megalithic wooden or stone structure built in a circular fashion. There are seven known timber temples and about 3,000 stone circles throughout Britain from this era, most located in southwestern England. These Stone Age monuments, including the awesome Stonehenge, served as religious meeting centers, as well as astronomical observatories. The ability of these cultures to accurately predict the movements of the heavenly bodies surely gave them a sense of communion with a larger and greater force in the universe. They may have felt an ability to control these natural forces by erecting their monuments.

### The British Isles have a long history of ancient lore and global significance.

The next great influx of culture started with the Celts, who brought with them the skill to use bronze and later, iron. Their lasting legacy is the languages they spoke, which can still be heard today in Wales (Brythonic), and Ireland and Scotland (Gaelic). In 43 CE the Romans crossed the English Channel and ruled in force for 370 years. The Roman legacy can still be found with some of their old roads and the 71-mile (115-km) long Hadrian's Wall, which extends across the country just south of the Scottish border. Christianity arrived in the third century CE with a new Germanic immigration, filling the vacuum left by the Romans. These Germanic tribes called themselves the English.

The next wave of invaders were the brutal Vikings from Denmark and Norway who briefly ruled various parts of the country. Several Viking ships were buried along with their king on eastern British beaches, and the relics excavated are some of the finest that survive today. The Normans of France (descendants of the Vikings) conquered England in 1066 and established the feudal system. This divided Britain into small territories, and imposing castles were constructed all over the country for individual protection of autonomous kingdoms.

During the Middle Ages numerous power struggles took place between English kings, overseas nations, small dynasties, and finally, the first Tudor king, Henry VII. Great cathedrals were constructed, and the Bible was translated into English. The 16th century was a golden age; Shakespeare wrote his plays, Francis Bacon laid the foundations for modern science, and the European powers explored the world and became fabulously rich through trade. The foundation of an empire began in 1649 when Oliver Cromwell assumed dictatorial powers and modernized the army and navy.

The British Empire was at its height in 1770 when France ceded all of Canada and all but two trading stations in India, while Captain Cook sailed the world and claimed Australia and several other new colonies for the British Crown. A decade later the Industrial Revolution began in Britain. Soon, Midland country towns became industrial cities. When Queen Victoria took the throne in 1837, the United Kingdom was the greatest power in the world. Factories were set up around the globe, all linked by its dominating fleet of ships. This virtual monopoly on world trade made Britain enormously wealthy, and literally thousands of monuments, palaces and stately buildings were constructed worldwide as a testament to this period.

## Avebury

The assorted monuments around the small English village of Avebury are among the most important Neolithic ruins of the British Isles. They include England's tallest artificial hill, the foundations of a monumental stone circle much like Stonehenge, several preserved prehistoric tombs, and the remnants of two 1.5-mile (2.4-km) long stone avenues. One menhir-lined avenue reaches out southeast and terminates in another stone circle called the Sanctuary. Viewed from above, the Sanctuary circle on Overton Hill and the avenue leading to it resemble a serpent. The Avebury monuments were not just a concentration of elaborate ruins, but also a prehistoric staging ground for seasonal rituals and courting dramas. An underground stream, two rivers, and a bubbling spring were also part of the ritual-religious structure. Depending on the season and festival at hand, each worship ritual moved from location to location during the course of a year.

### The henge surrounding Avebury village is the largest Neolithic monumentt in Britain.

The scale of the Avebury henge is breathtaking. Covering 28 acres (11.3 hectares), the henge is defined by a boundary ditch 50 feet (15 m) deep, which runs between two high banks. The original henge once contained 100 standing stones, of which only 27 remain. Enclosing two smaller circles are a bunch of random stones. The village of Avebury grew up inside the henge at a much later date. Within sight of the Avebury henge are most of the other associated religious sites. The other major Neolithic monument in the area —Stonehenge —lies 17 miles (26 km) due south on the Salisbury Plain.

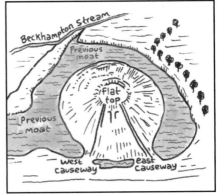

▲ Silbury Hill near Avebury. In ancient times it was part of a larger ritual complex.

Perhaps the most extraordinary monument near Avebury is Silbury Hill — the largest humanmade mound in Europe, whose shape was chosen to resemble a pregnant goddess. Her womb is the mound, 130 feet (40 m) high and measuring more than 550 feet (165 m) in diameter. The rest of her body was defined by a water-filled moat suggesting she is in a squat position, ready to give birth and complete the life cycle. From her head to her thigh, the Mother measures almost 1,400 feet (420 m). On the flat top of the mound, fertility rituals were likely performed to ensure the longevity of the tribe. Built by hand thousands of years ago, Silbury Hill was put together in sections of chalk-mud much like a pyramid. Centuries after its construction, a Viking bride was laid to rest just below the summit. The Viking bride discovery in 1723 led archaeologists to believe Silbury Hill was intended as a burial mound. This view has been changed in modern times. Two powerful ley lines intersect underneath the hill, producing a node of very strong energy. Some of the first contemporary crop circles were discovered near Silbury Hill, and continue to manifest nearby on a regular basis.

Other important sacred sites close to Avebury include: Windmill Hill, a causeway camp built in 3350 BCE before Avebury was constructed; West Kennet Long Barrow, England's largest prehistoric tomb, which extends 340 feet (104 m) in length; and the Devil's Chair, a huge stone that was one of the few megaliths to survive the near-destruction of Avebury by the Puritans in the 17th and 18th centuries. The main sites, including the Processional Avenue, the Sanctuary, Avebury Henge, Silbury Hill and several long barrows (underground tombs), are all within a few miles of each other, and make for splendid hiking and discovery. Many mysteries remain, but certainty Avebury was a known center of much religious activity in prehistoric times.

### Getting to Avebury

The mighty Neolithic ruins of Avebury are located on the beautiful rolling downs of southwestern England. Avebury was once linked by a sacred track to Glastonbury, which is now a narrow country highway. Follow directions to either Glastonbury or Stonehenge to find Avebury. From Salisbury the #5 bus to Swindon passes through Avebury four times daily. Once located, it is well worth a day or more wandering the countryside to see the various monuments around Avebury.

# Glastonbury

The region surrounding Glastonbury was not only an important Neolithic site, but also the reputed home of King Arthur and Camelot. Although little remains physically of either, prehistoric religion and Arthurian legend are just another aspect of Glastonbury, which makes this small town in Somerset so spiritually magnificent. In fact, many proponents of the New Age regard the entire area as an acupuncture point of the earth body—the heart chakra—and one of the most powerful energy centers on the planet.

The charming atmosphere of Glastonbury and the surrounding countryside has encouraged much folklore and legend. King Arthur, for example, was probably a prominent chief who helped to defend this part of England against the pagan Saxons. It is believed the bones of King Arthur and his Queen Guinevere are buried in the Glastonbury Abbey. However, no one really knows because the stories of Camelot and the Round Table came many years after their death. Tradition also relates that among the many esteemed visitors to this holy place was Jesus Christ himself. Jesus was a prolific traveler who likely went along with his uncle, Saint Joseph of Arimathea, on at least one trading mission to Glastonbury.

## Glastonbury has been a recognized religious center since pre-Christian times.

For many centuries early Christian pilgrims have made their way to Glastonbury. It is said that the oldest Christian shrine in England resides here. Remains of an old wattle (twigs and poles) church date back to 633 CE. Successive churches were built on the exact site of the wattle church, later to be surrounded by a medieval abbey, now in ruins. On the Abbey grounds is the Glastonbury Thorn, which allegedly sprang from Saint Joseph's staff and blooms every Christmas. Throughout modern history Christians have yearned to make a pilgrimage to the Holy Land where Christ was born and died. Yet, most had to be satisfied with a pilgrimage to one of the Stations of the Cross. The Glastonbury Abbey symbolically represents one of the 14 Stations, each of which represented part of Christ's journey to his execution on Calvary Hill. His name "Jesus Christ" is engraved outside the Abbey, marking the pilgrim's final destination point.

Rising above the flat plains of Somerset Levels is the Glastonbury Tor, an unmistakable landmark hill with a ruined church tower at its peak. Excavations atop Glastonbury Tor in the 1960s revealed traces of earlier timber buildings, metal-working hearths, animal bones and pieces of pottery suggesting that Mediterranean wine had been drunk. The 500-foot (150-m) Tor could have served as a fortress, perhaps where Queen Guinevere was held captive by Melwas before King Arthur came to rescue her. The remains of the tower seen today was part of a medieval church dedicated

to Saint Michael the Archangel.
Monks built the Saint Michael's
church atop an existing church,
which was later left to ruin by an
earthquake. A medieval fair was held
at the foot of Glastonbury Tor every
year from 1127 until 1825 in honor of
Saint Michael. The Chalice Well
between the Tor and the Abbey was
said to contain the Holy Grail, the

▲ The tower atop Glastonbury Tor is all that
remains of a hilltop church.

elusive chalice used by Christ during the Last Supper and sought in vain by the
Knights of the Round Table.

Although Glastonbury was an ancient pagan and Christian center rich with folklore
and history, it has taken on a new role as the heart chakra of the planet by New Agers.
Accordingly, the cosmic vibration is clearly marked by a massive Zodiac surrounding
the Glastonbury area. Similar to the Nazca Lines in Peru, the 10-mile (16-km) wide
earthworks are only visible from the air. Hedges, woods, ditches and ancient footpaths were laid out in the Age of Taurus to form a ring of the twelve Zodiac signs, and
may have been used as a Temple to the Stars. The Zodiac is also representative of
King Arthur's Round Table. The Arthurian legends and the Zodiac signify our quest
for "the eternal self," also identified as King Arthur's Holy Grail. Grasping its significance requires much patience and imagination because the Zodiac is based largely on
associations and legends rather than known historical facts.

### Getting to Glastonbury

The small town in Somerset is most easily reached by private car. Glastonbury is on
Route 4 from London, and can be accessed from the M5 out of Exeter. The ancient
Roman town Bath is about 30 miles (50 km) from Glastonbury. Tour groups frequently visit Glastonbury from London, yet local buses and trains can be difficult to
navigate because several transfers need to take place.

## Stone Circles of the British Isles

The United Kingdom contains some 1,000 ancient stone circles scattered across
the countryside. Most are located in the southwest quadrant of the country, with the
famous Stonehenge as the apparent center. Upright stones are associated throughout
the world as a representation of the sun as supreme deity and the power of life it
bestows upon the planet. British Isle henge circles were devoted to sun worship, symbolized as the giver of light in our solar system and the ultimate source of information. Incorporated into the stone circles are sophisticated astronomical alignments.
By understanding the relationship with the cosmos, humans could comprehend the
eternal rhythms of nature and the very order of our existence.

Within a five-mile (8-km) radius of Stonehenge itself lie more than 500 stone, wood and earthen monuments. Construction of these huge monuments continued for almost 3,000 years, from the fifth to the second millennium BCE. Two miles from the solar capital Stonehenge is Woodhenge, a wooden circle whose timber has long disappeared over the centuries, where a large circular ditch and embankment still exists. Woodhenge is believed to have been laid out according to a plan derived from the coordinates of Mercury, the nearest planet to the Sun, and connected to Stonehenge in this respect. 17 miles (27 km) north of Woodhenge is the famous stone circle at Avebury called Sanctuary—its two circles of sarsen stones were likely erected during the building phase of Stonehenge and could represent another planet in our solar system. Also within a few miles of Stonehenge are more than 350 barrows, or ancient burial mounds.

**Stone Circles of the British Isles represent a profound understanding of our solar system and the cosmos above. Callanish, for example, has several astronomical alignments, including one with Pleiades.**

The Callanish circle lies at the center of three single and one double set of convex stone rows each within the other. The inner circle consists of a modest diameter at 37 x 43 feet (11.3 x 13.1 m), yet the stones are unlike other circles. Callanish stones are tall and thin and made of gneiss stone quarried only a mile to the northeast. The central stone of the circle is more than 14 feet (4.5 m) tall. Near the cardinal points of the Callanish circle are several lines of stones leading away from the monument. The northern line is the most prominent avenue. It is a double row forming a processional approach to and from the center. Viewed from above, the Callanish arrangement resembles a Celtic cross. There is also a chambered barrow burial at the site. The amazing Callanish circle and standing stones reside 12 miles (20 km) west of Stornoway village in the Outer Hebrides Isle of Lewis off the coast of Scotland. Separated a mile or so from the main Callanish site are several other stone circles named: Cnoc Ceann a'Gharaidh (Callanish II); Cnoc Filibhir Bheag (Callanish III); and Ceann Hulavig (Callanish IV).

A rather crudely cut stone circle, Duloe is unique because it is the only circle in Cornwall made entirely from quartz. Seven protruding boulders create a circle with intense energy, perceptible to sensitive people. Modern dowsers claim there is a natural psychedelic larder within this site, which keeps food preserved longer than normal. Duloe is rarely visited and finding the site can be difficult. The best way is to arrive in the town Duloe, Cornwall, and then inquire about directions in a pub or petrol station. Check reference SX/235583 on a map of England, or travel to the south end of the B3254 and ask the first person you come across. Everyone in the immediate region knows where the Duloe circle is located, just as they would the Callanish site in Stornoway village. Duloe is located in the Bodmin Moor area between Liskeard and Looe.

Almost all the stone circles of Britain are enclosures that share a curvilinear plan: either circles, "flattened" circles, ellipses, or egg-shaped rings. All consist of free-standing stones, except the two inner rings of Stonehenge, which include "trilithons," meaning two standing stones supporting a lintel. Mathematicians and astronomers have recently deduced that many of the British stone enclosures were laid out with a sophisticated standard unit of length according to the rules of geometry. Furthermore, it is accepted that the henge builders incorporated a solar calendar in their designs and recorded some of the movements of the moon.

## Stonehenge

The impressive Stonehenge is one of the most famous sacred sites in Europe, if not the world. Built around 4,200 years ago on the Salisbury Plain in Wiltshire, it is the best example of a megalithic circular-cross arrangement. Wealthy Wessex chieftains likely built the sophisticated site as an agricultural calendar and worship center. The first Stonehenge consisted of a circular ditch dug sometime between 2,600 and 2,200 BCE, and was followed by the construction within the ditch of two concentric circles of 60 "Blue Stones," quarried in the Presili Mountains of southern Wales. At least 200 years elapsed before the two great inner circles of standing stones were constructed. The outer circle and inner horseshoe sarsen stones were cut from a local Wiltshire quarry. How these 20-foot (6-m) upright slabs—topped with perfectly fitted horizontal slabs (lintels)—were put into place at such a distant time in history remains a mystery. Stonehenge originally consisted of one perfect ring and a horseshoe-shaped ring of huge stones arranged in concentric circles, outside the older circular embankment and wooden wall. In another building phase the Blue Stones were removed and 19 of them were brought into the center of the henge. The Heel Stone to the north-east aligns to the exact point where the sun rises on summer solstice, with another marker indicating the shortest day, the winter solstice. On these significant mornings, the rays of the sun stream through the arches to the inner circle where high priests would bless the coming and going of the seasons. Also calculated by this monumental observatory are eclipses of the

▲ The circular ditch surrounding Stonehenge is a prominent feature when seen from above.

sun and moon, the northernmost setting of the moon, the midwinter sunrise and indications of lunar phases from new to full.

### Stonehenge is the most famous prehistoric megalith in Europe. Still one of the earth's great mysteries, Stonehenge was an ancient Druid temple and astronomical observatory, among other functions.

What remains of Stonehenge today is a mere shell of its former glory, so the full understanding of its alignments and computations is still being revealed. There are several astronomical truths that can be derived from Stonehenge. For example, there are 19 of the huge Blue Stones around the inner horseshoe which could represent the 19 years between the extreme rising and setting points of the moon, which also suggest the 19 years before another full moon occurs on the exact same day of the year. Also, there are 19 eclipse years (or 223 full moons) between similar eclipses when the sun, earth and moon return to their same relative positions. It is exactly 29.53 days between full moons, and in the outer Sarsen Circle there are 29-and-one-half monoliths. Discovered recently, 56 is the number of Aubrey Holes set around the outer circle. The number 56 is significant because it corresponds to a 56-year cycle of the rising of the full moon nearest the winter solstice over the Heel Stone, allowing for a successful prediction of an eclipse. Interestingly, less than half the eclipses that Stonehenge predicts can actually be viewed from England! The five large trilithon archways may represent the five planets visible to the naked eye: Mercury, Venus, Mars, Jupiter and Saturn. The other planets' positions may factor into even larger cycles.

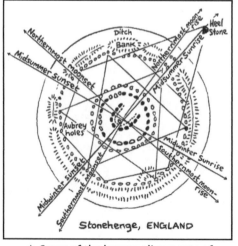

Stonehenge, ENGLAND

▲ Some of the known alignments of Stonehenge.

Several powerful ley lines intersect at Stonehenge, with the ultimate power days falling on the longest and shortest days of the year. The mysterious Druids, an order of priests that began in the age of the Gauls, continue to worship at Stonehenge during the summer and winter solstices. This communing with nature and the cosmos represents one of the longest preserved religious rites in the world. Incidentally, most English crop circles appear in the Wiltshire and Hampshire regions of southern England, with Stonehenge at the presumed center of activity.

### Getting to Stonehenge

Stonehenge is on the Salisbury Plain in southern England. It is easily reached by road from the nearby towns of Amesbury or Salisbury. Public buses leave from Salisbury to Stonehenge on an hourly basis every day. In recent years, Stonehenge has been fenced off and the Druid rituals are permitted only on the winter and summer solstice days. From London, Stonehenge is only a few hours' drive along the 303 roadway southwest to Exeter. Stonehenge is located 8 miles (13 km) north of Salisbury.

# FRANCE

In medieval times, France was a critical crossroads for commerce and Christian pilgrimage. Middle Age pilgrims soon carved out a network of new roads in France known collectively as the Santiago de Compostela routes, so named because they all headed to Compostela, Spain, where the body of Saint James (apostle and cousin of Christ) was reputedly buried. Like Hindus venturing to the Ganges River, medieval Christians seeking repentance would travel to either Rome or Compostela. All along the many French routes great cathedrals were constructed and new cities emerged. Major pilgrimage routes developed within France to various locations. The first travel guide of Europe was Aimery Picaud's *Guide du Pelerin*, a book on good and bad places along the various pilgrimage routes.

# Carnac

The world's largest concentration of megalithic standing stones cluster around a small coastal village named Carnac. Surrounding the region are henges (circular ditched enclosures), stone alignments in circle or arch form, and the famous menhirs (single upright stones) standing in long rows. The long avenues of solitary stones, numbering 2,934 in all, may have been part of an observatory to determine sun and moon alignments. Carnac reached its most completed development around the middle of the second century BCE. In the greater Brittany region there are several rectilinear or semicircular enclosures bounded by long rows of menhirs, but with the exception of Er Lannic near Carnac, none of the stone alignments form a complete circle. Carnac was erected during the Stonehenge era—two impressive megalithic sites divided by the English Channel. Few doubt the ancient culture in northwestern France had strong cultural ties with religious practices similar to those of megalithic builders on the British Isles.

The age of megalith building in northwestern France lasted from 3500 to 1500 BCE, and since then the stones have inspired much speculation about their origin. Local legend says that a marching Roman legion was cast to stone after a fugitive saint made the sign of the cross and faced down the mighty army. Another story associates the stones to a Celtic cattle cult that lasted into Christian times. In the Middle Ages, the stones were viewed as the work of demons, of wizards, or built by giants who walked the earth before the biblical flood. Many of the megaliths were destroyed or defaced by early Christians, but estimates predict that some 50,000 of them once stood in Northern Europe. Now less than 10,000 remain. Though many have been pillaged as ready-quarried stone, Carnac remains one of the best-preserved Stone Age ritual centers in Europe.

**The elaborate stone rows at Carnac form part of an impressive group of ritual monuments, the largest concentration of megaliths in the world.**

The immediate region around Carnac is a diverse landscape of menhirs and monuments. The famous Grand Menhir Brisé of Locmariaquer, which once stood 66 feet high (20 m) and weighed about 380 tons (344,660 kg), is the king of all menhirs. At one time it likely served as a sighting point in astronomical observations for the whole Carnac complex. Today it is cracked in several parts lying on the ground. The Ménec alignments near Carnac consist of no fewer than 11 nearly parallel lines of menhirs extending more than 3,200 feet (950 m) between two fragmentary enclosures. The Ménec Lines, named for a nearby hamlet, consist of 1,099 individual menhirs. The Gavrinis Passage Grave is one of the most beautiful in the world and is also aligned to the midsummer solstice. The long tumulus features spiral and abstract line carvings. The Gavrinis mound likely predates the creation of the stone rows. The expansive ritual center had four alignments and also included huge burial mounds. Carnac was likely a large outdoor worship center, though no altar stones have ever been found. The lines of the tallest stones produce astrological information, specifically pertaining to lunar movements.

The small town on the southern coast of Brittany has become a favored destination for New Agers. Dowsers report the stones of Carnac are charged with a discernable magnetic force. Experiments prove the area north of Carnac has a magnetic or electrical force that may have affected the early builders to choose the site. History repeats at Carnac: young brides and barren couples come for fertility worship. They dance around the stones naked just as their ancestors did thousands of years ago. New Agers come for the reported healing powers of the stones. As is common with indigenous religions worldwide, the mere touching of sacred stones can heal a sick person with their power. Such are the ancient memories of festivals enacted to bring the protection of fertility gods—reenacted then and now.

### Getting to Carnac

Carnac and most of the great megaliths of France lie on the southwest Brittany coast facing the Gulf of Morbihan. The three main sites in this region are Carnac, Locmariaquer and Gavrinis. Most travelers make their way to the French port cities of Quiberon, Vannes or Lorient and take the bus or train to the ruins from there. In the village of Carnac there is an excellent Museum of Prehistory and a viewing platform of the fenced-off menhirs.

## Chartres Cathedral

Most travelers to the Loire Valley west of Paris are headed for the medieval town of Chartres, graced by a magnificent Gothic cathedral. The Chartres Cathedral ranks with Notre Dame, Amiens and Reims as the finest examples of Gothic architecture in France. It is particularly noted for its exquisite stained-glass windows. The renowned windows, some 130 in all, are nearly all originals dating from the 12th and 13th centuries when the cathedral was constructed. The windows feature more than 5,000 figures

▲ Chartres Cathedral is one of the most unique cathedrals in Europe.

depicting the lives of saints and various biblical scenes. The radiating symmetries of the stained glass, as well as the light coming through the famous rose windows, are the true marvels of Chartres Cathedral. Also popular with travelers are the treasury and the climb to the top of the north tower.

Chartres Cathedral and its location hold many unique distinctions. The structure spans the development of the Gothic style of architecture in France. The facade and right tower, completed around 1150 CE, shows the difference between the massive and heavy Romanesque style and the lighter Gothic on the left. The circular rose window in the front is a perfect example of a Gothic motif. The builders of the cathedral were master monks who followed laws of sacred geometry, incorporating various ancient "cubits" of measurement. The hill position where the cathedral stands corresponds to major ley lines connecting Glastonbury, Stonehenge and the Great Pyramids. It was built upon a sacred pagan mound with a grotto, known in antiquity as the "pregnant Virgin," which had first housed a Druid temple then was replaced by a Roman temple. The geometry of Chartres Cathedral resembles a cross-shaped mandala, and is based upon the nine gates of the human body. The cathedral is unique in being virtually unaltered since its consecration in 1260.

## Chartres Cathedral is one of the finest examples of Gothic architecture in Europe and has more than its fair share of mysteries and wonders.

Legend speaks of the Knights Templar as recovering the lost language and treasure of King Solomon, and hiding it within Chartres Cathedral. The Templars were keepers of eternal wisdom dating back to early Egypt, and were predecessors of the Freemasons. The secret society of Freemasonry is the oldest known existing organization in the world. The legend tells of nine French Knights Templar excavating Solomon's temple in Jerusalem around 1100 CE, returning with its engineering secrets and placing the treasure under the stones of Chartres Cathedral. To some who believe in a lost language of Solomon and Jesus, Chartres Cathedral is the "Rosetta Stone" for decoding the language. With the help of the brilliant French abbot Bernard de Clairvaux, the nine knights, directed by the Count of Champagne, formed the Knights Templar and assisted in the building of Chartres Cathedral upon their return from the Holy Land.

Catholic tradition relates the story of Holy Roman emperor Charles the Bald giving the Sancta Camisia, or Holy Veil of the Virgin Mary, to the old church on the same site. The old church was replaced by Chartres Cathedral, but the Holy Veil remained and is still on display today. The veil is believed to be the same veil Mary wore when she gave birth to Jesus. The attraction of the veil made Chartres one of the major pilgrimage sites in Europe during medieval times. The veil is in a chapel near the choir.

234

### Getting to Chartres Cathedral

The city of Chartres is about 60 miles (97 km) southwest of Paris, and 20 miles (35 km) from the famous Palace of Versailles. Apart from the Cathedral, Chartres is a small and somewhat undistinguished town. Most travelers who come to Chartres arrive from Paris, which is about an hour away by train or bus. The cathedral dominates the oldest center of town and is easy to find.

## Lourdes

Lourdes was hardly more than a hamlet until 1858, the year a 14-year-old peasant girl named Bernadette Soubirous had the first of 18 visions of the Virgin Mary at a location called Grotte de Massabielle, by the Gave de Pau. Over a period of several months the young girl and many townspeople gathered at the riverside grotto and viewed an apparition of Mary, or the "Immaculate Conception" as she described herself. After the girl's visions were recognized by the Catholic Church, Lourdes experienced a building boom and is now one of the most visited sites in southern France. Bernadette was beatified in 1925 and canonized a Saint in 1933.

**Lourdes attracts more than 5 million Christian pilgrims every year, making it the most visited pilgrimage destination in Europe.**

Most of the visitors who come to Lourdes are hoping for a miraculous cure for their pain and suffering. Some 70,000 visitors are handicapped or have serious physical ailments and are given preferential treatment at the site. Lourdes has been called a "city of miracles" or "capital of prayer," which does correspond with a tangible reality. Well over 5,000 cases of spontaneous healing have been reported, and of those, 65 have been declared miraculous by ecclesiastic authorities following long and precise procedures. Such recognized miracles by the Catholic Church have undoubtedly necessitated the steady increase of pilgrims.

Along the river is the *Cité Réligieuse*, the object of desire for the throngs of faithful flocking to Lourdes. Tucked alongside the river is the moisture-blackened grotto, which predictably houses a statue of the Virgin Mary. Suspended in front of the grotto are rows of rusting crutches offered

▲ Lourdes, France is considered a city where healing miracles occur.

up by the hopeful. Rising above the grotto is the first church built on the site in 1871. Below the church is a massive subterranean basilica, which can house some 20,000 people at once. On site is a natural spring that formed during one of the apparitions. The water clustered from the spring is used for blessings and healing. Because of its famous reputation, many modern Christian pilgrim routes in Europe now lead to Lourdes.

### Getting to Lourdes

Lourdes is just north of the Spanish border and about 75 miles (120 km) southwest of Toulouse. Lourdes is about 20 miles (30 km) southeast of the city Pau, but has its own train station for the multitude of visitors. The train station is on the northeastern edge of town and the grotto is easily located by following the crowds past the many kitsch religious shops. Pau is one of the best places for setting off into the highest parts of the Pyrenees Mountains. There are three trains daily from the Gare d'Austerlitz station in Paris, as well as trains from larger cities around France and buses from regional towns.

# Mont Saint Michel and the Saint Michael's Line

The most famous site on the Normandy coast, just where it joins the peninsula of Brittany, is the island monastery of Mont Saint Michel, an extraordinary Gothic abbey complex that crowns the pinnacle of a steep rock. According to Celtic mythology the sea-surrounded outcropping was one of the sea tombs where recently deceased souls were conveyed to the afterlife. The first chapel on the mass of granite was built in 709 CE for Saint Michel and quickly became the goal for Christian pilgrims, as it remains today. The Gothic abbey was started in 1020, the cathedral was established early enough to host Harold the Saxon and William the Conqueror in 1058, yet it took until 1230 to complete the entire religious complex. Mont Saint Michel is also known as *La Merveille*, meaning the "The Marvel," because of its awe-inspiring qualities and geographical positioning. The unusual tide surrounding the island withdraws as far as 10 miles (16 km), leaving Mont Saint Michel rising majestically on a smooth and sandy plain. At any given time the fog comes back to fill the bay and the sea eventually returns, racing toward the shore at an astonishing 210 feet (63 m) per minute! With that in mind, it would be wise to know the direction of the tide before embarking on a walk across the vast plain to the island. People unaware of the high tide fluctuations have drowned near Mont Saint Michel.

Anyone who sees The Marvel knows Mont Saint Michel is an extraordinary work of human ingenuity. The abbey's granite was sculpted to match the exact contours of the rocky pinnacle, and even though space has always been a factor, the complex has grown in an inventive geometric fashion. Benedictine monks prayed, studied and worked on the monastery for many centuries. Guy de Maupassant called it "the most wonderful Gothic dwelling ever made for God on this earth." Indeed, Mont Saint Michel looks like a castle out of a fairy-tale book and is one of Christendom's premier pilgrimage sites.

**Mont Saint Michel has been described as a compact Gothic version of Heaven where land meets the sea. It is positioned on an important energy location along the Saint Michael's Line.**

Modern dowsers describe ley lines as precise locations of potent earth energy, analogous to veins on a leaf or any living entity, including Gaia the living planet. The scientific Gaia hypothesis proposes that the whole earth behaves like one self-regulating organism wherein all of the geologic, hydrologic, and biologic cycles of the planet mutually self-regulate the conditions on the surface of the earth so as to perpetuate life. Along the ley paths, especially at intersection points, humans detected the energy and erected primitive shrines that later became great cathedrals. Great Britain has two central ley lines named after Saint Michael and Saint Mary, which dissect the country and connect major sacred sites. Another noted ley line in Europe is also named after the archangel Saint Michael, the heavenly defender and guardian against Satan. Arching across Europe is the Saint Michael's Line starting at Skellig Michael in Ireland, crossing Michael's Mont in Cornwall to Mont Saint Michel in France, then across the European mainland to the Monte Sant'Angelo grotto in Italy, through the ancient Greek sanctuaries of Delphi and Delos until it reaches the Holy Land. All across the route are shrines, temples and statues dedicated to the highly venerated Saint Michael the Archangel.

### Getting to Mont Saint Michel

The nearest train station to Mont Saint Michel is 4 miles (6 km) south at Pontorson —a lackluster town for tourists. There is an expensive connection bus to the Mont when the train arrives, or bicycles can be rented at the station for an interesting ride to the sea. An alternative train stop is Avranches, where hotel prices are more reasonable. Paris is about 180 miles (290 km) to the west. Travel time is halved on a new high-speed train from Paris to Rennes, then a one-day sightseeing tour of Mont Saint Michel, including a stop in Saint Malo and Dinard.

# GREECE

Just the name of this ancient country conjures up images of powerful gods, spectacular architecture, religious movements and the beginnings of civilization. The historic sites of Greece span four centuries of Western development. Greek gods and goddesses merged into similar religious depictions in the Roman era. Greek and Roman monuments are both well represented throughout Greece. Scattered across the country are numerous pagan temples and shrines. Of the 166 inhabited islands in the Aegean Sea, the island of Delos was considered the most sacred in times of antiquity, being the birthplace of Apollo and home to his famous sanctuary. The first Christians developed the new faith while residing in Greece. The saints of early Christianity proselytized from the secluded Aegean islands to the mainland cross-

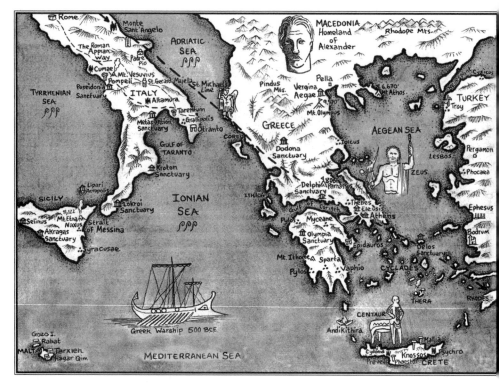

roads of Europe. The predominant national religion remains Greek Orthodox, represented by thousands of monasteries nationwide, including more than 400 on the island of Kyos alone.

The oldest Greek literary creations come from the eminent poet Homer—scribe of *The Iliad* and *The Odyssey*—both stories passed down orally for generations. *The Iliad* narrates the circumstances and events of the Trojan War, which in the end, precipitated the destruction of a civilization. After the Greeks sacked Troy by hiding in a wooden horse, *The Odyssey* continues the tale of the hero Ulysses' long return to his home island of Ithaca. Homer's epic poems, describing the devastating feud between ancient Greeks and Persians, remains a potent warning to all humankind that war is both tragic and futile.

## Acropolis of Athens

The Acropolis is perched upon a limestone hill towering above the city of Athens. The ruins of the Acropolis consist of the Erechtheum, the Propylaea, the Temple of Athena Nike and the magnificent Parthenon. The name Parthenon means "virgin's chamber," and was dedicated to the virgin Athena, goddess of wisdom, and patroness of Athens. The Parthenon was erected between 447 and 432 BCE by order of Pericles, and is considered one of the most perfectly proportioned buildings of all time. So precise was the architect Ictinus who designed the Parthenon that a discernible indent was incorporated into the straight lines of its long sides to lend the effect of appearing even straighter from a distance.

The ruins of the Acropolis are considered the most outstanding relics of the Classical era Greeks. They are the primary focus of Athens and remain the principal tourist attraction in the

▲ No ancient building in Greece matches the grandeur of the Parthenon.

country. The centerpiece of the Acropolis is the Parthenon, a temple dedicated to Athena after whom the city was named. According to legend when the ancient Greeks were planning to name their city, they called upon their two most potent gods, Athena and Poseidon, to hold a contest challenging each to procure the finest gift. Poseidon, god of the sea, struck open a wall on the Acropolis with his trident and water poured out, bestowing a well. Athena acted quickly and formed an olive tree to grow from the well. The olive tree was considered a symbol of peace, and so taken with this gift the Greeks declared Athena the winner and named their city after her. The visible marks on the Acropolis wall are Poseidon's trident, and below them grow Athena's many olive trees.

Long before the ruined buildings on the hill were constructed, the site was considered a sacred place. Around 3500 BCE Neolithic people settled upon the hill and built small shrines. By 1400 BCE it had become the residence for all subsequent kings of Athens. In the sixth century BCE, the first temple honoring Athena was constructed here, and henceforth the "Citadel of the Gods" was considered a goddess shrine for many centuries. Pagan worship was banned in 429 CE by the Christian Roman Emperor Theodosius, but it was not long before Byzantine era priests began to utilize the temples of the Acropolis for Christian worship. The last foreign occupiers, the Turks, established a garrison on the hill and converted the Parthenon into a mosque, replete with a call-to-prayer tower, which has since been removed.

**Downtown Athens is dominated by the lofty heights of the Acropolis. This sacred city appears to be floating on clouds above the modern city, especially during heavy smog days.**

Some of the greatest damage to the 2,500-year-old Acropolis complex took place only in the last 350 years. In 1677, hostilities between the Ottoman Empire and Venice spiked when the Venetians lay siege upon Athens and scored a direct artillery hit on the Parthenon which, at the time, contained a Turkish ammunition dump. The explosion sent the roof and many of Phidias's pediment sculptures flying over Athens. The goddess Athena undoubtedly wept on that infamous day when her Parthenon was largely destroyed by the folly of war. In the 1820s the Greeks had been waging a violent War of Independence from the Turks, who again used several buildings of the Acropolis to store gunpowder and ammunition. Another explosion reduced the grand Erechtheum to a mere shell of its former self. Today, the greatest threat to the Acropolis complex is modern fossil-fuel emissions. Like the Taj Mahal in India, the corrosive effects of air pollution threaten to undermine these magnificent world treasures.

### Getting to the Acropolis

The Acropolis hill, or the "Sacred Rock" of Athens, is the most important site in Greece's capital located in the oldest section of the city. The site is a bustling tourist destination all year round, and is visible for many miles in all directions. A General Admission ticket is valid for all the archaeological sites of Athens: the Acropolis site and museum, Ancient Agora, Theatre of Dionysos Kerameikos, Olympieion, and the Roman Agora.

# Delphi

In the fourth century BCE, Greek pilgrims rode wooden carts to Delphi seeking the oracle and a higher meaning of life. The Delphi religious complex contained more than 235 buildings and monuments, set beautifully overlooking the sea at the base of Mount Parnassus. Individual temples at Delphi were ascribed to different Greek gods, including the Tholos dedicated to Athena. The most significant building was the Temple of Apollo bearing the famous inscription "Know Thyself." The Apollo temple dominates the Sacred Precincts area of the city, which was considered the center of the earth. Greek mythology relates how the god Zeus released two eagles from the eastern and western edges of the world and waited for the result. The two birds flew at exactly the same speed and met over Delphi. The spot is marked in the temple *omphalos*, meaning "navel." Along with its abundance of temples, Delphi was renowned for the oracle, presided over by a priestess of the Delphic mystery school. The oracle was legendary for its accuracy of prediction.

**Delphi was the most famous pilgrimage destination in classical Greece. Ancient pilgrims sought a chasm of vapors where a priestess would recite divine direction.**

Candidates seeking the enigmatic oracle, including foreign rulers, powerful generals, and everyday commoners would make the pilgrimage to Delphi from all parts of the classical world. They sought the Temple of Apollo, dramatically set beneath towering cliffs on the slopes of Mount Parnassus, and the oracle's advice on important matters such as war, worship, business, love and vengeance. Following a ritualistic cleansing in a nearby spring, pilgrims would sacrifice a goat in Apollo's name before entering the temple. Inside, they were directed into a subterranean vault where a local priestess (usually a young virgin) called the Pythia sat suspended over a gas fissure in the rock. The foul smell of the gases, combined with the dim lighting and the multitude of high priests present in the chamber must have been quite an amazing spectacle. Pilgrims would pose their question to the priestess, who would enter into a trance and communicate with Apollo. Her answer, it would seem, came directly from the god Apollo himself through the fissures in the rock — from the very bowels of the earth. The priestess would utter a response and the assembled priests would translate her answer into pithy rhymes for the awaiting pilgrim. Those who purportedly consulted the Delphic oracle range from Oedipus and Agamemnon to Croesus and Philip of Macedon, as well as Philip's famous son Alexander the Great, who was told, "My son, none can resist thee."

As classical Greece culture flourished in the Mediterranean region Delphi became the premier pilgrimage destination for much of the ancient world. Festivals accompanied by athletic competitions took place regularly at the complex. Although Apollo was the primary deity worshiped at Delphi, many came to praise the goddess Venus.

A festival was held at the temple complex every eight years to mark the completion of a "rose mandala" pattern made by the planet Venus. With each completed conjunction (a coming together with the sun), the planet Venus traces a five-pointed star within a circle pattern. The powerful connection ancient Greeks held with the cosmos climaxed in the eighth year at Delphi when Venus completed her cycle. The goddess of love presided over lavish celebrations enjoyed by all.

▲ The Sphinx of the Naxians from Delphi has a distinctive Egyptian appearance.

Worship at the various Delphi temples lasted for a thousand years before yielding to Christianity in the fourth century CE. In the following millennia the old pagan sanctuary fell into decay. French archaeologists began to uncover Delphi in the late 19th century. They found the Sacred Precincts forming a square in the heart of Delphi, a place where the ancient Greeks believed gods and mortals could co-mingle. The Temple of Apollo dominates the Sacred Precincts, while the original theater, the stadium and several various altars complete the square. Near the site is the Museum of Delphi containing more than 7,000 objects, including the bronze Charioteer, carved pieces from the Athenian Treasury and the mysterious Sphinx of the Naxians.

### Getting to Delphi

Delphi is conveniently located only 90 miles (150 km) northwest of Athens, situated on the north shore of the Gulf of Corinth. The site is located on the lower slopes of 8,061-foot (2,420-m) Mount Parnassus. Athens is a major transportation hub with one of the busiest international airports in Europe. Buses and taxis ply the route every day from Athens, which is along the well-traveled road from Thebes (Thirai) to Amtissa. Local buses run regularly from the nearby train station Livadhia to the Delphi archaeological complex.

## Knossos

At a time on mainland Greece when the warlike Mycenaeans were fighting themselves into oblivion, another culture was blossoming on the island of Crete. They were the peaceful Minoans, who, along with the Mycenaeans, represent the last of the glorious Aegean Bronze Age civilizations. Many similarities exist between the two classical Greek predecessors, whose histories hark back to accounts given by Homer. The Minoans, named after their legendary King Minos, prospered on Crete between 2000 and 1400 BCE, and built thriving communities across the island. The foremost European city of its day was Knossos, of which Homer praised: "One of the 90 towns on Crete is a great city called Knossos, and there, for nine years, King Minos ruled and enjoyed the friendship of almighty Zeus."

**Nature and god were one and the same to ancient Minoans, where everything contained aspects of the divine spirit. Knossos was not a religious building — instead, small chapels were located within natural environments, especially caves.**

The Minoans were a creative people and a maritime force on the high seas. They ruled the seaways from Asia Minor and Africa to Italy, and started the first major civilization in Europe. The legacy of the Minoans was their assimilation of great technological advancements made earlier in the East, particularly Egypt. They invented a written language of picture writing much like Egyptian hieroglyphs. Their two linear scripts called Linear A and B were found on clay tablets at Knossos. Linear A, presumably the Minoans' own language, remains undeciphered, while Linear B was deciphered in 1952 and found to be an extremely archaic form of Greek. The Minoans at Knossos are credited with creating the oldest European alphabet discovered to date.

▲ Knossos was an open air palace on the sun drenched island of Crete. It was positioned with views out to sea and located uphill from a natural harbor. An extensive network of roads linked Knossos to outlaying cities.

While similarities exist with Egypt, the Minoan civilization was essentially Mediterranean, and is sharply distinguished from any other culture of the Near East. Before its quick decline the Minoan civilization largely shaped the development of archaic Greece.

The real glory of the Minoan people is found in the charred ruins of Knossos. Unlike the Mycenaean chieftains who lived in heavily fortified citadels, Minoan kings built the Palace of Knossos unfortified, brightly colored and open to the air. Devoid of the symmetry dear to the later Greeks, Knossos was a maze of apartments, corridors, colonnades, staircases and light wells interconnecting over six acres and rising at least three stories tall. From its labyrinthine complexity came the myth of the Minotaur, a lurking half-man, half-bull monster slain by the legendary Theseus.

As puzzling as the Minoan civilization began, mystery also shrouds its demise. Sometime around 1400 BCE most of its buildings were burned, destroyed, and abandoned for good. Possible explanations include a devastating earthquake, a seaborn invasion, or inundation by a tidal wave after a colossal volcano erupted on nearby Thera, also inhabited by Minoans. Archaeologist K. T. Frost sums up the mysterious demise of the Minoans well: "As a political and commercial force, therefore, Knossos and its allied cities were swept away just when they seemed strongest and safest. It was as if the whole kingdom had sunk in the sea, as if the tale of Atlantis were true."

## Getting to Knossos

The ruins of Knossos are easily located, only three miles (5 km) uphill from the busy Cretan port city Iráklion. Buses and taxis ply the route to the site daily, and it is also a pleasant walk. The partially rebuilt Palace of Knossos is well worth a full day of exploring and wonder. What's left of Minoan culture on Crete can be found in an excellent museum in Iráklion, Crete's largest city.

# IRELAND

For a country about the size of Maine, Ireland is a destination rich in history. Scattered across the emerald green countryside are huge monolithic stone circles, lone towers, Middle Age monasteries, and romantic castles. Devout Catholics climb the summit of Croach Patrick, Ireland's holiest mountain, where pilgrims gather at dawn on the last day of July marking Saint Patrick's fast of 441 CE. Tourists flock to the Blarney Stone at Blarney Castle, known for the eloquence it is said to impart on all those who kiss it. More subtly, the sacred hermitage of Skellig Michael was a monastery of early Christian monks with strong Celtic ties. The legendary hill of Tara is another important site, where in ancient times people came from all over Ireland to join celebrations, coronations, or simply for devotion.

## Newgrange

In the verdant green Boyne Valley are three huge earth mounds, the most impressive is called Newgrange. The two other nearby mounds are named Knowth and Dowth, and all three are said by dowsers to intersect at key "telluric energy" points, as well as being situated in perfect alignment with seasonal points of solar movements. Newgrange and the other megaliths in the valley were created some 5,000 years ago by a puzzling group of kinsmen known as the Beaker People, who built in the Boyne Valley and nowhere else in Ireland. To add further mystery, the Beaker People also constructed monuments on the Mediterranean islands of Malta and Gozo. No direct traces of these people have been found anywhere else in the world.

▲ The entrance to Newgrange is surrounded by giant boulders containing the spiral motif. Nearly identical designs are also located on the Mediterranean islands of Malta and Gozo.

244

Conventional archaeologists regard the mounds in Boyne Valley as part of a prehistoric cemetery, largely because charred human remains were found deep inside their chambered passageways. The Boyne Valley passage graves are fine examples of megalithic culture construction, but Newgrange is more than just a burial tomb. On the days around December 21st each winter solstice, the entrance passage is in exact alignment with the rising sun, illuminating a triple spiral relief sculpture in the farthest recess of the chamber. The construction of Newgrange was once surrounded by 38 enormous pillars, but only 12 survive. The site was built to mark the turning point in the sun's cycle.

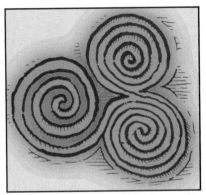

▲ The spiral pattern at the end of the Newgrange passage.

**The inner sanctuary of Newgrange is illuminated by rays of the sun only during the few days before and after the winter solstice, making it the largest and oldest sundial in the world.**

Surrounding the exterior of the Newgrange mound are images of spirals, chevrons and other symbolic forms carved on the huge stones. There are a total of 97 curbstones lying on their sides around the mound, and the carved patterns also appear inside the passage. The carvings are believed to be recordings of astronomical and cosmological observations. The internal "beehive" chamber has a funnel-shaped roof and is externally connected by a long passageway. Whatever rituals or activities the Beaker People may have performed in this internal chamber remain a mystery. The mound covering the internal passage is more than 40 feet (12 m) in height and covers an acre (.4 hectare) of ground. The egg-shaped mound is called a tumulus, rising above the flat meadow and surrounded by a stone curbing. Over 20,000 cantaloupe-size stones were brought in from 75 miles (120 km) away to create the bulk of the tumulus. The entrance to Newgrange is marked by the elaborately carved Threshold Stone featuring carved spirals framed by concentric circles and diamond shapes.

### Getting to Newgrange

Newgrange is located in the Boyne Valley, seven miles (11 km) south of the picturesque Irish seaport town Drogheda, which has a train station and local bus service directly to Newgrange. The site is well marked along the main N1 Belfast road if driving by car. The Knowth and Dowth mounds are both found on the nearby road to Slane. All can be visited quite easily on a day trip from Dublin, which is 28 miles (45 km) due south.

# ITALY

T he boot shaped peninsula jutting into the Mediterranean Sea was geographically ideal for cultural dissemination. Starting with the artistically gifted Etruscans co-existing with Greek colonists, to mighty Rome and then the seat of the Holy Roman Empire, much of Western culture passed through Italy. In Roman times the statesman Julius Caesar praised his countrymen for "imitating whatever was worthwhile in the culture of other nations." From the early inhabitants of Italy, particularly the indigenous Etruscans, the Romans inherited a taste for honest portraiture, superb metalwork and lavish jewelry. The Romans admired and copied Greek settlers south of Rome who imported their heritage of architecture, marble sculpture and mural paintings. Benefiting from the rich culture that Rome absorbed from its empire, Roman art and architecture took on an integrated look that became uniquely Roman. Italy today has a common language, Italian, developed directly from the Latin of Imperial Rome. The religion is Roman Catholic.

## Pompeii

Nearly 2,000 years ago Mount Vesuvius violently erupted over a period of two days and buried everything in its cloud path. Several Roman towns to the south of the volcano — Herculaneum, Boscoreale, Oplontis, Stabiae, and Pompeii — were completely covered in volcanic debris. The volcanic cataclysm occurred so suddenly that the activities of thousands of people were abruptly interrupted. Many escaped by boat into the Bay of Naples, but others stayed in the city and were buried alive. Pompeii is a snapshot of a Roman city whose daily life in August, 79 CE came to an instant standstill. Illustrating the suddenness of the deathly catastrophe, modern archaeologists created plaster casts of Pompeii citizens as they fell gasping for air attempting to survive.

**The well-preserved city of Pompeii gives the visitor a vicarious feel of what it must have felt like to walk down an urban Roman street and visit its many sacred sites.**

According to Roman city design Pompeii centers itself around a large rectangular open-air plaza called the Forum. This square denotes the center of the city, in most cases founded at the confluence of important old communication routes. The Forum in every Roman city played a fundamental role in politics, economics and religion. Situated prominently around the Pompeii Forum are most of the important religious buildings in the city, including the Temples of Apollo and Jupiter. Near the Forum are the opulent baths, the House of the Vetii and the Villa of Mystery where pagan cults met and mysterious rituals took place. The unusual Temple of Isis is located in a sacred area bounded by a high wall near the large theater and the rectangular Forum. Inside the Doric-pillared temple are the statues of Harpocrates and Anubis, divinities connected with the cult of Isis. The walls are frescoed with five panels of sacred subjects in Egyptian style with dual representations of Io in Egypt and Io in Argos. The

246

large hall in the temple is where the cult of Isis met and initiations were performed.

The Mount Vesuvius eruption that destroyed Pompeii also buried Herculaneum — two cities persevered in their near entirety. Great care has been taken in the excavation of the two cities and the outlaying villas. Herculaneum was a residential suburb of Naples, rather than a resort, and because it was buried in mud lava it remained in a better state of preservation than Pompeii. About 5,000 people lived in Herculaneum at the time of the eruption. In total for all locations, about 3,360 people died in the eruption from poisonous gasses, ash flows, and falling rocks. 90% of the population impacted by the

Pompeii Goddess

explosion survived by leaving in time. Those left behind were prisoners, slaves, children or adults who refused to vacate.

All trips to Pompeii should include a visit to the famous museum, where exhibits include plaster casts of people and animals found during the excavation of the ruins. Archaeologists created the casts by pouring liquid plaster into hollow cavities containing bones. When the plaster dried a near-perfect rendition of the deceased person or animal emerged and could be excavated. Also on display in the museum are stoves, altars, cooking utensils, tools, coins, fossilized bread loafs and many accessories from everyday life in a Roman city.

### Getting to Pompeii

Pompeii is about 10 miles (16 km) southeast of the city Naples. Public buses and trains access Pompeii with Naples and most southern Italian cities. Pompeii is now a direct train stop and, like so many other famous archaeological sites, a modern tourist town has developed around the ruins. Herculaneum, once a seaside resort, is now surrounded by the modern city of Ercolano. If possible, visit Pompeii on a night when is the site illuminated.

# ROME

Rome did not become Italy's capital city until 1871, yet remained an influential political metropolis for many millennia. Some of the most important ancient treasures in Italy are within the city of Rome. The ruins of Rome are of extraordinary archaeological, cultural and artistic value — the Coliseum, the Roman Forum, and the Imperial Forum just to name a few, give a glimpse of its former splendor and glory. Thousands of years of continuous occupation allow Rome to live up to its nickname "Eternal City."

# Saint Peter's Basilica

The autonomous state of Vatican City (Holy See) has been the focus of Catholic pilgrims for many centuries. Crossing the Tiber River on the Ponte Sant'Angelo bridge, the visitor is welcomed to the world's smallest nation (106 acres/43 hectares) by beautifully rendered marble angels. Soon the visitor enters the Piazza San Pietro fronting Saint Peter's Basilica, which was created by renaissance sculptor Bernini and is one of the most renowned squares in the world. Twin colonnades featuring statues of various saints and martyrs flank either side of the square, with an 85-foot (26-m) obelisk rising from the center. It is the Piazza San Pietro where the masses gather to receive the pope's blessing every Wednesday.

**The Vatican City is its own autonomous political entity within Rome. At its center, the towering Saint Peter's Basilica is the heart of Christianity to the Catholic faith.**

Standing before Saint Peter's Basilica, the largest and most awe-inspiring church in Christendom, it is easy to grasp the enormous spiritual history of this site. Here is the church that kept alive the flame of Western civilization long after the demise of the Roman Empire in Italy. In the greatest pagan city, Christians believe Jesus sent the apostle Peter to Rome, the "rock" upon which his church would be built. When Europe descended into the Dark Ages, it was the ecclesiastical scribes who patiently copied manuscripts to preserve Western culture. During the Italian renaissance, when Saint Peter's was constructed on the exact spot where a fourth century church built by Constantine stood, a rare configuration of brilliant minds gathered to add their gifted influence. The fathers of the church, the visionary Saint Ignatius Loyola, Saint Francis Xaviar, and the eminent poet of mysticism Saint John of the Cross, are all represented as marble statues inside the church. These statues, and the church itself, were designed by leading artists of the age. Bernini, Raphael, Michelangelo, Borromini and Bramante were indeed renaissance and baroque masters who dedicated much of their lives to Christian art and architecture, including Saint Peter's magnificent church.

Many people believe Saint Peter's Basilica contains the most beautiful collection of artwork ever assembled in one place. Inside and out, thousands of magnificent pieces of art and sculpture decorate the walls, floors, and halls of the church. Most famous are Michelangelo's Pietà, the highly adored statue of Saint Peter, and the spectacular papal altar. The Pietà, just within the entrance of the basilica to the right, is an exquisitely rendered sculpture of Mary grieving over the body of Jesus after the crucifixion. In the central nave is the statue of the seated apostle Peter whose one foot is worn thin from the faithful kissing and touching it over the centuries. Front and center in the basilica is the high altar where the pope celebrates Mass.

The most outstanding aspect of Saint Peter's Basilica is the dome. Designed by Michelangelo and finished 24 years after his death by Fontana and Della Porta, it holds reign over the enormous interior of the church, which at capacity can accommodate 100,000 standing people. Four massive pentagonal pillars support the dome. Each gilded pier is a reliquary, containing very sacred Christian objects. The colossal space created by the dome allows spectacular shafts of light to flood into the basilica. Vatican City's other attractions include galleries, museums, the papal library and the amazing Sistine Chapel adorned with famous Michelangelo frescos.

### Getting to Saint Peter's Basilica

Saint Peter's Basilica comprises a sizable amount of the tiny autonomous state of Vatican City. After several days of sightseeing in Rome, be sure to save at least a full day for the Vatican City. Like most of the attractions in the old section of Rome, *Citta Del Vaticano* is easily reached by bus or by walking. From the center of Rome, where the first century CE Coliseum is located, head east and cross the Tiber River. The dome of Saint Peter's dominates the eastern skyline and is easily located. Most visitors arrive at Saint Peter's in the morning for the elevator tour to the top of the dome and the commanding views of Rome.

# MALTA

Malta loans its name to the entire Maltese archipelago, a string of islands that consist of Malta, Gozo, Comino and two uninhabited rock outcroppings. Centrally located in the Mediterranean Sea, about 50 miles (80 km) south of Sicily, the Maltese Islands hardly seem far from civilization. Yet 5,000 years ago this must have been a rather isolated location. Scattered across Malta and Gozo are numerous megalithic temples dating from 3600 to 2200 BCE. The earliest arrivals were the puzzling tribe of skilled masons known as the "Beaker People." How these early people learned to move massive slabs of stone and build enormous circular temples remains unknown. There is evidence of a cataclysm (perhaps linked to Atlantis) from the layers of sediment found during excavation, which could only have been deposited by a great flood. To add further mystery, the only other place where buildings of this design were constructed is Ireland's Boyne Valley. The mound temples of Newgrange, Knowth and Dowth in Ireland are remarkably similar to those found on Malta and Gozo.

▲ Ancient spiral motif of Malta.

## Tarxien

One of the earliest flourishing cultures of Europe took place on the Maltese archipelago. The most impressive communal activity of the megalithic builders was the construction of large and elaborate stone temples. Among the most important temples are Mnajdra, Hagar Qim, Mgarr and Skorba on Malta, and Ggantija on Gozo. The Tarxien megalithic temple complex on Malta is perhaps the oldest and best preserved of all. The interior chambers of most Maltese prehistoric temples are decorated with numerous spiral carvings and contain elaborate altars for animal sacrifice. An unknown, yet highly organized religion was clearly at hand, whose practice included worship of fat-bodied asexual statues and naturalistically rendered female goddesses. Like other ancient religions, one or a few high priests likely controlled the population. The priest held the key to health and prosperity on the island, and thus wielded great power. A tremendously organized work force must have come from a blend of individual vision and communal effort to create the various temple complexes on Malta.

The Tarxien sanctuary was completely buried under field soil until 1914, when a farmer mentioned to the curator of the museum that his plow continued to hit rock at a certain depth. While nothing on the surface pointed to its existence, the site was excavated completely in six years. What emerged was an age-old temple that may well in fact be the oldest stone ruin in the world. The Tarxien monument is composed of three interconnecting main temples, and the remains of an older temple. The older temple represents the first purpose-made religious structure in Europe, and the whole complex is one of the largest ancient monument sites in Europe.

## The high altar of the south temple at Tarxien is decorated with a motif of spiral designs. These designs may represent the eyes of the Earth Mother goddess or the cosmos.

▲ The prehistoric temples of Malta are some of the oldest ever discovered. The megalithic architecture and elaborate religious practices only enhance the mystery.

At Tarxien, ancient Maltese inhabitants worshiped an overabundant female deity—called the Earth Mother, or Great Goddess. She is represented in many statues across the islands, with similar characteristics such as wide hips, bulbous legs and a single folded arm. One statue depicts her as a giant, standing 8 feet (2.4 m) tall, that is, judging from what's left —only the lower part of a pleated skirt and two massive legs remain. This mysterious cult of the Earth Mother may be a result of the Maltese people's fear of starvation, a depiction of an earthly Venus, a fertility symbol, or simply a profound respect for powerful women. Whoever she was, the Earth Mother was highly venerated for about 800 years before the Maltese temples were abandoned and their users vanished. Drought, plague, famine, relocation and invasion are among suggestions as to the cause of their disappearance. Others say it was the planetary cataclysm associated with the sinking of Atlantis that destroyed the culture. Nevertheless, successive settlers used the ruins of Tarxien as a cemetery for cremated remains, and the Romans used part of the temple as a wine cellar. Shortly after the Roman era it was covered with topsoil and forgotten.

### Getting to Tarxien

The island of Malta is rather small, only 16 miles (25 km) across at its widest point. The nearby island of Gozo is even smaller, and is accessible by a regular ferry. The dozen or so ruins on Malta and Gozo are easy to locate and accessible by road. Most of the ruins, including Tarxien, are scattered around the suburbs of the capital Valletta. From Valletta city center, take a local bus or taxi to Tarxien. There are regular flights to Valletta from Italy and most European cities. The most popular Maltese route for backpackers is the ferry from Sicily and Tunisia.

# PORTUGAL

Portugal has always been a country turned toward the sea. Since early times, fishing and overseas commerce were the main economic activities. Prominent explorers such as Henry the Navigator, Bartolomeu Dias and Vasco da Gama left the shores of Portugal to establish global trade routes. Following its heyday as a world power during the 15th and 16th centuries Portugal lost much of its wealth and status with the destruction of Lisbon in the earthquake of 1755, occupation during the Napoleonic Wars, and the loss of its Brazilian colony in 1822.

## Fátima

As World War I was devastating Europe, three illiterate children in a poor village started experiencing multiple visions of the Virgin Mary in an isolated ravine called Cova da Iria. As the news spread quickly from Portuguese village to village, soon thousands of townspeople also experienced aspects of the apparition and the legend of Fátima began. Despite only three children as direct witnesses, thousands of others experienced a variety of miracles and strange sightings. Perhaps the most astonishing was when 70,000 people filled the valley for the sixth apparition during a heavy downpour and became miraculously dry as the sun suddenly burst through the clouds concluding the sightings. After this event the three youngsters became world-renowned and the atmosphere of their peasant village would never be the same.

The story begins early in 1916 when nine-year old Lúcia Santos was sent by her parents to tend the family's sheep in the hills near the village of Fátima. Her cousins Francisco Marto, aged eight, and his six-year old sister, Jacinta, also accompanied her. The children were walking along a hillside when they saw a vision of a human figure. Writing many years later of the event, Lúcia remembers, "It was a figure like a statue … a young man, about fourteen or fifteen, whiter than snow." The figure spoke to the children, directing them to pray three times with him, "My God, I believe, I adore." Yet the children kept their first encounter a secret. The next year, in 1917, the Marian series of apparitions appeared to the children near the same place. The children first saw two flashes of lightening and then a "Lady, brighter than the sun, shedding rays of light" who said she was from heaven. Lúcia—the only one of the three children who ever spoke to the visions directly—asked, "What do you want of me?" The Lady answered, "I want you to come here for six months in succession. Then I will tell you who I am and what I want." The Lady also directed the children to pray every day for peace before she departed in a blinding light. The children, unsure of what had happened to them again, promised to keep quiet as they had before, but later Jacinta let the subject slip to her parents. Soon the entire village knew of the supposed apparitions and started making fun of the children. Yet the children knew the apparitions were to continue through October, always on the 13th day of each month. The second vision came to the children again on the prophesied date in front of 60 onlookers. After the second sighting the apparitions were reported widely.

> **Fátima is among the most visited shrines in the world devoted to the Virgin Mary. The site draws some five million visitors a year, putting it on par with Lourdes in southern France.**

The information Mary conveyed to Lúcia during the apparitions remains a mystery. The three secrets of Fátima came during the July appearance when the lady prefigured the coming of World War II, another identified Russia's "rejection of God," and the final secret became a "sealed message" recorded by Lúcia, for the pope's eyes only. Church officials opened the third secret in 1960, but only the pope knows the letter in its entirety. Part of the third message describes the 1981 assassination attempt on the pope. Also prophesied by Mary, both Francisco and Jacinta died soon after the apparitions ended during the worldwide influenza epidemic of 1918–1920. One of the final requests of the Virgin Mary was to have a place of worship devoted to her in the valley. A small chapel built at Cova da Iris to commemorate the apparitions was destroyed by skeptics in 1922, only to be replaced by a massive square and towering church. Uncomfortable with all the attention, Lúcia left Fátima to become a nun in 1926, and in 1948 joined a Carmelite monastery in Spain where she still lives. She has only returned to the shrine a few times since it was built. In 1930, after thoroughly investigating the events of 1917, the Vatican authenticated the apparitions.

### Getting to Fátima

Located in west central Portugal, in the region of Leiria and approximately 87 miles (140 km) north-northeast of Lisbon, Fátima is a small rural village in a rocky region whose main export product is olive oil. A train runs daily from Lisbon to Chão de Maças, 12.5 miles (20 km) outside Fátima. From there a 30-minute bus ride takes passengers from Chão de Maças into Fátima.

# SPAIN

R ichly endowed by both nature and history, Spain is a sun-baked land of castles, dramatic coastlines, snow-capped mountains, lively festivals and proud traditions. The Pyrenees form its mountainous backbone with France, and Portugal is the only other country Spain borders on the Iberian Peninsula. From prehistoric cave dwellers, numerous empires and invaders, to eight centuries of Moorish (Muslim) occupation, Spain has been influenced, and has influenced much of Western civilization's development. Spain was a first-rate power in developing the New World and Spanish remains one of the top spoken languages worldwide.

## Prehistoric Caves

The first modern humans in Europe, the hunter and gatherers of the Upper Paleolithic period (35,000-30,000 BCE) produced the continent's earliest recorded art. This art, mostly found on cave walls in northern Spain and southwest France, is believed to have played an important role in religious rituals involving hunting, fertility and the initiation of young tribal members. The cave art of this period is often located in extremely inaccessible parts of the cave, where few could have viewed them and lighting and scaffolding would have been required in its creation.

**Paleolithic cave art of northern Spain is an evocative monument to early humanity and represents the earliest explorations of the sacred.**

The painted ceilings and walls in Altamira Cave depict near life-sized animals and strange symbols throughout its labyrinths. This 14,000-year-old masterpiece collection was discovered in 1879, but its authenticity was not recognized until 1902. Altamira is regarded as one of the best-preserved and most prolifically painted prehistoric caves in Europe. Bison dominate the animal compositions, but other interesting depictions include horses, boars, stags, felines and mammoths. The narrow corridor at the back of the cave was crowded with images, suggesting that this was an area of special significance. Portable art of figurines have also been found at the site. Altamira cave is near of the Bay of Biscay coast and the town Santander, Spain.

Although most cave art is found in the fertile valleys of the Vèzére and Dordogne in southwest France, the Pyrenees, and the Cantabrian Mountains of Spain, cave paintings and engravings are found throughout Europe. Apart from animal representations, wall art also includes abstract images such as lines, dots and combinations of these. Human figures are rarely depicted. There are hand stencils in some caves, made by painting around a spread-out hand, and these are thought to represent male and female symbols used in fertility and initiation rites. Footmarks and fingerprints of young children have been found at certain sites, suggesting rite of passage rituals for younger members. Some images appear to represent people wearing masks, animal skins and antlers. These latter may be camouflage for hunting or ceremonial dress for hunting rituals worn by shaman.

# Montserrat

The Montserrat monastery in the Pyrenees Mountains is a sacred Christian site of religious legend. It is here that Saint Peter is said to have deposited a statue of the Virgin Mary, which had been given to him by Saint Luke and hidden in the mountains for 50 years. The latter-carved 12th century "Black Madonna" statue earned fame for being the catalyst of many miracles. So popular was the sculpture that several of the first Spanish missionary churches in Mexico, Chile, Peru and a Caribbean island of the same name were dedicated to the Virgin of Montserrat. In King Arthur legend, Montserrat is where Parsifal discovered the Holy Grail after an arduous quest to Spain. The famous Ignatius Loyola spent much of his life in the monastery writing spiritual exercises and founding the Jesuit order.

Because of its reputation, Montserrat is one of the most popular pilgrimage sites in Spain. This spiritual community outside of Barcelona resides near the top of a 4,200-foot (1,300-m) mountain. The saw-toothed mountain surrounding the monastery is popular for hiking, biking, spelunking and rock climbing, but the real attraction is at the top of the peak. There can be found the 11th century sanctuary of Our Lady of Montserrat. This pilgrimage destination is home to the 12th century statue of *La Moreneta,* meaning "Black Madonna." The statue is now located above the high alter in a mountain top basilica. The statue used to be housed in the *Santa Cova* "Holy Cave" located nearby. Both statue and basilica are blackened by the smoke of countless candles. Many miracles have been attributed to the statue, and it has attracted untold millions of pilgrims over the centuries.

## The legendary Montserrat is a famous mountain, sanctuary, monastery, and spiritual community attracting more than a million visitors per year.

Among its many mysteries, Montserrat is reputed to contain the biblical Ark of the Covenant. The powerful and ultra-sacred Ark of the Covenant first appears in the story of Exodus and appears some 200 other times in the Old Testament. Sacred to Jews and Christians alike, the Ark is said to possess supernatural powers and is where Moses symbolically placed a copy of the Ten Commandments. Around the time of Christ's crucifixion, an earthquake and a hurricane hit Jerusalem and exposed the Ark inside Solomon's Temple. As the Montserrat story goes, it was taken to the Phoenician port of Catalunya, were it was transported by the Essene Brotherhood to a secret cave underneath the monastery. Indeed, the symbol for the monastery is three mountain peaks with a box at the top of the center peak.

▲ Montserrat is clustered atop a mountain plateau surrounded by serrated sandstone cliffs.

### Getting to Montserrat

Montserrat is 35 miles (56 km) northwest of Barcelona. The best approach from the city is the *Ferrocarriles Catalanes* trains, which connect with a cable car for an exhilarating ride to the top. The trains to Montserrat leave Barcelona from beneath the Placa de Espanya five times daily and take about 90 minutes each way. Tour buses also make the round trip from Barcelona along the A2 road toward Tarragona, then turning west on the N11 and following the signs to the monastery.

# Santiago de Compostela

In the far-western Galicia region of Spain is a mystical land predating the Christian era. The countryside of Galicia features impressive megalithic dolmens, similar to Britain's Stonehenge and France's Carnac. The original settlement of Santiago de Compostela attracted pagan worshippers in the same way that it later drew medieval

Christians, who made overland pilgrimages there to honor the remains of Saint James the Apostle. The large amount of megaliths and rock engravings near the town suggests that it was a sacred place throughout ancient times. It is believed that the earliest pilgrims would have been able to find this farthest point on the continent by taking bearings from the Milky Way galaxy. Interestingly, Galicia is also renowned for its numerous UFO sightings. In the age of flat earth believers, Galicia was literally considered Land's End, and the actual end of the world was supposedly visible from nearby Cape Finisterre.

Biblical tradition tells us the story of Saint James the Apostle traveling to Galicia in 40 CE to spread the gospel of Jesus to the west as far as possible. He died a martyr's death upon returning to Jerusalem, and his remains were eventually returned to Spain and placed in the sacred cathedral of Santiago de Compostela. Through the many centuries his shrine has attracted more pilgrims than that of any other Christian apostle. The endpoint of Christian pilgrimage is the cathedral where the relics of Saint James reside in the high altar. Devout pilgrims can follow the centuries-old tradition of climbing the stairs behind the altar to kiss the bejeweled cape on the golden statue of the saint. Directly below the statue is the crypt that contains his bones in a silver reliquary.

## The monumental cathedral at Santiago de Compostela was the terminus of the most important pilgrimage destination of medieval Europe, outside of Rome.

Santiago de Compostela is the third most significant holy city in Christendom, after Rome and Jerusalem. Because of its enormous significance to Christians over the centuries, all of the earliest European roads led there via "The Compostela Way." So popular was the pilgrimage in the Middle Ages that in the 16th century, more than 200,000 pilgrims on average made the journey every year. Some pilgrims were convicted criminals who had to bring back a certificate of arrival so the judge would abdicate their sentence. Certificates in Latin called a *Compostela* are still given out at the shrine to Saint James. Pilgrims today can enjoy a wealth of medieval art inside the cathedral, treasury, various cloisters or ascend the cathedral towers to gain a fine panoramic view of the city. Near the holy city is a lone mountain peak known as Pico Sagro, another venerated site from pagan times. The Compostela cathedral is supposedly laid out in accordance to the angle of the sunlight as it shines across the lone mountain peak.

### Getting to Santiago de Compostela

Santiago de Compostela is located in the northwestern corner of Spain, about 30 miles (48 km) southwest of La Coruña. The cathedral, located at the Plaza de Obradoiro, is considered one of the finest architectural achievements in Europe and can be seen from miles away. Anyone in the city of Santiago knows the way to the famous plaza. Bus, airlines, and trains service the city.

# TURKEY

T he ancient civilization of Turkey has long been a gateway for cultural dissemination. A blend of Occident and Orient, East and West, Christian and Muslim
—Turkey played host to mighty empires. Throughout the country are ruins and sacred
sites from various periods of time. The earliest known city, even pre-dating those in
Sumer, is the archaeological site Catal Hüyük, located 200 miles (320 km) south of the
capital Ankara. After these earliest dwellers came the war-like Hittites, who left
behind a mountain citadel called Boghazkoy and a form of writing very similar to
Egyptian hieroglyphics. Along the Aegean Sea are sites from classical Greek mythology, such as Homer's Troy. Roman cities are scattered across Turkey, with Ephesus
being the most famous. The ancient city Byzantium became the Roman Empire's second capital, renamed Constantinople, today named Istanbul. The Ottoman Turks
arrived in the 14th century CE and ousted the last of the long-standing rulers of the
Byzantine Empire. Istanbul became the Ottoman capital where the sultan ruled with
his harem at the Topkapi Palace.

## Cappadochia (Göreme)

The lunar landscape surrounding the Cappadochia region is spectacular, but the
area is most renowned for its underground cities and churches carved directly into
the soft rock. The whole region is scattered with unusual chimney-like rock formations and sculpted sanctuaries. Several impressive underground cities exist at
Derinkuyu and Nevsehir Kaymakli near Göreme. Early Christians expanded these
subterranean suburbs to protect themselves from invading Arab armies. It is known
that Saint Paul and several of the original followers of Jesus Christ came to
Cappadochia and established a Christian colony. The cities were inhabited from the
second century CE until the 12th century. In all, the massive underground cities of
Central Anatolia once held a population of approximately 50,000 residents.

**There are more than 1,000 rock-hewn churches
in Cappadochia, some dating from the earliest
days of Christianity.**

Cappadochia is located 31 miles (50 km) to the south of Mount Erciyes (Argaeus), a
former volcano. The violent eruptions of Erciyes covered whole areas with a thick
layer of volcanic ash, which solidified over time. Many millenniums passed and the
hardened tuff became bizarrely eroded by the natural elements of wind, water and
earthquakes. The first settlers to the area were the Hittites who cultivated the
exceedingly fertile soil and burrowed into the soft rock. The small caves were later
enlarged by Christian communities who created missionary schools, churches, homes
and wine cellars. A total of 40 cities have been discovered, ranging from small under-

Cappadochia, TURKEY

▲ The burrowed cities of Cappadochia are remarkable in design and scale.

ground villages to vast cities, but only a few are open to the public.

One of the oldest settlements in the Cappadochia region is the still occupied town of Göreme, and the nearby El Nazar valley. Although little is known of the original occupants, Göreme grew to a 30,000-person spiritual settlement in the seventh century CE. Saint Basil established the first monastery to educate missionaries, whom would proselytize Christianity to the largely pagan population at that time. During the expansion period of Islam the Christians dug even deeper, creating a labyrinth of defensive tunnels and traps to detour the invading forces. Göreme is home to the fairy chimneys and some of the finest early-era Christian churches. Maps of the dozen or so churches are available in the village of Göreme, as well as guided tours to the most important sites.

### Getting to Cappadochia (Göreme)

Cappadochia is located about 93 miles (150 km) southeast of Ankara, the capital city of Turkey. Because of its popularity, several bus companies service the Cappadochia region, but only the bus lines *Göreme* and *Nevtour* actually travel direct to Göreme, while the rest will drop off at Nevsehir or some other surrounding village. Several local bus or the dolmus minibus routes bisect the surrounding villages and offer a good opportunity to discover the less visited sites of the region. Further south is Konya, best known as the birthplace of the Sufi Muslim sect and a good stopover between Cappadochia and the coast.

## Ephesus

The seaport city of Ephesus was a pilgrimage city to the Greeks and Romans, and was also important to early Christians. Centuries after being abandoned, Ephesus is among the best-preserved archaeological sites in the Mediterranean region. Ephesus is renowned for its history and beauty. It has been described as the "Paris of the Ancient World" with much accuracy. During its Greek heyday only Athens was more magnificent, yet Ephesus served more as a spiritual location than a political center. It was to worship Artemis, the goddess of fertility, later renamed Diana by the Romans, that pilgrims came from all over the empire to this sacred city. The Temple of Artemis (Diana) was ranked as one of the Seven Wonders of the Ancient World. The temple was located just outside the city. Unfortunately there is little left of the Temple of Artemis—the foundation stones are all that remain.

## Apart from Pompeii and some inaccessible ruins in Libya, Ephesus is the largest ancient city preserved nearly intact.

The founding of Ephesus, which dates back 4,000 years, represents influence from several civilizations. The original inhabitants were called the "Lelegers and Karers" who had cultural ties with the Hittites. Very little of this culture remains, but according to historians, on the western slope of the castle hill above Ephesus once stood an ancient temple devoted to the earth goddess Cybele. The Ionian Greeks changed Cybele to Artemis and erected a fantastic temple in her honor. During Greek and Roman times the temple was so revered that even marauding armies would not harm the citizens taking refuge inside the temple. Ephesus and the temple precinct were without defensive walls, or a protecting army. The city survived and thrived because of the reverence to Artemis, the virgin goddess of the hunt and the moon. The pilgrim trade played a role in the growth of the city as a prosperous trading center. The majority of buildings remaining are either Greek or Roman. They include the famous statue of the Mother Goddess; the Temple of Hadrian; the Arcadian Way leading to the now dried-up seaport; the Marble Main Street; a 24,000-person capacity amphitheater; several fine floor mosaics; the Fountain of Trajan; and the Celsus Library.

Surrounding and within the ancient city are several monuments from early Christianity, when Ephesus was its religious center. The Basilica of Saint John is said to be the actual tomb of biblical Saint John, who is buried beneath a lavish church built by Emperor Justinian. This classic edifice provides an interesting contrast to the neighboring early Turkish citadel and the 14th century Mosque of Isa Bey, with its exquisite marble door and richly ornamental windows. Five miles (8 km) outside Ephesus is the square where Saint Paul preached. The Shrine of Our Lady of the Assumption is built on the site where, legend claims, the Virgin Mary spent her last years, died, and was buried. Nearby the Mary shrine are the remains of an early Christian cave settlement. Modern Christians flock to Ephesus for the strong connection to Saint Paul and the Virgin Mary.

### Getting to Ephesus

The archaeological park of Ephesus, or Efes as the Turks call it, is located 50 miles (80 km) southeast from Izmir, a major port city located on the Aegean Sea. Izmir is serviced by ferries from Greece and bus routes extending all over Turkey. Izmir is close enough to visit Ephesus on a day trip, but it is more practical to stay in the town of Selcuk near the ruins. Several days are necessary to fully explore Ephesus and its surrounding sites. From Selcuk it is a hot 40-minute walk to Ephesus, or taxis and most dolmus minibuses leave from the bus station upon demand.

# Hagia Sophia

At the junction of Europe and Asia, with only the narrow Bosporus waterway as a division, the Roman outpost Byzantium occupied a superb position for a trading city. Surrounded by water on three sides including the Golden Horn, the Bosporus, and Sea of Marmara, its position was favorable as a naturally defended city. Emperor Constantine moved the Roman capital there in 330 CE, and in so doing renamed the city after himself. Constantinople prospered as the capital for Byzantine emperors until 1453, when the last of the Roman influence finally ended.

The most illustrious Byzantine emperor was Justinian, whose reign from 527-565 CE was marked by many achievements. Justinian was a devout Christian, a legal reformer, a renowned military leader and a builder of magnificent public buildings. His most famous building was Hagia Sophia (meaning Holy Wisdom), the largest dome structure in the world. Built on the sacred grounds where another church had stood, Hagia Sophia was constructed by the greatest mathematicians, masons and mosaic artists of their time. Long to become the spiritual focus of Christendom, Hagia Sophia inspired millions as the church of divine wisdom.

**Hagia Sophia became the spiritual center of Eastern Orthodoxy before Muslims captured the city. The Orthodox faith spread from Constantinople to Greece, the Balkans, and Russia, where it remains today.**

Upon capturing Constantinople on May 28, 1453, the Ottoman Turks smashed their way into Hagia Sophia the next day and massacred the many faithful praying for the deliverance of their Christian city. The Turkish sultan Mehmet II converted the church into a mosque to symbolize his victory. After 900 years the ancient church began a new life dedicated to a new god. The second age of worship enhanced the converted mosque by adding a tall minaret, a marble throne, and six large green medallions. These medallions bear the name of Allah, the prophet Mohammed, and various founders of the Islamic faith. The mosque remained for five centuries until it was converted into a museum in 1935, just over a decade after the collapse of the Ottoman Empire and the establishment of a secular Turkish state. The spectacular structure has gone through much since Justinian first entered his church and declared, "O Solomon, I have surpassed thee!"

Pilgrims from around the world continue to make their way here to be awed by its presence. The dome of the church and the architectural style it represents influenced

▲ Hagia Sophia can be seen from afar in Istanbul.

260

Christian and Muslim building practices for centuries. Its lasting legacy is the Byzantine church, whose offshoot religion was Christian Orthodox—a faith still practiced in neighboring European countries. Still, today, it is not difficult to be awestruck by Hagia Sophia's massive proportions, even though the Muslims converted the church into a mosque.

### Getting to Hagia Sophia

The church-mosque-museum Hagia Sophia is located in the center of the old city of Istanbul. The city has an international airport with modern and efficient public transportation. Justinian's great church is visible from all over Istanbul, which makes it very easy to locate. Near the Topkapi Palace in the Sultanahmet section of the city rises the majestic Hagia Sophia.

# ACKNOWLEDGMENTS

THIS WORK WAS GREATLY ENHANCED by the exceptional suggestions from the following editors: William J. Sullivan (Read by Bill), Randall Lyman, Beverly Cambron, Edward "Mr. T" Taylor, Marc "Mr. Beans" Olson, Tom Loftus, Michael McColl, Bruce Northam, Carolyn Durkalski, and family members Chris Olsen (brother), Marsi Olsen (sister) and Elaine Olsen (mother). Book design and production art by Mark Maxam, book cover assistance from Eric Stampfli, gratuitous support came from author Karen Tate, Trevor Zimmer, Harry Pariser, Joe Firmage of Many One, Michael O'Rourke, Justin Smith, Justin Wiener, and David Templeman from the Peace Tour. Special thanks to Stewart Fallon, Calum Grant, Heinz Orsatti, Peter Bartsch, Jerry Nardini, Kun & Erika, Tanya Serova, and the wonderful books, inspiration and advice from maverick archaeologist David Hatcher Childress.

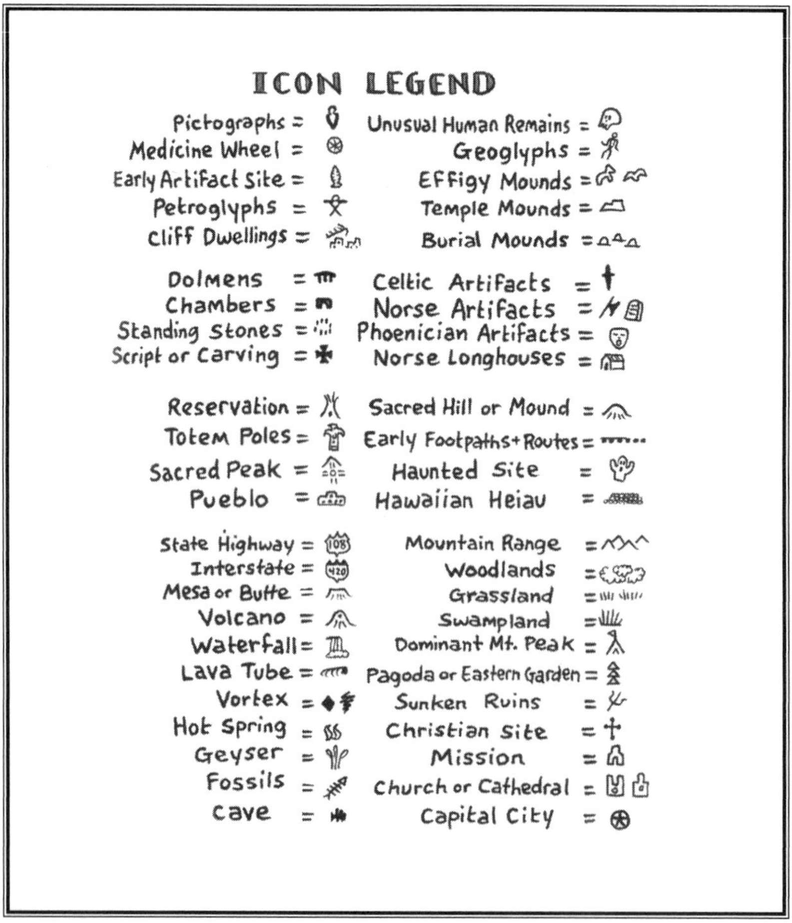
ICON LEGEND
Pictographs =
Medicine Wheel =
Early Artifact Site =
Petroglyphs =
Cliff Dwellings =
Unusual Human Remains =
Geoglyphs =
Effigy Mounds =
Temple Mounds =
Burial Mounds =
Dolmens =
Chambers =
Standing Stones =
Script or Carving =
Celtic Artifacts =
Norse Artifacts =
Phoenician Artifacts =
Norse Longhouses =
Reservation =
Totem Poles =
Sacred Peak =
Pueblo =
Sacred Hill or Mound =
Early Footpaths+Routes =
Haunted Site =
Hawaiian Heiau =
State Highway =
Interstate =
Mesa or Butte =
Volcano =
Waterfall =
Lava Tube =
Vortex =
Hot Spring =
Geyser =
Fossils =
Cave =
Mountain Range =
Woodlands =
Grassland =
Swampland =
Dominant Mt. Peak =
Pagoda or Eastern Garden =
Sunken Ruins =
Christian Site =
Mission =
Church or Cathedral =
Capital City =

# BIBLIOGRAPHY

## Author's Karma Statement

Dillard, Annie, "The Wreck Of Time: Taking Our Century's Measure." *Harper's*, (New York), January 1998.

## Introduction

Adams, Russell B., Series Director, *Mystic Places: Mysteries of the Unknown*. Alexandria, VA: Time-Life Books, 1987.

Childress, David Hatcher, *Anti-Gravity & The World Grid*. Stelle, IL: Adventures Unlimited Press, 1995.

Metzner, Ralph, *The Unfolding Self*. Navato, CA: Origin Press, 1998.

Westward, Jennifer, Editor, *The Atlas of Mysterious Places*. London, UK: Weidenfeld & Nicolson, 1987.

## North Africa and the Middle East

Aldred, Cyril, *Egyptian Art*. Oxford, UK: Oxford University Press, 1980.

Brosnahan, Tom, et. al. *Middle East on a Shoestring*. Hawthorn, Australia: Lonely Planet Publications, 1994.

Campbell, Jonathan G., *Dead Sea Scrolls*. Berkeley, CA: Ulysses Press, 1998.

Childress, David Hatcher, *Lost Cities & Ancient Mysteries of Africa and Arabia*. Stelle, IL: Adventures Unlimited Press, 1997.

Esposito, John, et. al. *The March of Islam*. Alexandria, VA: Time-Life Books, 1988.

Noone, Richard, *5/5/2000 Ice: The Ultimate Disaster*. New York, NY: Three Rivers Press, 1982.

Roberts, David, R.A., *The Holy Land: Yesterday and Today*. New York, NY: Stewart, Tabori & Chang, 1994.

Smyth, Piazzi, *The Great Pyramid*. New York, NY: Bell Publishing Co., 1880.

Steiner, Margreet, et. al., "David's Jerusalem: Fiction or Reality?" *Biblical Archaeology Review*, (Washington DC), July/August 1998.

Wareham, Norman, Gill, Jill, *Shrines of the Holy Land*. Liguori, MO: Liguori, 1998.

## The Far East

Childress, David Hatcher, *Lost Cities of China, Central Asia & India*. Stelle, IL: Adventures Unlimited Press, 1991.

Doubleday, Nelson, Editor, *Encyclopedia of World Travel Volume 2*. Garden City, NY: Doubleday & Company, 1967.

Frank, Irene M., et. al. *To the Ends of the Earth*. New York: Facts On File Publications, 1984.

Hausdorf, Hartwig, *The Chinese Roswell*. Boca Raton, FL: New Paradigm Books.

Malik, Michael, Editor, *All-Asia Guide Compendium*. Hong Kong, China: Far Eastern Economic Review Publishing Co. Ltd., 1991.

Rampa, Lobsang, T., *Third Eye: The Autobiography of a Tibetan Lama*. New York, NY: Ballantine, 1956.

Stolper, Jordan, "The Battle for Russia's Lake Baikal." *Blue*, Dec. '02, Jan. '03.

Sullivan, Walter, et. al, *The World's Last Mysteries*. Pleasantville, NY: The Reader's Digest Association 1981.

Wilson, Colin, *The Atlas of Holy Places and Sacred Sites*. New York, NY: DK Publishing, 1996.

## India and the Sub-Continent

Bayly, C. A., et. al. *Light in the East*. Alexandria, VA: Time-Life Books, 1988.

Longhurst, A. H., *Hampi Ruins*. Delhi, India: Asian Educational Services, 1982.

Moloney, Norah, *The Young Oxford Book of Archaeology*. Oxford, England: Oxford University Press, 1995.

Wheeler, Mortimer, Editor, *Splendors of the East*. New York, NY: G.P. Putnam's Sons, 1965.

Wheeler, Tony, *West Asia on a Shoestring*. Hawthorn, Australia: Lonely Planet Publications, 1990.

# SACRED PLACES AROUND THE WORLD

## Southeast Asia

**Belliveau**, Jeannette, *An Amateur's Guide to the Planet*. Baltimore, MD: Beau Monde Press, 1996.

**Hofer**, Hans, *Insight Guides: Thailand*. Boston, MA: Houghton Mifflin Co., 1993.

**Malik**, Michael, Editor, *All-Asia Guide Compendium*. Hong Kong, China: Far Eastern Economic Review Publishing Co. Ltd., 1991.

**Tingley**, Nancy, et. al. *Southeast Asia Galleries*. San Francisco, CA: De Young Asian Art Museum, 1997.

## Australia and the South Pacific

**Childress**, David Hatcher, *Ancient Tonga & the Lost City of Mu'a*. Stelle, IL: Adventures Unlimited Press, 1996.

**Childress**, David Hatcher, *Lost Cities of Ancient Lemuria and the Pacific*. Stelle, IL: Adventures Unlimited Press, 1988.

**Childress**, David Hatcher, "Nan Modal: Ancient City of Mystery." *World Explorer*, (Kempton, IL), Vol. 2, No. 1.

**Howell**, Clark, F., *Early Man*. Alexandria, VA: Time-Life Books, 1968.

## South America

**Bahn**, Paul G., Editor, *100 Great Archaeological Discoveries*. London, UK: Barnes & Noble Books, 1995.

**Brockman**, Norman, C., *Encyclopedia of Sacred Places*. New York, NY: Oxford University Press, 1997.

**Brooks**, John, Editor, *South American Handbook*. Chicago, IL: Rand McNally and Company, 1986.

**Heyerdahl**, Thor, *Aku-Aku, The Art of Easter Island*. New York, NY: Doubleday, 1975.

**Lewan**, Todd, "Half of Amazon Jungle Ready To Go Up in Smoke." *Associated Press* (New York), December 10, 1997.

## Central America

**Brosnahan**, Tom, *Guatemala, Belize & Yucatan*. Hawthorn, Australia: Lonely Planet Publications, 1994.

**Childress**, David Hatcher, *Lost Cities of North and Central America*. Stelle, IL: Adventures Unlimited Press, 1992.

**Eiseley**, Loren, Editor, *The Epic Of Man*, New York, NY: Life Books, 1961.

**O'Reilly**, James; Habegger, Larry, *Travelers' Tales Mexico*. San Francisco, CA: Travelers' Tales, Inc., 1994.

**Sullivan**, Walter, et. al, *The World's Last Mysteries*. Pleasantville, NY: The Reader's Digest Association, 1981.

**Van Auken**, John; Little, Lora, *The Lost Hall of Records*. Memphis, TN: Eagle Wing Books, 2000.

## North America

**Barlow**, Bernyce, *Sacred Sites of the West*. St. Paul, MN: Llewellyn Worldwide Ltd., 1997.

**Childress**, David Hatcher, *Lost Cities of North and Central America*. Stelle, IL: Adventures Unlimited Press, 1992.

**Coronel**, Antonio, *Tales of Mexican California*. Santa Barbara, CA: Bellerophon Books, 1994.

**Doubleday**, Nelson, Editor, *Encyclopedia of World Travel Volume 1*. Garden City, NY: Doubleday & Company, 1967.

**Guiley**, Rosemary Ellen, *Atlas of the Mysterious in North America*. New York, NY: Facts On File, 1995.

**Wright**, Ralph B., *California's Missions*. Covina, CA: Herbert A. Lowman, 1950.

## Sub-Sahara Africa

**Childress**, David Hatcher, "The Search for the Ark of the Covenant" *World Explorer*, (Kempton, IL), Vol. 2, No. 2.

**Frank**, Irene M., et. al. *To the Ends of the Earth*. New York: Facts On File Publications, 1984.

**Ingpen**, Robert, et. at. *Encyclopedia of Mysterious Places*. New York: Viking Penguin, 1990.

## *Europe*

**Ellingham**, Mark, Series Editor, *Rough Guide Europe*. London, UK. Penguin, 1998.

**Hamlyn**, Paul, *Greek Mythology*. London, UK: Westbook House, 1964.

**Hartt**, Frederick, et. al. Art: A History of Painting, Sculpture, and Architecture: Second Edition. Englewood Cliffs, New Jersey: Prentice-Hall, 1985.

**Meehan**, Cary, *Sacred Ireland*. Glastonbury, UK: Gothic Image Publications, 2002.

**Michell**, John, *Sacred England*. Glastonbury, UK: Gothic Image Publications, 2003.

**Scarre**, Chris, General Editor, *Past Worlds: The Times Atlas of Archaeology*. London, UK: Times Books Limited, 1988.

**Wright**, Kevin J., *Catholic Shrines of Western Europe*. Liguori, MO: Liguori, 1997.

**Whitehouse**, David & Ruth, *Archaeological Atlas of the World*, San Francisco, CA: W.H. Freeman & CO., 1975.

# TOUR OUTFITTERS TO SACRED PLACES

Many of the selected outfitters below specialize in one or a few sacred site regions of the world. Call for a free brochure and more information about the destinations they serve.

### Adventure Center
1311 63rd Street, Suite # 200, Emeryville, CA 94608, PHONE: (800) 227-8747
*Specializes in affordable group travel to especially adventurous destinations.*
WEB: www.adventurecenter.com

### Amazon Tours and Cruises
8700 W. Flagler Street, Suite # 190, Miami, FL 33174, PHONE: (800) 423-2791
*Largest tour and boat operator on the Peruvian Amazon River.*
WEB: www.amazontours.net

### Canterbury Tours, Inc.
PO Box 783, Pawling, NY 12564 USA, PHONE: (800) 653-0017
*Leads pilgrimage groups to European shrines.*

### Circle the Planet
PHONE: (800) 799-8888
*Lowest-cost tickets for round-the-world destinations and most sacred sites worldwide.*
WEB: www.circletheplanet.com

### Deja Vu Tours
2210 Harold Way, Berkeley, CA 94704 USA, PHONE: (800) 204-TOUR
*Tours to sacred sites led by graduates of the Berkeley Psychic Institute.*
WEB: www.berkeleypsychic.com

### Geographic Expeditions
2627 Lombard Street, San Francisco, CA 94123, PHONE: (415) 922-0448, (800) 777-8183
*Specializes in hard-to-reach sacred places, such as Mount Kailas in Tibet.*
WEB: www.geoex.com

### Global Exchange REALITY TOURS
2017 Mission Street # 303, San Francisco, CA 94110, PHONE: (800) 497-1994
*Educational, interactive and inspiring excursions dealing with provocative themes, such as peace and conflict, human rights, revolution, history, culture, art and the environment.*
WEB: www.globalexchange.org

### Holy Pilgrimages
PO Box 177, Atkinson, NH 03811, PHONE: (603) 362-4793
*Small pilgrimage groups to European shrines.*

### IMC Pamir
133 Kievskaya Str. # 30, 720001, Bishkek, Kyrgyzstan, PHONE: (996-312) 66-04-64, 66-04-68
*Leads expeditions along the Silk Route through several countries.*
EMAIL: imcpamir@imfiko.bishkek.su; WEB: www.bishkek.su/IMCPAMIR

# TOUR OUTFITTERS TO SACRED PLACES

### Key Tours
11096B Lee Hwy. Suite # 104, Fairfax, VA 22030, PHONE: (800) 576-1784
*Specializes in tours to the Eastern Mediterranean region.*
WEB: www.keytours.com

### Maya Tour
2608 N. Ocean Blvd., Suite # 8, Pompano Beach, FL 33062, PHONE: (800) 392-6292
*Leads tour groups to Maya cities in Central America.*
WEB: www.mayatour.com

### Mediatrix Tours
PO Box 941371, Plano, TX 75094-1371, PHONE: (800) 555-9480
*Tour outfitter to sacred Christian sites.*
WEB: www.mediatrixtours.com

### Power Places Tours & Conferences
116 King St., Fredericksted, Virgin Islands 00840, PHONE: (800) 234-8687
*Tours led by modern-day luminaries to power places around the world.*
WEB: www.powerplaces.com

### Somak Safaris
2700 E. Imperial Hwy., Suite #N, Brea, CA 92821, PHONE: (800) 757-6625
*African outfitter covering the entire continent.*
WEB: www.somaksafaris.com

### World Explorers Club
PO Box 99, 403 Kemp Street, Kempton, IL 60946, PHONE: (815) 253-9000
*Tours/Expeditions/Conferences to more remote sacred places.*
WEB: www.wexclub.com

SPECIAL PROMOTIONAL THANKS to the Israel Ministry of Tourism 1-800-782-4360, www.infotour.co.il; Costa Rica Tourism Board 1-800-343-6332, www.tourism-costarica.com; and the Austrian National Tourism Office 1-212-944-6880, www.anto.com; and the ASEAN Tourism Forum.

**WWW.CCCPUBLISHING.COM    WWW.STOMPERS.COM
WWW.PEACETOUR.ORG    WWW.BRADOLSEN.COM**

Angkor, CAMBODIA

# INDEX

# INDEX

# INDEX

# ABOUT THE AUTHOR:

BRAD OLSEN's *World Stompers: A Global Travel Manifesto*, now in its fifth edition, was lauded by film director Oliver Stone as a "subversive masterpiece of travel writing," and *Publisher's Weekly* as a "quirky pleaser." He is Contributing Editor for *World Explorer* magazine and the author/illustrator of *Extreme Adventures Hawaii* and *Extreme Adventures Northern California* (Hunter Publishing). His popular travel website stompers.com was Microsoft Network's 'Site of the Week' and ranked as a Lycos 'Top 5%' Website. Brad is the President of CCC Publishing in San Francisco, which publishes the *Sacred Places: 108 Destinations* series and *In Search of Adventure: A Wild Travel Anthology*. His commentaries have appeared on National Public Radio, CNNfn and the Travel Channel. Brad enjoys lecturing on the subject of journeys to sacred places and extended global travel.

In between jaunts around the world, Brad usually spends his summers in the Midwest and the rest of the year in sunny California. Brad is an expert downhill skier, scuba diver, and ultimate frisbee player. He goes to the Burning Man festival every year and occasionally builds an art project to burn. While researching *Sacred Places North America: 108 Destinations*, Brad wrote his first historical screenplay entitled *Voyage to Vinland*. The true story chronicles the Greenland Viking excursions to North America. The film treatment can be read on the cccpublishing.com website. In between projects, or when the weather is really nice, he can usually be found playing frisbee or volleyball with his friends on San Francisco's Baker Beach. Brad is

Executive Director of the World Peace Through Technology Organization, a 501 (c) 3 nonprofit corporation, and the founder of the *How Weird Street Faire*. Both projects are based out of San Francisco. He is 38 years old.

To learn more about this contented world explorer and passionate peace activist have a look at his websites:

**www.bradolsen.com**
**www.cccpublishing.com**
**www.stompers.com**
**www.peacetour.org**
**www.howwierd.org**

▲ Brad Olsen clicked this shot of himself in June, 2002 at Dreamer's Rock, Canada while on a solo cross country roadtrip developing his North America guide.

# In Search of Adventure
## A Wild Travel Anthology

*In Search of Adventure* celebrates the wild side of contemporary travel writing. This epic collection of 100 traveler's tales applauds the roving prose of Tim Cahill, Marybeth Bond, Jeff Greenwald, Robert Young Pelton and Simon Winchester. Revealing, humorous, sometimes naughty stories by acclaimed authors. Written and compiled by Bruce Northam and Brad Olsen.

*"Today's Pick:* In Search of Adventure *is an engrossing read. And, for anyone who has ever dreamed of escape or imagined a wilder existence, this refreshing and sometimes over-the-top compilation will not disappoint."* —Newsweek.com

*"The anthology is a fresh, irreverent look at international travel, and delves into areas often glossed over, including experiences with crime, sex, and religious fraud."* —San Francisco Chronicle

*"Lovers of storytelling and anyone looking for summer vacation inspiration shouldn't miss this (book.)"* —Bay Guardian

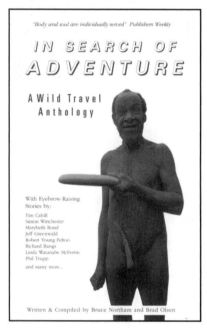

*"Body and soul are individually served" Publishers Weekly*

**IN SEARCH OF ADVENTURE**

A Wild Travel Anthology

With Eyebrow-Raising Stories by:
Tim Cahill
Simon Winchester
Marybeth Bond
Jeff Greenwald
Robert Young Pelton
Richard Bangs
Linda Watanabe McFerrin
Phil Trapp
and many more...

Written & Compiled by Bruce Northam and Brad Olsen

*"You don't have to read a traditional guidebook to gain an understanding of a destination. This compilation of 100 eclectic essays takes readers into the hearts and minds of the authors and the destinations in which their adventures take place. Whether clients are headed to Bhutan or their favorite chair, they will be entertained, enlightened and sometimes shocked by these honest slices of life on the road."* —Travel Weekly

*The editors had the courage to embark on this border-crossing adventure in publishing and lived to bring back a collection of extraordinary memories, memories that conjure our own most moving journeys and make us hunger for more."* —Salon

ISBN 1-888729-03-1    465 pages    $17.95
Available from: Independent Publishers Group (800) 888-4741
or online www.amazon.com or www.stompers.com

## EXTREME ADVENTURES
# HAWAII

Take in the most the Hawaiian Islands have to offer. This travel guide supplement offers radical excursion options to all the islands. Includes: trekking, surfing, diving, windsurfing, biking, waterfall jumping and much more!

ISBN 1-55650-809-3    238 pages    $13.95
Maps and photos by Brad Olsen

## EXTREME ADVENTURES

## NORTHERN CALIFORNIA

A fun-lovers' guide to the many exciting adventures in Northern California. Includes: bungee jumping, ghost town adventures, ski resort ratings, rock climbing, trekking, skyboarding, hot springs & many more extreme excursions!

These books contain hundreds of supplemental adventures not included in many standard travel guides. Includes adventure ratings for *Risk* and *Adrenaline*.

ISBN 1-55650-808-5    238 pages    $13.95
Written and illustrated by Brad Olsen

*Extreme adventures are individual sports and outdoor activities, like rock climbing, parasailing, mountain biking, skyboarding, disc golf, and snowboarding, that contain a certain degree of risk and excite an adrenaline rush. Olsen, author of* World Stompers, *surveys extreme adventures in Northern California and Hawaii. Each adventure, organized by region or island, is rated on a scale measuring the risk factor and the adrenaline rush. Replete with practical advice "the best being to avoid any activity you have the slightest degree of uncertainty about" each section contains a selective list of guides, suppliers, and information sources. —Library Journal*

Both *Extreme Adventure* titles are only available from:
www.amazon.com or www.stompers.com
*Extreme Adventures Northern California & Hawaii* ($13.95 / 236 pp.)
are only available through CCC Publishing.

# SACRED PLACES NORTH AMERICA
# 108 DESTINATIONS

"Author, photographer, and cartographer Brad Olsen reveals the many spiritual sites that abound in North America. *"Pilgrimage is one way we can find ourselves and this book will provide a guide,"* raved the **Twin Cities Wellness** paper. The venerable **Midwest Book Review** said: *"Sacred Places North America is a revealing, useful, and enthusiastically recommended guide."* **Spirituality and Health** noted: *"In this handy and helpful resource, Brad Olsen demonstrates his respect for sacred places."* And the **Orlando Sentinel** reviewed: *"He offers information on each site, juxtaposing local folklore and Native American legend with scientific theories or physical evidence to provide context."* Read the critically acclaimed North America guide to 108 Destinations. *Want to visit wondrous, exotic, incredibly gorgeous locales and experience a sense of mystical transcendence? You don't need a plane ticket, a passport, or even a psychedelic drug. In fact, there's probably such a place within driving distance of your home."* observed **Fearless Books**.

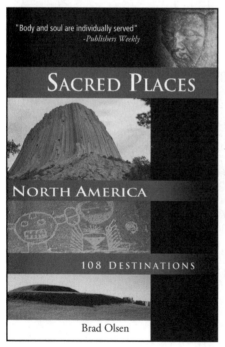

■ Who were the first Europeans in North America: the Vikings, Celts, or ancient Phoenicians?

■ Why did Native Americans revere certain mountains?

■ Where are the most frequent sightings of Bigfoot and UFOs?

■ Why does attendance at Graceland increase every year?

■ Where do people of the New Age movement convene to experience Earth energy?

■ How did certain prehistoric civilizations mark seasonal equinoxes and solstices?

108 B&W Photographs / 66 Maps and Graphics

ISBN 1-888729-09-0     304 pages     USA $17.95     Canada $26.95
## Travel / Spirituality / History

# WORLD STOMPERS
## A GLOBAL TRAVEL MANIFESTO
### (FIFTH EDITION)

When you are ready to leave your day job, load up your backpack and head out to distant lands for extended periods of time, Brad Olsen's "Travel Classic" will lend a helping hand. It will save you hundreds of dollars in travel expenses, prepare you for an extended journey, keep you safe & healthy on the road, find you a job overseas, and get you psyched to travel the world! For a good time, read the book *Publishers Weekly* called a "Quirky Chain Pleaser" and *Library Journal* recommended as "A great addition to your collection.'

*"Travel can be a nightmare when you find yourself in the wrong place at the wrong time. This subversive masterpiece of travel writing might just save your sanity the next time you go out there. Get it. It makes life fun!"* —film director Oliver Stone

*"Twentysomethings, especially those who would really hate to be known by that moniker, will love this irreverent, low-gloss guide that intersperses witty cartoons & quotes from such wise sages as Mr. Roarke from Fantasy Island with advice on how to crash for little cash; health tips; & detailed realistic descriptions of work possibilities abroad."* — Bookpaper

*"A traveling guide for a new generation"* —Last Gasp

*"This brightly colored post-psychedelic cover conceals what may be more than you ever knew existed about (travel)."* —Chicago Tribune

*"Some travelers like it a little wild. If you do,* World Stompers *is a great travel book to buy - it is an impeccably honest description of the world."* —Student World Traveler

### 65 Line Drawings, 10 Maps and 7 Charts

ISBN 1-888729-05-8  288 pages
USA $17.95  Canada $26.95

Maps and illustrations by
Brad Olsen

# THE *SACRED PLACES: 108 DESTINATIONS* SERIES CONTINUES!

CCC Publishing's critically acclaimed *Sacred Places 108 Destinations* series continues with "Sacred Places of Goddess" by Karen Tate in 2005, and "Europe" by Brad Olsen in 2007.

*Sacred Places of Goddess: 108 Destinations* escorts the reader on a pilgrimage that reawakens, rethinks, and redefines the divine feminine in a multitude of sacred locations on every continent. Goddess

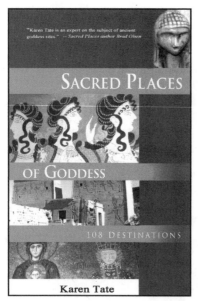

expert Karen Tate takes her audience on a journey of discovery from the Indus Valley, to the Middle East, Europe, Africa, the Americas and beyond, introducing the feminine face of God, sometimes forgotten for centuries or repressed. Visit shrines, springs, temples, yoni stones, archaeological sites, museums and labyrinths. Come along and examine the spectrum of evidence as the author dispels myths, and documents the long history of goddess reverence in many cultures. Tate outlines worldwide locations devoted to goddess worship, from the moment self-awareness crept into the collective spirits of our ancestors, to the living traditions of goddess practitioners today.

## SACRED PLACES OF GODDESS: 108 DESTINATIONS
### ISBN: 1-888729-11-2    $17.95    by: Karen Tate

## FOLLOWING IN THE 108 DESTINATION SERIES:
*Sacred Places Europe* * *Sacred Places Central America & the Caribbean*
*Sacred Places South America* * and *Sacred Places Southeast Asia*.

## OUR DISCOUNT SCHEDULE:
**Retailers:** 40% on quantities up to 30, free shipping. You can choose any selection of books from our catalog. Our pricing is 52% discount on quantities of 31 or more, *and* for each 31 you order, we'll send you the 32nd book FREE.

## SEND A CHECK AND QUANTITY ORDERED TO:
**CCC Publishing,** 1560 Howard Street, San Francisco, CA 94103; *or order online at:* www.cccpublishing.com; or www.bradolsen.com

**All Consortium of Collective Consciousness books are distributed to the trade by:**
Independent Publishers Group (800) 888-4741: www.ipgbook.com